practically perfect in every way

practically perfect
{ in every way }

My Misadventures Through the World
of Self-Help—and Back

Jennifer Niesslein

G. P. PUTNAM'S SONS
New York

G. P. PUTNAM'S SONS
Publishers Since 1838
Published by the Penguin Group
Penguin Group (USA) Inc., 375 Hudson Street, New York, New York 10014, USA •
Penguin Group (Canada), 90 Eglinton Avenue East, Suite 700, Toronto, Ontario M4P 2Y3,
Canada (a division of Pearson Penguin Canada Inc.) • Penguin Books Ltd, 80 Strand,
London WC2R 0RL, England • Penguin Ireland, 25 St Stephen's Green, Dublin 2, Ireland
(a division of Penguin Books Ltd) • Penguin Group (Australia), 250 Camberwell Road,
Camberwell, Victoria 3124, Australia (a division of Pearson Australia Group Pty Ltd) •
Penguin Books India Pvt Ltd, 11 Community Centre, Panchsheel Park, New Delhi–110 017, India •
Penguin Group (NZ), 67 Apollo Drive, Mairangi Bay, Auckland 1311, New Zealand
(a division of Pearson New Zealand Ltd) • Penguin Books (South Africa) (Pty) Ltd,
24 Sturdee Avenue, Rosebank, Johannesburg 2196, South Africa

Penguin Books Ltd, Registered Offices:
80 Strand, London WC2R 0RL, England

Library of Congress Cataloging-in-Publication Data
Niesslein, Jennifer.
Practically perfect in every way: my misadventures through the world of self-help—
and back / Jennifer Niesslein.
p.   cm.
Includes bibliographical references.
ISBN   978-0-399-15391-4
1. Niesslein, Jennifer.   2. Self-help techniques.   I. Title.
BF632.N537   2007   2006037341
646.7.092—dc22

Printed in the United States of America
1   3   5   7   9   10   8   6   4   2

BOOK DESIGN BY AMANDA DEWEY

Some names and minor details have been changed to bring this
manuscript in compliance with the Golden Rule.

For Brandon and Caleb

practically perfect in every way

The Challenge

ARE YOU READY FOR the porch swing ride of your life?" I ask Caleb, my five-year-old son. We're killing time before dinner.

He nods and scrambles up onto the swing with me. "I'm holding on to the side," he tells me before I can ask him. "I'm crisscross applesauce."

I swing back and catch the ground with my feet. My sandals slide a little as I push the swing, lopsided with his weight, up toward the railing as far as it can go. "Seriously, Caleb," I say. "Are you *ready* for the porch swing *ride* of your *life?*"

"Yes! Yes! I *am* ready for the porch swing ride of your life!" he shrieks. "Daddy, look at us!"

Brandon's carrying the Styrofoam boxes of tonight's takeout up the stairs. He gives Caleb a thumbs-up. I lift my feet, and Caleb and I whoosh through the sticky summer air.

It sounds like good times, but I'm still obsessing about the recycling bin.

. . .

WE LIVE IN a neighborhood that's a planned unit development, which means that our houses are crammed close to one another and the roads are unspeakably narrow. The roads are so unspeakably narrow that the trash and recycling trucks can't get down them. So each Thursday morning, we neighbors drag our trash cans and recycling bins down to the end of the street and each Thursday evening, we drag them back.

Brandon's a recycling enthusiast. We moved here last year and he endured a hardship, waiting a good nine months for the city to deliver our curbside recycling bins to us. When they came, I plucked two from the city truck: one for the bottles and cans, another for the paper. (Let it be noted that we also recycle plastic and other materials, but then it doesn't get picked up curbside.) The bins were red and shiny and ours.

One Friday, Brandon mentions that when he made the evening trip to get our bins the night before, there was only one red bin left. That, and an ugly, scuffed green one.

Oh, I thought generously, someone will realize their mistake in picking up an extra red bin. Because surely it was a mistake.

A week goes by. The ugly green bin is still down at the end of the road, unclaimed. Recycling day comes again. No one claims the green bin. No one offers up the second red one that is rightfully ours. The paper is mounting in our home. I am having an injustice overload.

I fire off a polite e-mail to all the neighbors on our street, asking them if they picked it up by accident. I see my next-door neighbor on her porch when I come back from grocery shopping. She calls to me that she doesn't have our recycling bin and I believe her. Through a scientific process of elimination, I narrow down the suspects.

My message goes unanswered for a few days, although I start checking e-mail compulsively. I become vocal with anyone who dares to listen. One day at work, Debie asks me, "Hey, any news about the recycling bin?" No, I reply darkly. One evening, Brandon walks into the kitchen and catches me, while I load the dishwasher, playacting the scene that will happen when the recycling bin thief is confronted. You had to have known that that wasn't your recycling bin, I snap. That nasty-ass green one is. My ire is contagious, and soon Brandon and I have, together, painted a devastating picture of the perpetrators' moral vacuum.

Finally, the suspicious neighbor e-mails back. "I suggest you take the green one and paint it red!" he writes. Hah. He adds that they don't have it. I don't believe him, but I don't know what to do: You cannot accuse someone of lying in this tiny neighborhood, even if you are 80 percent sure they are.

When I see the suspicious neighbors, I can barely look at them. I curse the fact that they are almost always home—guarding the recycling bin, I imagine. I just want my bin back. Plus, at this point, an apology. I will not be nice to them until I get one, I swear to God.

OH, IT'S FUNNY. But, oh ho, it's not. At the same time I'm stewing in my outrage, I'm also wondering, Isn't this a little petty? Shouldn't I be a better person than this?

It's not just the recycling bin, either. Here in early summer 2004, I'm plagued with what seem like a mess of unrelated questions regarding the details of my life.

Tripping over a herd of shoes in the kitchen, I wonder, Doesn't this mess seem a little, well, teenager-y? But I don't clean it up.

Or, grocery shopping with Caleb, I gaze at the checkout belt, rolling forth another shopper's purchases—fresh vegetables, an organic roaster chicken, and two tubs of no-fat yogurt—and I think, Now that's some wholesome goodness, before Caleb tugs on my sleeve and asks, "What if I picked out a candy bar?" I say go for it.

Or, watching TV one afternoon, I hear my lady Oprah tell a guest, "The first thing about fixing your life is honoring the truth about your life." To which I say out loud, "Honoring the *truth* about your *life?* Oprah, what the hell is that supposed to mean?" And then I wonder, Maybe this is what's wrong with me—that I'm so dismissive of things that I haven't even tried.

This time, though, is different. This will be my first nudge toward what will become a quest. As I remember it, sometime before five o'clock, it's as if Oprah turns her head to the camera. I'm sitting in the living room, iced tea in hand, and Oprah is not just looking into the camera, but looking at me—a longtime viewer, although not necessarily a big believer in self-help. Practically a self-help virgin, really. As I remember it, Oprah simply asks: "Are you happy?"

THE NEXT MORNING I feel vaguely dissatisfied, with an unspecified yearning located somewhere in my abdomen.

Am I happy? I ask myself this as I make Caleb some oatmeal. It is not something I ask myself often. It's the sort of question that, to me, is in the same league with "How are you?" The answer is always "Fine!" Or, if things are not going so well "Fine."

I'm not happy all the time or even a lot of the time. By happy, I mean that I don't feel as if I'm holding a warm puppy or enjoying a first kiss or dancing wildly to my favorite band at a bar. Or, even to take it down a notch or two, I don't feel as if I'm eating delicious soup or driving home with the windows open at dusk in the summer. Mostly, I feel mildly harried, my emotional state just on the positive side of neutral. This life of mine makes me feel, if not happy, then lucky.

I take Caleb's bowl of oatmeal into the living room where he sits sorting his rubber lizards into families. "Would you not mind getting me a paper towel?" he asks.

"I would not mind at all," I tell him.

There are times when I'm on the negative side of neutral. I don't cry or feel despairing. It's more of an uncomfortable feeling, anxious and out of sorts. The best way I can describe it is this: My body is a glove and my hand—my mind—can't get itself into the glove right. As if one of the glove's fingers got twisted funny in the wash. On these days, I'm in a low-grade funk. Brandon is more likely to ask me if I'm okay. Caleb is more likely to find a mother who's mildly distracted and restless. This feeling can last weeks.

Is this a problem? Or is this normal?

I bring Caleb his paper towel and unload the dishwasher while Brandon gets Caleb dressed. I put some water on for tea. I putter around the house, sweep the kitchen floor, write some bills. I drink the tea. I take a shower; I sort my laundry and some of Caleb's into three piles on the bedroom carpet. I listen to Caleb and Brandon gathering stuff to go on a reptile hunt, an activity from which I am mercifully excluded. I make the bed and stretch out on it, belly down. I am going to think about my happiness.

I have not done this much navel-gazing since I was in high school, when I would sit on my bed, play solitaire, and listen to tapes. *We were once so close to heaven,* the band They Might Be Giants would sing, *Peter came out and gave us medals, declaring us the nicest of the daaamned.*

That struck me as a good, modest thing to hope for, being the nicest of the damned. I thought then—and think now—that you cannot expect life to go wonderfully. Terrible things might not be happening now . . . but they will happen. Probably to you. Your job is to accept that and live a nice life anyway.

I roll onto my back, in the pose of someone deep in thought. Do people generally feel like this? Or am I wrong? I think of Oprah Winfrey and all her sincerity, her constant striving to change the populace. Oprah does not see bad things happening as inevitable. Last year, she started talking about how to "live your best life." I see the appeal: It's a lovely idea to think that there are all sorts of versions of your life available to you, if only circumstances were different. For example, if I had stayed with one college boyfriend, we could probably both be unemployed potheads with serious fidelity issues, whiling away the time by coming up with ways to make psychedelic drugs out of common grocery items. Or if I had bought that lottery ticket, I could have been the big winner, leading to all sorts of unforeseen events. Or, if I had a different upbringing, I might have become any number of things—an identity thief, a tightrope walker, someone who would consent to be somebody's third wife. I shudder.

Oprah doesn't work on the past much anymore; she trucks precious little in regret. But, the idea of living your best life is the same: If we consciously make decisions, our future is ours for the picking. If I made different decisions, would I lose the ill-fitting-glove feeling? If I changed, could I be happier? Could I be a better person?

I zero in on the clock. It's noon. Downstairs the front door opens. Caleb yells up the stairs, "Come see the salamander we caught!"

"Okay," I call. I do a quick happiness check before I leave the room, the quilt now rumpled, the laundry in still-life on the floor. Eh. I'm just fine.

THAT EVENING, I'm in the backyard with a tennis ball between my knees, trying to entice our dog Simon, the one who is well, to stay still while I brush him. This impromptu grooming was Caleb's idea, but he's off to find a jar for fireflies now. It would make sense to hold Simon's collar like I do with our other dog, but he twists and jumps and chokes himself in his excitement. He's an exuberant dog, blessed with the capacity to find unexpected joy in a tasty spot on the floor, a grubby tennis ball, his own penis.

"Simon," I say, "I think I'm ready to try to be a better person. I'm ready to take some advice."

He wags his tail.

I tell him about the ill-fitting-glove feeling. I also tell him my reservations about this. "I'm suspicious, Si, that people can just grab their own destinies and be whatever they want to be," I say. But then a vision of Abraham Lincoln pops into my head. He wags his long, Snoop-Dogg-like finger at me. *I was born in a log cabin.* I picture Thoreau, writing his tribute to self-examination in his little shack on Walden. He, too, looks disapproving. It occurs to me that maybe my problem has to do with a lack of exposure to small, ramshackle buildings.

"I know this sounds un-American," I say and smooth the loose fur off Simon's coat.

He wags his tail.

I have other reservations, I report. "Doesn't it seem unlikely that you can fix one thing in your life and everything else falls into place? It's never that simple."

The ball slips from between my knees onto the grass but I scoop it up before Simon can get it. He looks up at me, anticipating. *Can you believe she's going to throw the ball!* But the earnest look on his face also says: Who have you been listening to? Oprah never said that you fix *one* thing. It's a whole process. Remember "Get with the program"? It was called that because it's a *program.*

I throw the ball and he runs, grabs it up, and drops it at my feet. Tail wagging, he looks up at me again. His brown eyes seem more urgent now.

You are nowhere near as messed up as some people. But you owe it to yourself to make the glove fit. Make it fit.

And: Give. Me. The. Ball.

"Good boy," I say, "good Simon," and I throw it again. He tears across the yard, catches the ball on the first bounce, and jumps up against the fence for what appears to be the hell of it.

I'm ready.

. . .

LATER, after Caleb goes to sleep, Brandon and I creep back downstairs and settle in on the couch. I pull an envelope out of the recycling bin and write on it, "My Plan."

"What plan?" Brandon asks.

I tell him what's been going on with the plan for self-improvement. As I talk, I watch his face, shifting between half amused and half worried.

"When are you going to start this?" he asks.

"Don't know yet," I say.

"Am I supposed to be doing something?" he asks.

"I don't think so. Not yet, anyway. I'll let you know."

He massages my knee while he watches TV. I finish my list. This is what I write:

house
finances
marriage
mothering
community
health
spirituality

When I'm done, I read it over, assessing. I realize—with the shock of a person who was raised to believe she was special and unique—that I am completely average. In every category, I could use improvement, but on the other hand I feel like I'm not a worst-case scenario.

To put it another way: If I wanted to be a guest on *Oprah*, no producer would call me up. Although this perversely deflates me, it also gives me hope. Maybe a happier version of my life is within grabbing distance.

Next I come up with ground rules. I decide that I will not be a blank slate, lying prostrate as tons of unexamined advice gushes over me. I will be more like a liver, filtering out the patently insane ideas, keeping and using the advice that makes sense.

The liver has much to reject: any ideas that will harm or scare my son; any ideas that will harm or scare my husband; advice that is a thin veneer for a money-making scheme; anything that seems too good to be true. Also: I will take the types of advice that I might encounter in my life, as a married, middle-class mother. (Lucky for me, this is one of the biggest advice markets.) Also rejected: anything that seems physically dangerous. I am a liver with common sense.

I nudge Brandon. "Do you want to see My Plan?" He tells me that sure he does. He picks it up and reads.

Suddenly, I am seized with nervousness. It's a last-ditch panic. What am I *doing?* I study Brandon's face, his soft lips, the small scar on his forehead, the straight line of his nose. It occurs to me that things could get screwed up. We have made all our major life decisions—to live together, to get married, to move, to buy a house, to have a child, etc.—over a beer or three with, in hindsight, alarming casualness. Things have always worked out. But that doesn't mean they always will. I realize I'll be throwing straw after straw on the camel's back.

Brandon puts down the paper. "It looks like a lot of work," he says. It's a nice way of saying, "What's your problem?"

"I'm not unhappy. But I'm not super-happy either."

"I know what you're saying." He does; he spends his days at a job with a very stressful work environment largely for the money, which we like very much.

One of the dogs—Cleo, the one who is dying—starts barking. I know that she won't be quiet until we give her a treat. I get up, pad into the kitchen, and give her one of the spongy snacks that she likes. It's something I'm happy to be able to do, this hospice care for our first dog, our pound puppy. She dances around a little when she spots the treat, her nails clicking on the kitchen floor. The night we brought her home from the shelter, this is what I loved most about her—hearing those nails on the floor as she followed me, like the heels of a small adoring secretary.

Cleo gobbles her treat and five minutes later, I hear her throwing up on the rug. Brandon offers to get it, but he cleaned up the last mess—fair is fair, this one's mine. I clean the mess off the rug. She's been less and less able to keep things down lately, and so far the casualties have been the rug, my purse, and a stack of Caleb's drawings.

I spray the spot with carpet cleaner. I see that our lives are going to change anyway.

It is then, on my knees in our family room, I commit to My Plan. I will start with the house.

1

The House

I T SEEMS SIMPLE ENOUGH. To get a clean house, you clean house—action and result neatly bundled in two words. It also seems to be a reasonable enough suggestion that if my surroundings were pleasant, then I might feel more pleasant. As Julie Morgenstern, the well-known (and Oprah-approved) organization consultant, puts it: "No matter how hectic life gets, just knowing that this special place is waiting for you will help you let go of anxiety." It's a concept that falls squarely in the camp of Little Things Make a Big Difference. If a butterfly beats its wings and stirs all our dust bunnies out the door—so to speak—on the other side of my life, there will be a swelling of tidiness and peace.

I evaluate the house while Caleb and I play hide-and-seek. I hear him downstairs shouting numbers, and while he counts—*seven, eight*—I find a spot. I wedge myself between the bed and the wall in the guest bedroom. *Thirteen, fourteen.* This is, by far, the cleanest room in the house. We have few guests and the room is used mostly for conjugal visits while Caleb sleeps in our bed, sprawled in the middle. The bed is unmade, and on the floor is a bra and skirt I wore two weekends ago. It occurs to me that I'm living my childhood dream of keeping my house as messy as I want to. Ready or not, here I come!

I hear Caleb upstairs now opening closets and pulling back the shower curtain before his tread creaks near the door. I hear him hesitate, and then he appears smiling at the foot of the bed. Dispensing with the traditional *I found you!* he tells me, "Okay, now you go downstairs and count."

If I were smaller—much smaller, the size of, say, a leprechaun—it's conceivable that Caleb would be unable to find me, such is the jumble of our home. It's a shame. This is likely to be the biggest and best house we'll ever own, the one in which we'll notch Caleb's growth next to the furnace until he grows up and leaves Brandon and me to our own devices. Still, the house is an ongoing source of disappointment to me. It's not living up to its potential.

When we moved here just one year ago, I caught a glimpse of the house that it could be: vast open countertop spaces, a floor free of scattered dog fur, a family room that said *relax in me*, not *pick up all these damn stacks of papers and deal with them*. But like a rock star in decline, my house is becoming uncomfortable to be around. It's sloppy, a good third of its basement filled with materials to be recycled, a master bedroom littered with used dryer sheets, a dining room table hosting random camera equipment. The mess on top of the refrigerator, I can see in hindsight, was a gateway drug, the easy fix of where to put stuff. I know how this will end; I've watched it happen before. I think of this house in those early days, when our boxes were still packed and the stove was yet a stranger to burned-on food. Remember how everyone loved your backsplash, baby? Remember the compliments we used to get on the rug in the family room? I fear that unless something is done, I will detach myself from the house and simply watch as it slides into a miserable decline. We are not good at interventions.

Our problem is clutter.

I finish counting and go upstairs to find Caleb. Caleb's signature move is creating a pile of our belongings that looks like it might be hiding him . . . but what's this? *He's not there!* He's actually hiding somewhere nearby, so near in fact that you can hear him suppressing his laughter.

With my foot, I poke at the pile of laundry on the master bedroom floor, where he is not. "Hmm, where could that boy be?" I wonder aloud. He's under the bed.

"Found you!" I say. Caleb scooches out and I shoo him downstairs to count while I hide. I tuck myself in the shower in our bathroom. Standing there, it occurs to me that the reason Caleb can consistently perform his little trompe l'oeil is that there are always piles of things in our house that a five-year-old can fit under.

During this perfectly pleasant game with my son, an almost imperceptible urgency is growing under my skin. I could be Swiffering, I think as I step into the closet to hide. I could be cleaning out the microwave!

I won't Swiffer, though, until the next day when the sight of muddy paw prints on the door sends me into a cleaning frenzy. Brandon and I both experience cleaning fits, but mine get a little nasty, I'm sorry to report. I demand that the menfolk of the house do my bidding. Pick up your shoes! Put your bowl in the dishwasher! For Christ's sakes, why are there underpants in the living room? I never do get to the microwave and the frenzy lasts long enough to put us one notch above presentable. And that's why cleaning alone seems simple enough, but it never is. We need . . . organizing.

ONE STEAMY DAY after I pick Caleb up from camp, I stop at the mailbox. There is a sign: The latest issue of *Real Simple* has arrived and it promises on its cover, in nonconfrontational lowercase letters, to reveal both "the ultimate cleaning system" and "7 clutter-busting secrets of the pros."

I'm a sucker for this *Real Simple* vision of life, whether it's proffered by Time, Inc., Pottery Barn, or Martha Stewart. It says competency, efficiency—what biographers of aristocratic women or high-end real estate agents might call "gracious living." I would like to be gracious and relaxed, the very opposite of the resentful harpy who piles Caleb's toys into grocery sacks and, two weeks later, huffily deposits them at the door of his bedroom. I'd like to be in a place where Brandon and I can entertain guests just like the invisible homeowners in the Pottery Barn catalog do, with fluffed pillows and cold beers on ice in the special Cold-Beer-on-Ice Ceramic Tub. Where the three of us know the perfect location for any given item that comes into our home, where we stroll through the wide, clutter-free spaces of our hallways, confident that the floor holds nothing we could trip over. In this place, we sit on clean porch furniture, drinking lemonade and margaritas, our minds completely clear of what we should be really doing. Because, you see, *we are doing exactly what we should be doing*. We are *so* organized and *so* gracious that we have a completely crossed-off chore list and leisure time in spades.

Real Simple is the lone service magazine I subscribe to, and I enjoy reading it. Every criticism I've read about *Real Simple* is true. It *has* co-opted the simplicity movement for commercial gains; it *does* promise to help you simplify while also pushing more products at you; it *is* yuppie through and through. I don't care. It doesn't pretend to be more than it is, and I am hurting no one by sitting in my living room and looking at soft-focus photographs of bath towels.

I sit down with the magazine that evening while Brandon gives Caleb a bath. The clutter-busting section begins with a quote from Tina Turner: "Whatever is bringing you down, get rid of it. Because you'll find that when you're free, your true creativity, your true self comes out." Spice cabinet, I don't care who's wrong or right—I don't really want to fight no more.

I see that the seven tips are mostly sensible, if perhaps optimistic. *Act Like You're Moving*, for example, or *Clean Out for a Worthy Cause*. But we just moved and, frankly, we don't have the kind of discards people want.

These sorts of tips presuppose that we have lots and lots of stuff, that we go on buying orgies, that each Christmas, our family room is stuffed with a gluttonous mountain of presents, driving us further into credit card debt each year. I've seen those people on TV, and we are not them.

Am I in denial? I get up and do a quick clutter check. Aha—the coffee table in the family room. There is a stack of to-be-read magazines. Two library books on the subject of lizards. A ball attached to a jump rope that loops around one's ankle for exercise. A plate of creatures fashioned out of homemade Play-Doh (made at the home of a more ambitious parent). Some change, some crayons, and a variety of "maps" Caleb has made.

It's not the collection of items you'd get from a lifetime of desperate spending in an attempt to soothe the emptiness in your soul. I gloat about this for a moment. We are not caricatures of selfish, hollow Americans! We are caricatures of pack rats!

THAT EVENING, Brandon and I convene downstairs after Caleb falls asleep. It's a warm Friday night, and we head out to the front porch and talk quietly, so as not to wake Caleb or broadcast our thoughts to the neighbors. Brandon takes the rocking chair, and I settle in on the love seat under a blanket to protect myself from the mosquitoes.

"Did I tell you I might have to go to Italy and/or Germany for work?" Brandon asks.

"No, you didn't," I say. "Man, I don't want you to go."

"I don't want me to go either. I'll miss you guys."

There is quiet for a moment, and I realize we're acting right now—me trying to pantomime casual interest, him grumbling about it a little—so we don't reenact last year's drama, titled "What Did I Do Wrong? / Nothing, Just Shut Up About It." The last time he went overseas for work, it was Italy, and I had a freak-out. After he came back, there had been gnashing of teeth and angry putting away of dishes and wonderment, on both our parts, where this angry, angry woman had come from. I will die without ever having gone to Florence, I had cried, the lines of my lips blurred red. Then why don't you come with me the next time? Brandon had asked, reasonably.

But I wouldn't be consoled. I didn't really want a solution and I didn't really want to go to Florence, either. I had just realized all the lives that I would not be leading. This life I'd made with Brandon—with frequent dinners out at moderately priced restaurants and annual vacations in the mid-Atlantic region—was certainly good, but I had forgotten that there even *were* other ones I could have had. A life that included trips to Florence, say. What bothered me equally, though, was that Brandon actually got to lead both of these lives—the brisk, small-city one with me *and* the trips to Florence with languorous, five-hour dinners.

"Maybe it won't happen," I say, eager to bury this subject. I have made a temporary peace with it—*no, it's not fair and you can be a big girl about it*—but I don't want to look at it head-on. I tiptoe; I refuse to examine.

"Yep, maybe it won't," Brandon replies and lets it drop.

I tell him that I'm editing an essay by a woman who is the largest pain in the ass I ever encountered. "I sent her my edits and she started an e-mail with, 'Sigh.' She's on The List now. We will never work with her again."

"I wish I could have a list," Brandon says.

The night progresses like this, one petty thing after another. It feels delicious. What we're doing, it seems, is punching off the items to prepare for the organizing experiment ahead. The Italy conversation? Done. The electronically sighing essayist? In the past. The housing developer who still hasn't finished the common area? He'll get his.

I am also indulging all the bad parts of me—the grudge-holding, the passive aggression (infrequent), the out-and-out aggression (more frequent), the pettiness, the foul moods, the part of me that does not and will not play well with others. I indulge this tonight like a dieter gorging on doughnuts the day before he starts, like a smoker wheezing down his last pack of cigarettes, like a bachelorette flirting extravagantly before solemnly swearing to be true to her beloved. Because I think that I am at a crossroads here. If there was ever anything charming about a crotchety twentysomething, it becomes less so as time goes on. The cynical twentysomething becomes the glum thirtysomething becomes the dour middle-aged woman. Pretty soon, you're staring down bitter, complaining old-ladyhood. I can either become a better person, or I can continue indulging what I don't like about myself. And from past experience, I know that when I'm unhappy, I drag people down with me.

Brandon eventually moves from the rocking chair to sit next to me on the love seat, and I lean against his chest. He and I talk, knocking out one source of conflict after the other until we're yawning.

"Ready for bed?"

"Yepper pepper."

We fall into the lead-blanket sleep experienced by people who have technically everything they need, and for whom happiness is the last frontier.

THE NEXT DAY, I look a little closer at *Real Simple*'s tip number 4: *"Edit" Your Rooms.* It's appealing to me, as an editor. You "read" your room, upper left to lower right and think of the room as a book, the dresser as a chapter, etc. The tip is attributed to Alice

Winner, an inspiringly named organizing consultant in Pennsylvania. She hints at the happiness to come, advising, "Get rid of the extra words—*things*—that are making your life more complicated and unmanageable."

So I "read" the living room, tidying here, recycling a magazine there. I toss some Happy Meal toys into a paper bag, which makes me happy indeed. I stack throw pillows and fluff the couch cushions. I wipe off the baseboards, something I haven't done since the Saturdays of my childhood. I run a loop of masking tape over the love seat and chair where the dogs like to retire. Because *Queer Eye*'s interior design expert Thom Filicia is often concerned that the home reflects only the woman's tastes and hobbies, I designate separate shelves for my books, Brandon's books, and Caleb's books. I arrange some books in the manner of a Pottery Barn set: a few upright, a stack, then a few more upright. I'm feeling very Thom. I'm feeling close to gracious.

I'm trucking along when I come to a paragraph I did not write. Brandon did, and I'm afraid it's poorly constructed—a shelf full of random crap on the bookcase: miscellaneous screws, a stack of photos, a pile of ancient, rusted keys.

I call out the window to where Brandon and Caleb are throwing down grass seed in the yard. "Can you help me out?" They trudge up the stairs.

Caleb's eyes fall on the paper bag. "What are you doing with these?"

"You don't play with them anymore, right?" I say cautiously. "I was going to throw them out."

Caleb narrows his eyes. "You promised," he says in a low voice. "You promised me."

"What did I promise you?" I ask. Caleb has discovered the power of the word *promise*, and, as a result, we occasionally enact soap-operatic scenes like this, as if the backstory is my evil twin's making promises to my son that I will later break.

"You promised you would *never* take away toys that I love."

I never said any such thing—it's good to keep your options open, as a parent—but I hand over the bag. He takes it and deposits it in the family room.

I turn to Brandon. "Okay, I'm 'editing' here. I started up there"—I point to the top right shelf—"and I'm working my way over and down like I'm reading. But then I got to this." I point to the shelf of items in question.

"So what's your system?" he asks. "Where should I put them?"

He's right. We *don't* have a good place for ancient, rusted keys. If we were our *old* selves, we would buy a place to put them, a special ancient rusted key container. Instead, we wing it. Brandon takes the belongings from the shelf.

Soon after, my motivation dies. The living room looks fine— it wasn't the worst room in the house, anyway—and I call it a day, which turns into a weekend, which turns into a week without "editing" any of the rooms. Two weeks later I find the keys in the junk drawer. Some time from now, I will reread Barbara Ehrenreich's *Nickel and Dimed* and discover why "reading" the rooms—from top to bottom, left to right—sounded so familiar: It's how the maid service that Ehrenreich worked for mandated that they clean houses. The pros.

"DE-CLUTTERING really shouldn't be that hard," I say to Brandon. We're in the kitchen, side by side at the counter like two short-order cooks. Brandon's making Caleb some chocolate milk, and I'm cutting up hot dogs for Cleo. Last week, she stopped eating dog food, even the kind that looks like the yum variety of Chunky soup known as "sirloin burger." She is, we joke, completing her transformation from dog to human in these last months of her life.

"We're not good at it," Brandon says ruefully.

"Hey, are you an Ameri*can't?*" I put the plate of food on the floor. Cleo sniffs at it and turns her head. "But I do feel like I'm dabbling. I'm missing something."

"If we had more places to put stuff . . . ," Brandon says.

This is exactly the mistake Brandon and I made the last time we tried to confront the mess of our home: the consumerism route. We pored through the various catalogs (Pottery Barn, Crate & Barrel, Hold Everything, Restoration Hardware, etc.) and thought that we could buy our way to Taking Pride in Our Home. We tried it when Caleb was around two years old and wound up with way too many structures cluttering our space, all overflowing with the bounty of grandparental love. Blessedly, Caleb is now old enough now that his collections tend to be of small things. "We should have plenty of space now. We have a hundred times the closet space we used to."

I pick up the plate of hot dogs and microwave it for nine seconds. Cleo eats the warmed food but she does it warily, as if I laced it with sand.

Brandon shrugs like a man who is tired of talking about this.

I am tired of talking about this. At first, it felt like a lark, but now it's feeling increasingly ridiculous, thirty-one hundred square feet of disorganization hanging over my head. Thus far, I've been 95 percent talk and 5 percent action.

Normally, I would just out myself with this project. I work at home and I play little psychological games with myself—I said I was contacting potential illustrators, so that's what I must do!—to get things done. And I know just who to tell, who would be a wizard at this organization thing: my grandmother.

But I don't dare mention this to her, for a couple of reasons. First, let's just say that I have a reputation. My sister Erin has more exacting standards of cleanliness than a bottle of bleach, but in my extended family dynamic, I play The Egghead with Fancy Tastes. Which means that while I'm a good person to call if you, say, need to refinance your home or proofread an important letter, I'm not the sort of girl who can be counted on to get the dog hair off the couch before you come to visit. I will serve "strange" food, and when you decide to make yourself a sandwich instead, you will discover that I have neither peanut butter nor jelly in my pantry, only something called garlic jam. You will likely leave my house looking more disheveled than when you arrive. You'll want to stop at Wendy's when you leave.

One can understand why I wouldn't want to reinforce this reputation.

But more than that, I don't talk to my grandmother about the clutter situation because it would seem wildly, extravagantly spoiled of me to complain about it. She is literally a coal miner's daughter; her childhood and much of her adulthood were spent in a fog of back-breaking chores. When I talk to her about it, she moves into the second person, like a tour guide of a place people don't often visit. It's poignant, as if she doesn't want to remember that the person who lived through it was her.

Me:	Gram, I can't believe how much laundry Caleb makes!
Grandma:	When the kids were babies, you'd have to use the wringer washer and put the wet clothes up on the line. In the winter, you'd hang them in the house. And they didn't have disposable diapers then, either. You'd have to wash them every day because you didn't want that diaper bucket lying around. Your back would just ache by the end of the day. And then you'd have to do it all over again the next day.

It's humbling, yes, definitely. I *am* lucky that I didn't grow up in the sort of poverty my grandmother (and, for that matter, my mother) did. I'm lucky that, when I was a kid, girls weren't expected to whittle away their lives with this sort of labor—were, in fact, left free to study the liner notes of Olivia Newton-John albums and bicker with their sisters about who ate the lip gloss. I know my luck well.

But does it inspire me to just get up and organize? No. It doesn't.

I've lived all my adult life in the type of dwelling chaos I now find myself in. Brandon and I moved in together when we were twenty years old, both college students. His use of time was never more important than mine. We've muddled on this way—no one really in charge of the house upkeep—for more than a decade, despite his eventually making much more money than I, despite our splitting child care fifty-fifty. We do our own laundry, and whoever can't stand the mess first busts out the Swiffer. We're lucky this way: We can tolerate pretty much the same amount of mess. Although organizing is never presented as anything as lowly as *cleaning*, it's on the same order of home betterment.

Brandon gets the brunt of my organization fretting because it's his house, too, and, more to the point, I don't have anyone else to turn to for advice. Who are the people in my neighborhood? Mostly they're people who hire a cleaning lady to come once a week—her visits force them to organize. They clear the floor so she can mop it and they pick up the countertops so she can wipe them.

It works for my neighbors. I know one couple where the guy has more rigorous housekeeping standards than the wife does; she's home with the kids and he won't actually do the gruntwork when he gets home at 5:30, so their solution is a biweekly housecleaning service. Another husband and wife are both employed full-time, and when they married, the woman who cleaned the husband's house suggested to the wife that her services could enhance the marriage. None of this is my business, not if I want to maintain a relationship with any of these people, whom I consider friends. But I can barely figure out the tenor of my relationship with my editorial interns, much less with someone expected to scrub my toilet.

My other friends? Slobs, I tell you. None of us entertain much. We go to the park, meet at restaurants, or stay quarantined in the one room that the hostess has cleaned for the guests' visit. Avert your eyes from the family room, people—the guts of domestic life are spilled all over the floor.

"You know, Bran, there are professional organizers," I say, floating the idea. I read about them in *Newsweek*, these organization consultants with their own national association. They run $50 to $200 an hour.

"You think we're that bad off?" he asks, surprised.

"No, probably not. It seems like the province of the superrich or completely desperate," I say. "And we're not either."

Cleo barks again and refuses more hot dogs; Simon swoops in and gets them. I give Cleo a treat. She eats it, this time with gusto, and looks up at me. Her tail is wagging and her black-ringed eyes say, *Simon was right. It's a program, not one thing.* They also say, *Another treat. Now. Now. Now. I'm hungry.*

THERE IS GOOD NEWS and there is news of indeterminate goodness. The good news is that I have found a book—a program!—to help me with my clutter. It's a best seller, which leads me to believe that many people have found this book helpful. The book is called *Clear Your Clutter with Feng Shui: Free Yourself from Physical, Mental, Emotional, and Spiritual Clutter Forever* by Karen Kingston. My knowledge of feng shui is limited to the idea that one's furniture needs to be placed in a certain way. This sounds good, I think. This sounds a million miles away from cleaning.

The news of indeterminate goodness? Kingston is a big proponent of New Age thinking. This, in itself, isn't a problem. I believe that there is, you know, energy attached to people and other creatures. I believe in the good vibe, the bad vibe, the power of intuition.

It's just that New Agers in general have this tendency to take it one step too far and lose me. Again and again, it's happened: Energy—yeah! Synergy—yeah! The healing power of crystals? Um, wait. No.

My first year in college, my roommate and I took a short course called Psychic Development. We signed up, believing that perhaps we could develop our own psychic powers, which would presumably head off occurrences like my falling down the stairs at a fraternity house, badly spraining my ankle, and starting my first week of classes on crutches. One evening each week, my roommate and I would head off for a classroom emptied of academics, and a strange, intense man in his thirties would lecture us on chakras, energy, and life after death. At first, we were a little disappointed to learn that we would not actually become psychic friends. But as a treat at the end of the semester, the Psychic Development lecturer promised that he would channel a spirit who was several thousand years old. The spirit would talk to each of us personally, imparting the wisdom one gets from being dead.

We looked forward to this last class. And we truly did entertain the whole energy/chakra/etc. idea as a conceivable one, despite the uncomfortable gaze of the lecturer (who seemed stranger and more intense with each class), despite the guest lecturer, who explained that in one of her death experiences, she saw . . . dinosaurs. Okay, okay, we thought. We were still going to meet this ancient spirit and we were still going to witness a channeling.

On the last day of class, the lecturer prepared us to meet the ancient spirit. And his name was—and here he wrote it out on the blackboard—"Jerhoam."

I looked at my roommate. *Jerhoam?* Pronounced *Jerome?* She raised her eyebrows. I immediately envisioned the weird lecturer channeling not an ancient spirit, but a man with a moist Jheri curl, maybe a slender mustache and dreams of a career in R&B.

The detail of the ancient spirit's name slammed down a mental gate for me. It didn't matter that when the strange lecturer spoke next, his voice was completely different, strangled-sounding, or that his posture was changed, more elderly. When Jerhoam got around to me and gazed upon me, he asked what I had done to my mouth (had braces somehow eluded his consciousness for the past several decades?) and my chest (gee, could he smell the cloud of clove cigarette smoke enveloping me most of the time?).

I didn't respond. Jerhoam then told me, "You are an old soul, and you will find what you've been looking for in this lifetime."

This last gave me pause. But then, as I found myself smiling and giving voice to the words, "Thank you, Jerhoam," I realized that I could no longer suspend my disbelief. *Jerhoam.*

Now, I have a similar feeling of disbelief when I crack the spine on Karen Kingston's book—my initial reaction is that she might be taking it a little too far for most people. For one, she says that clutter—"stuck energy"—feels like cobwebs. It has a musty smell that a person's aura will absorb, making his or her aura smell musty as well. In another chapter—"How Clutter Affects You"—she claims that having clutter can make you feel tired and lethargic, affect your body weight, confuse you, make you feel ashamed, dull your sensitivity and enjoyment of life, and have other unpleasant effects.

These ramifications of clutter make a sort of intuitive sense to me; in fact, they're why I'm doing this clutter experiment in the first place. But Kingston doesn't stop there. Reading *Clear Your Clutter* one evening, I get the sinking feeling that this is a woman who has a lot of faith in the Amazing Coincidence. For example, she tells the story of one of her workshop participants who decluttered so vigorously, she had just "five items of clothing left." The next week, the woman got an $8,000 check from her mom—all because she "released huge amounts of stuck energy."

Five items of clothing?

This, I read aloud to Brandon, who's thumbing through a photography magazine on the couch next to Caleb.

"No wonder her mother sent her money," Brandon says. "She was probably worried about her giving all of her clothes away."

"I cannot imagine having only five items of clothing," I say.

We sit for a few minutes in silence, each of us, I think, picturing our closet emptied out to such anorexic proportions.

"*This* will be fun," he says. "Let me know what I have to do."

Immediately, I decide not to share with him how much further than the Amazing Coincidence Kingston takes it. In fact, she moves quickly from the realm of the house into places where you might be uncomfortable having her. For example, in your head: She devotes a chapter to clearing mental clutter, which includes things like gossiping (stop it) and worrying (also stop it). Or, another example, up your ass: I am haunted by her chapter on colon clearing—colon decluttering, if you will. She seems to have saved her most vivid prose for this chapter, harnessed all her writing prowess in her description of the bowels and related matter. I will leave it at that.

I sit there in the living room, becoming increasingly alienated from Kingston, but just as I'm about to dismiss her, there it is—her carrot at the end, her version of ancient spirit-channeling.

When the house is clutter free, I can then perform a spiritual cleansing of it.

Yes! My very own exorcism! Although no one has lived in this house but us, it's probably fair to say that we've left some negative energy lying around. This carrot, combined with the belief that I can take what I need from *Clear Your Clutter*, seals the deal.

I tell Brandon the good news. "Guess what, babe! We get to do a little exorcism after we clean!"

"Hmm!" he says and looks back at his magazine. I take it to mean that, strangely enough, the spiritual cleansing/exorcism doesn't seem to up the fun factor for him.

THE THING IS, though, it *is* fun, in the same way that horoscopes are fun. Kingston writes of the feng shui bagua, which is an ancient

Chinese blueprint: a grid of nine squares, like a tic-tac-toe board. It's something like this:

Prosperity Wealth/Abundance Fortunate Blessings	Fame Reputation Illumination	Relationships Love Marriage
Elders Family Community	Health • Unity	Creativity Offspring Projects
Knowledge Wisdom Self-Improvement	Career Life Path The Journey	Helpful Friends Compassion Travel

You superimpose this grid over the floor plan of your house (matching it up with your front door), and you can then tell which areas represent what in your life. So, for example, my prosperity, wealth, abundance, and fortunate blessings are in my kitchen. If I let my kitchen (top left square) become a complete wreck, according to Kingston, I can expect my prosperity, wealth, abundance, and fortunate blessings to suffer. If I let my bookshelves in the living room go to hell, well, there goes my creativity, offspring, and projects. (The bagua, in other feng shui tomes, looks more like an octagon, but the placement is pretty much the same.)

The bagua can be shrunk to accommodate an individual room or enlarged to fit your whole property. This is how feng shui (or Kingston's version of feng shui) closes its loopholes. "Forget any ideas you might have had about secretly shifting your junk to a shed at the bottom of the garden," Kingston writes. "There is nowhere you can put clutter where it will not affect you!"

This is bad news. Right now, Brandon keeps stacks of clutter on a windowsill, smack in the middle of our fame, reputation, and illumination. I have a collection of clutter in our prosperity section, and Caleb has taken to abandoning his plastic swords in our relationships, love, and marriage area. But for this particular project, I am most concerned about the dining room. My self-improvement is located somewhere underneath Brandon's camera equipment and my back issues of *Brain, Child*. And, Kingston warns, "Clutter in this area limits your ability to learn, make wise decisions, and improve yourself." Digging it out will be my first priority.

But not so fast, missy. If the New Agers tend to take it one step too far for me, they tend to go about three steps too far for Brandon, he of the scientific mind.

We go out to a bar one Saturday while Brandon's parents watch Caleb, and I start in on the bagua. Specifically, I'm a little bummed that our health and unity are located in a dusty corner right outside the downstairs bathroom and in front of the entrance to the basement.

"Do you think that maybe the builders should be aware of this sort of thing?" I wonder. "They put the *toilet* right next to the core of our *existence*."

Brandon gives me a look.

"What?"

"Do you believe that? Really?" he asks, taking a sip of his Manhattan. "I can see the energy, but the grid, I don't know. I'm not trying to discourage you. . . ."

This is the first time Brandon has really weighed in on the experiment, and I can see him wrestling with himself about it. He's open-minded, but also practical and grounded. For a couple of years, he played trumpet in a band that performed at communes and had a big following with the patchouli crowd; the band played upbeat, danceable music with lyrics about, for example, poverty and apartheid. Brandon undoubtedly liked the scene, but he was also the one who did a lot of the hard business for the band, the booking of gigs, the negotiating of the cut, the persuading of the club manager to put down the bong and pay up. It's hard to find a place of moderation with Kingston—she *begins* with a sort of fringe philosophy. (For example, she genuinely believes that since she advised a single woman to get rid of all her lone duck décor, the woman found a man and was no longer a lone duck herself. Yeah.) It appeals to my superstitiousness, and I certainly like the novelty of it, but I see where Brandon's coming from.

"Well, we haven't tested it yet," I say, both appealing to his appreciation of the scientific method and parroting Kingston herself, who writes (somewhat unconvincingly, but in the spirit of being a regular gal), "I am a great skeptic and I wholeheartedly encourage you to test the validity of this information before accepting it."

"But does it even make sense enough to test it?" he asks.

I take a slurp of my cosmo and try to channel a little Karen Kingston: He's still bargaining with the power of feng shui, I tell myself. He'll come around.

The next day while Caleb is at a friend's house, I urge Brandon to help me declutter the dining room. "You don't have to believe in it," I tell him. "You just have to do it."

For all of her wacky ideas, Kingston's actual methods of decluttering are surprisingly conventional, the same system found in sources from *Real Simple* to the TV show *Clean Sweep*: You take four boxes and label them something like *Trash, Repair, Recycling, Transit* (stuff that needs to go to another room). You work from there, only keeping things that you truly—*truly*, people—need. Kingston encourages one junk drawer and a filing system to deal with the reams of paperwork every household has. I don't have a filing cabinet (yet), but I set about organizing paperwork into files that will someday go in a filing cabinet. Brandon works on the camera equipment. We work and talk and throw empty cardboard boxes down the basement stairs. Brandon carries the boxes of *Brain, Child* up to my attic office. We rediscover the George Foreman Grill and the breadmaker, hidden under some dust bunnies on the bottom of the baker's rack. As we come upon every single decorating magazine that we ever purchased, we reminisce about buying the house. It's a lovely stroll down memory lane, and when we're done, we are filthy, achy . . . and the owners of a surprisingly bare dining room.

"Hey," Brandon says loudly. "Is my voice echoing in here? Whose dining room is this?"

"Wooo-hoo!" I yell.

Caleb comes home and can't resist the echo chamber that is the dining room either, so we all spend a little more time in there, repeating, "This is what the dining room sounds like" in funny voices.

Could it be that we're all feeling the buzz of our energies whipping around unimpeded? Could it be that our energies, previously attached to so much crap in the dining room, are now, as Kingston would say, more centered and focused?

I'm not going to call it an amazing coincidence, but that evening, the neighbors across the street—and not even the ones I suspected— return our missing recycling bin. Kingston, I know, would be happy for us, despite the fact we still have all of our clothes.

AFTER THE BIG dining room triumph, it's hard to believe that there would be obstacles, but alas there are. I quickly realize that we have a lot of house. What this means in Kingston terms is that, sure, our knowledge, wisdom, and self-improvement are just dandy on the main floor, but I still have our bedroom, the basement storage room, and the bottom left sector of the attic to declutter—and that's just one-ninth of the whole bagua. No wonder I always imagined feng shui devotees living in huts in Hawaii. It's a daunting method to undertake in multistory homes.

I also quickly realize that Brandon is just not getting excited by the bagua, and Caleb's too young to grasp the concept, even if it were one I wanted to impart to him. I'm in this alone. I look to Kingston for advice and she's got it: "NEVER, EVER EVER clear their clutter for them unless they specifically ask you to. . . . Understand that you can never change anyone else. The only person you can change is yourself." She offers up two remedies: education (what I've been trying and failing at) and leading by example.

So I lead. I set a goal to get the main floor done, which is ambitious in and of itself, what with magazine deadlines looming and regular life besides. After I get finished with the last room, the first one's a wreck again. I start feeling like a cartoon character, zipping from room to room, running full blast into what looked like a clean kitchen—only to smack into the evil musty energy of unread mail and Caleb's dandelion bouquets disintegrating in small cups of water.

To be honest, I feel like I'm improvising a lot. Kingston offers the basic four-box method, but a lot of her advice is focused on resisting going on a free-for-all at the mall or a garage sale. In practical terms, this means I have learned from her to avoid starting a collection of cookie jars with pigs on them, but what about the review copies of books that stream in through the mail? Or Caleb's many drawings of dragons? Do I have to go to the recycling center every day? What about the rocks Caleb painstakingly washes and calls crystals? I'm not supposed to touch the coffee table that's becoming increasingly igneous in nature?

As I stand in front of a cluttered countertop, I think, there are questions, *urgent* questions, and here Kingston is frittering away paragraphs with descriptions about how her author photo is "specially produced" to raise my energy. I sense that Kingston is the friend who, when you go to pick her up, has formed intricate and fun-sounding plans but hasn't showered yet and is, in fact, in the middle of giving her dog a bath.

My organizing improv goes on for a few weeks until I volunteer us to host one leg of a neighborhood progressive dinner. I clean the whole main floor; Brandon shops and barbeques and mows the lawn; Caleb sets out bowls of Goldfish and juice boxes. Much clutter remains, but the difference between before and after is still startling enough to make me proud. The house, for us, looks pretty good.

The party goes off without a hitch, but better yet, I look around the next morning and it hits me that it's now or never: All the rooms are clean(ish). I am neither pregnant nor menstruating and am not sporting an open wound. I'm feeling dandy, both mentally and physically. Brandon and Caleb will be out of the house, fishing for a few hours. With all of Kingston's requirements fulfilled, I can now spiritually cleanse the first floor.

TO SPIRITUALLY CLEANSE your house ("for personal everyday use—not for the purposes of exorcism," says Kingston), you need the following: candles, incense, flowers, bells, and holy water.

Anticipating this day a week ago, I told my mother about it on the phone. After I read her the two pages of instructions, she paused for a moment and asked, "Where in the hell do you buy holy water?" Indeed.

Next, I called a local store owned by an ashram. "Do you sell holy water?" I asked. My voice sounded high because I was nervous. Apparently, it also sounded as if I were disguising it, crank caller style.

"No," the man who answered the phone said, with some disgust.

Blushing, I hung up. Clearly, the average consumer in an average-sized southern city can't just purchase some holy water, so I started working my connections to see where I could get my hands on some. I began with Debie, whose father is a minister and who has the most direct line to a holy man of anybody I know. She didn't know. "We're Presbyterian," she apologized. "You're probably going to have to try the Catholics."

Brandon asked the guy with whom he carpools—a guy who's Catholic enough to send his two kids to Catholic school—where a person might get some holy water. He told Brandon that he didn't know. Apparently, Brandon reported back, most users of holy water are content to do so within the confines of Mass.

Then I asked Stephanie, my co-editor, who has a degree in religious studies but who has no religion affiliation per se. "Can't you just go into a Catholic church and dip a little cup in the font?"

"What would I say?" I asked.

"That you wanted some holy water to sprinkle around your house," she said. "Or you could just take some while no one's looking."

I have enough Sunday school and vacation Bible school under my belt to blanche at this. "Oh my God, Steph," I said. "I'm not religious, but I'm superstitious enough to think that stealing holy water just might put me on the fast track to hell."

Still, something about the idea stuck with me, and at the progressive dinner, I asked two of my neighbors. "Could it be as easy as just taking some?" I ask them. "Or would that be totally offensive to churchgoers?"

Janet referred me to a mutual Catholic acquaintance. "You could ask her—she really likes her priest."

Kathleen told me that, actually, her husband's grandmother takes holy water from her Catholic church all the time. "But maybe it's because she's so respected there that they don't say anything," Kathleen said. "She's always blessing us, though, when we go to visit."

I very much liked the idea of being blessed by someone's beloved grandmother. Much less so, a Catholic priest, who, here, will be loosely based on a priest who officiated at a wedding I attended—a humorless man with steel-framed glasses, conflicted about even whether birth control is okay. I tried to picture the exchange between us, but the furthest I could get was a cartoon version of me standing before a cartoon version of him. We would have thought bubbles above our heads.

Mine: Has he *ever* had sex? Like, *ever?*
His: Does she know she's supposed to be obeying her husband?

I realized then and there that this was not the sort of energy (as depicted in an imaginary cartoon, I realize) that I wanted in my home. I'm not Catholic. More to the point, this was not the time to explore my religious options or even to reexamine my religious stereotypes.

And so I find myself standing in front of the sink this Sunday afternoon, a glass of water in hand, blessing it my own self. "I bless you, water," I mumble. "I fill you with calmness and relaxation and fun." I feel I should say more, so I explain to the glass of water my qualifications for blessing it. "I'm qualified to bless you because, uh, I'm part of the universe, and so are you."

Then, reading my instructions out of the book, I walk around the kitchen and open some windows. I light the incense and the scented candle I bought at Kmart that morning. I take a pot of begonias off the front porch and plunk it down on the living room table. And I begin.

As Kingston advises, I work in my bare feet and "attune to the space." I mentally announce my intentions, which are to have only good, peaceful energy on our first floor. Starting at the front door, I make my way around the interior perimeter of the house, holding my hands out since I'm supposed to use them to "sense the energy." I don't feel anything, good or bad.

After that, I make another pass, this one for the guardian spirit of the house and for the spirits of earth, air, fire, and water. Since I can't possibly carry the candles, the incense, the flowers, *and* the holy water, I verbally direct the spirits' attention to the other items while I sprinkle the water. As I pass through the dining room, I see there are neighbors gathered in front in the street chatting among themselves, and I desperately wish we had window treatments on this floor.

I make another pass around the house, this time clapping my hands in the corners to disperse stagnant energy. I really try to focus. I hope to feel something sort of cobwebby, but I don't. When I get to the family room, where Cleo and Simon are dozing on the couch, they both look up at me with interest. As I clap near his corner, Simon jumps up and wags his tail. Cleo snorts at me and lays her head back down. *You look ridiculous.*

I wash my hands in running water after the clapping—"very important to remember to do this," according to Kingston—and make another pass to purify the space with bells. I had some difficulties finding a bell that morning, so I wind up using a handful of small cheap bells made for adorning wedding gifts. (It was either that or the bell from Caleb's bike, the use of which would raise this ritual from kind-of-surreal to flat-out-Dada.)

The next step is to "shield the space." That's all the description Kingston gives, so I improvise. I push my hands toward the walls in what I hope negative energy recognizes as a shielding motion.

Then I sit down and I fill the space with good thoughts—as Kingston puts it, "intention, light, and love." I do this for a while, closing my eyes and working on the frame of mind I want here. It's not easy, not like sitting back and listening to Jerhoam. It's work, getting myself in a mood, and blowing away the parts of me that tut-tut, that are laughing at my earnestness. I have to try very hard to radiate goodness. It does not come naturally.

I'm not sure if I accomplish the spiritual cleansing. On one hand, as I bustle about, putting out the incense and tossing the holy water down the drain, I do feel conscious of the mood of the room. On the other hand, I feel vaguely fraudulent, with my homemade holy water, my Martha Stewart candle, my acting out of a ritual that made me feel goofy.

That evening, I tell Brandon, who has been sneezing at the incense in the house, that I bought a new pepper mill at Kmart. "Where is it?" he asks.

"I can't find it. I looked in the trunk and all over the house."

"Maybe the spirits took it," he says. "Maybe they didn't like the incense either."

"Hey," I say sharply. "Come on now—I just got rid of all the bad energy. Don't make me ring a bell at you." I'm partly joking, but I don't want the experiment messed up. What if the guardian spirits—in case they exist—can't take a little joshing?

As it turns out, I will always remember the spiritual cleansing with these twin feelings, the vaguely peaceful and the vaguely abashed.

IT'S AMAZING, though, how fast we descend back into our mess. Since I'd been thinking of the spiritual cleansing as the pinnacle of my Kingston experiment, I don't keep up with any of her advice, and we are soon, well, not back to where we started, but we're pretty far from the evening of the progressive dinner. I don't even think about the upstairs.

And looking back on *Clear Your Cutter with Feng Shui*, I realize that while Kingston was big on philosophy, there wasn't much in the way of nitty-gritty details in her advice, no daily lessons learned. The details that there were—the holy water, the colon cleansing, the statement that sometimes your significant other can actually be the clutter you need to dump—were not much use to me. I realize that what I need is not an overarching philosophy so much as steps. Small, habit-forming steps. I am, after all, looking to simply organize my house at this stage of my quest to make myself better.

I start casting about for advice that's bare bones, detail-oriented. Matter-of-fact would be refreshing at this point.

I find it on the Internet. I hear mentions of someone called The FlyLady on discussion boards. She's mentioned in a sheepish way, the way one might admit a sexual attraction to Dick Cheney. *It's goofy*, the posters admit. *It works, though*, they insist. They cannot explain her magic.

The FlyLady's website (flylady.net) offers a pretty good indication of what I will be getting myself into. The FlyLady—whose real name is Marla Cilley—is fond of acronyms: FLY (Finally Loving Yourself), CHAOS (Can't Have Anyone Over Syndrome), and SHE (Sidetracked Home Executives). She has the sort of earnest motivational tone that I suspect is genuine. She peppers her missives with LOL, which leaves the unfortunate image of a woman cackling madly in front of her monitor. She thinks of a clean home as a sign of self-worth.

And to the FlyLady, we're all worthy. She's a salesperson, and her product is my potential, which is presumably lurking somewhere underneath all my clutter. "FLINGing gets you ready to FLY!!!" she promises. "Cause once the clutter is gone; the Sky is the LIMIT!!"

The FlyLady's method is basically a list of simple rules and steps— tips elevated to a regimen. My first step is to sign up for her e-mails— usually around a whopping fifteen a day. If I apply myself, I can develop FlyLady habits in just twenty-seven days. Until then, I am a "FlyBaby," and my very first baby steps are "shining" my sink, getting completely dressed first thing in the morning, and making my bed ("first wait until everyone is out LOL!"). If I cannot remember these things, no worries. I will receive an e-mail to remind me. Each e-mail will end, "You are not behind! I don't want you to try to catch up; I just want you to jump in where we are. O.K.?"

Okay.

On one June day, I sign up. That afternoon, while Caleb watches TV, I shine my sink. When I am done, the sink smells like bleach and it is white as snow. Later, I notice I have a line of bleach on my dress. She told me that I should wear an apron, but I flouted her advice. Damn it. It's the first sacrifice I will make to FlyLady.

I GET USED TO the routine after a while. In the summer of 2004, we all have new projects dolloped on our regular lives. Caleb's learning to swim. Brandon's putting together a hardwood floor out of scrap flooring for his workshop in the basement. I'm checking e-mail, cleaning, organizing. Unlike Kingston, FlyLady is never short on specific things to do. And by doing these tasks, I'm creating pathways in my brain, neurological trails that never before existed. Like a pioneer, I'm bushwhacking blindly, optimistically, hoping that the trails lead me to a better place.

Something about FlyLady feels comfortable to me; she would never tell me to declutter my colon or send me on a scavenger hunt for a bell. Actually, she sells almost everything you need for her program, although it seems wildly marked up and I don't buy any of it.

At her insistence, I douse my home's "Hot Spots"—the surface areas where clutter tends to collect. I make sure I have an evening routine and wake up to a clean kitchen. I think about the next day's clothes the night before. On occasion, I do a "27 Fling Boogie"—a frenzied race through my home in which I pick up twenty-seven items and throw them into a trash bag, never to be seen again.

I'm finding it do-able, this experiment coinciding with an energetic period for me—these periods come and go for reasons I don't quite understand. Maybe it's the cycle of magazine publishing, the crescendo of activity up until the last deadline, repeated again and again with each issue. Maybe it's life with a child, riding hard until simple exhaustion forces me to get to bed at a decent hour. I don't know, but I am grateful that the energy has hit me now during the FlyLady routine. Because I'm doing it and, if I do say so myself, doing it well.

My house is realizing its potential, with a lot of tedious and constant work on my part. But living there is undeniably a good feeling. Can I describe the peace that comes from waking up to a clean kitchen? Is there a better feeling than a clean expanse of living room floor? Is this happiness? In this moment—let's say the moment is 7:30 in the morning in a perfectly tidy house with no other people around to mess it up—the answer is yes, this *is* happiness.

I admit that I wasn't, in the beginning, always a good student. I had trouble with the FlyLady's corny tone. Also, I had decided to sign up when various events—a fair at Caleb's camp, a visit from my in-laws, a special magazine project—were converging. But I muddled through, and now I am, perhaps, a FlyToddler, levitating a few feet off the ground like a domestically compulsive David Blaine. I feel that I may be on my way to gracious living.

I'M AT MY SISTER ERIN'S surprise birthday party, thrown by Erin's husband and our sister Krissy. Erin was surprised, in a good way. I had been a little worried about the event, that she'd take one look at the fifty unexpected guests in her town house and faint. Brandon stayed home with the dogs.

Erin doesn't need the FlyLady; she's a born organizer, and stress only makes her house cleaner. The day she quit a job with no other job to replace it, she called and told me that she had buffed her floors on her hands and knees. She was getting ready to peel off the old wallpaper in her son's bathroom.

It's loud and I don't know many people here. My three sisters, their significant others, people I remember from Erin's wedding last year. Earlier in the evening, our youngest sister, Jill, took her daughter Amara and Caleb out for milk shakes after Amara's first dance recital. The kids are back now in full force, playing with some other children. It appears to be a game in which they examine dead bugs, brought in from the outside. Mom stayed for a little while. We'd all been to the dance recital—all four hours of it—and she begged off, in need of some quiet time.

"Jenny!" Erin calls. "Come meet some people!"

I amble out onto Erin's deck. Someone has removed the sliding screen door and someone else has put on some dance music. Erin's wearing a tiara from Jill's twenty-first birthday and is in her bare feet. "How's it going, lady?" I ask her.

"Good." She smiles. "Jenny, I want you to meet . . ."

There is a long string of people and I know I will never get them straight. Small talk is not my forte, and as the night progresses, it doesn't take me long to feel lonely, aimless, and hermity. I miss Brandon. I wander to the steps and watch Caleb and the other kids catching lightning bugs at the edge of the woods. I pet one of Erin's gigantic dogs.

Erin sees me sitting on the edge of the deck, sipping on a mixed drink called a Blue Lagoon. "What are you doing over there by yourself?"

"I'm having fun! Don't you worry!" I call back.

I make my way back inside. It's starting to look messy. Aha! I think. I've found my calling tonight! I know that Erin cleans so she can relax. If everything is in order, only then can she feel justified in doing what she wants to do. She's been like this since she was a little kid, the girl with the organized dresser drawers and neatly stacked board games. When she shared a bedroom with Krissy—they were seven and four—she says that she cut Krissy a little slack because Krissy's side of the closet had a big, unwieldy toy in it. But just a little slack. Erin really can't understand how people can live in mess. I'm now able to see what she means.

So I pick up abandoned plates and toss them in the trash, run the dishwasher, gather up bottles and cans in the recycling bin. I wipe down the counters. Every few minutes I make a sweep through the house, keeping it all under control. It will be my gift to Erin: a mess-free party.

Someone has switched the music to an eighties mix. As I put another glass in the dishwasher, the music gets louder. *Dun-dun-dun-dah-dah-dun-dun.* It's Vanilla Ice's "Ice, Ice, Baby," a song that—I have admitted to my sisters—inexplicably gives me chills and puts me in a good mood. ("Baby Got Back" used to do the same before I abused it and listened to it too much in an effort to be in a good mood all the time.)

Jill runs into the kitchen and grabs me by the arm. She gathers up the four of us, and in Erin's living room, we dance, yelling the lyrics. *Girlies on stand-by, waving just to say hi.*

"*Did you stop?*" Krissy asks.

"*No. I just drove by,*" I respond.

People start to dance with us, and Caleb and Amara run in from outside. Amara busts some moves, still in her hula-girl costume. Caleb throws his arms around my legs and pauses to do some donkey kicks. "I love this song!" he shouts.

"Me, too!" I say and pick him up to dance with me. He lets me, and I press his sweaty cheek against mine. This is good times.

ON SUNDAY, I return to our little spic-and-span world. I trudge up the steps, carrying my overnight bag and Caleb's little suitcase. I am weary and Caleb is cranky. I hear Simon and Cleo barking, excited at our return. On the porch are the newspaper and an empty glass. I open the door, walk in, and pet the dogs. I look up.

Crap.

The house is not a complete wreck. But it's not how I left it. If Brandon had gone missing, let's just say that I would have a very good idea of what he did while we were away. He had an omelet with American cheese (evidence: pan and spatula on stove, cheese wrapper on counter). He cleaned up where Cleo threw up a couple of times (evidence: carpet spray and paper towels on floor). He got the mail (evidence spread all over kitchen table). And he . . . what? Detonated his camera case in the living room? My sleuthing skills would be inadequate. I might need George and Bess to crack this one!

Brandon comes up from the basement, spackle flecking his shirt. "Hi there," he says.

"We're home," Caleb says glumly.

"Oh, babe," I blurt out. My voice is thick with disappointment, and I can't help but crane my head around, as if taking in all the weekend's Fly-sins.

It's a lovely homecoming.

As I fall asleep that night, I replay walking into the house, Brandon's appearance at the basement stairs, the sinking of my heart, my voice in slo-mo, *Oooooooooh, baaaaaaaaabe*, my face looking jowly and sad. I barely recognize myself.

While I love the tidy house, I conclude, I am not Finally Loving Myself. In fact, this vision of me so dismayed, so hyped up over forty-five minutes' worth of work, makes me dislike myself quite a bit. Is the FlyLady exacerbating my pettiness? My bossiness? I think so. Brandon and I had a careful, nearly egalitarian division of (minimal) household labor, and with the FlyLady's help, I messed it up.

On Monday, I backtrack. Clearly, I need to better understand the program. Because this can't be just my crusade, can it? That can't be sustainable, and it can't be good for my ability to have a harmonious marriage. Despite what organizing retailers tell you, organization is constant upkeep, and maybe because I was the one receiving all the reminders, I was the only one keeping up.

I reread some of the testimonials the FlyLady sent my way and find that none of them include even one man lifting a finger. Worse, Cilley herself even makes the case that marriages go south because of clutter, and this is the woman's fault. She puts it this way:

Now let's discuss what happens to our husbands and children when the house is cluttered.

Husbands hid[e] in the bedroom, the family room in front of the TV or tinkering in the garage. These are places of refuge. As a result of husbands protecting themselves from the clutter, you feel abandoned. Lines of communication become broken because clutter can push people apart. You all know about this.

(Well, *now* I do.)

I can only recall one letter from a man. He sent in some verse that his wife penned, an homage to the FlyLady. His letter begins: "I want to thank you for teaching my wife how to clean house. I have been married to her for 14 years and have felt so overw[h]elmed at times. I just couldn't say the right thing or show her how to do all that needed to be done."

Mr. Management Material wasn't the only one reaping the benefits of Cilley's missives. I read in e-mail after e-mail about how *happy* FLYing efforts made the guys. Some of them, in a fifties-style gesture of appreciation, bought the gals jewelry for making the house look so nice. More often, they proffered a compliment/insult combination, along the lines of Our Dinners Aren't as Disgusting Anymore, Darling!

Clearly, the FlyLady sees this as a women's thing. And, I thought as I deleted another stream of e-mail reminders and testimonials and special challenges, a *creepy* women's thing, using the language of empowerment ("FLY! Get rid of CHAOS!") for the old-fashioned timesuck of housework.

Listen, I know that other people have different divisions of labor in their marriages than Brandon and I do. What bothers me is the implication that this FlyLady scenario is what I, and the thousands of other women (I imagine) receiving FlyLady's e-mails, should be striving for. Putting out hot spots, flinging twenty-seven things at regular intervals, going gonzo in the house just so our dear husbands will give us a wink and perhaps a new necklace.

It's not just the unfairness of it, and all the baggage of biological imperatives that's inherent in any discussion of gender and housework. It's also that this is a lot of work. Doing half might be sustainable, but doing all of it . . . I'm beginning to see why the FlyLady methods are broken down into tiny steps, like the proverbial journey of a thousand miles.

But I can't really let go of the dream of egalitarian, clutter-free living just yet, so I give it another shot.

I decide after one afternoon, when I find myself making two tidy stacks of papers belonging to Brandon (on the windowsill in the kitchen) and to Caleb (in the drawer in the coffee table), that I will not aspire to fly higher for a while. I'm not going to take any more of the challenges, like "boogying" my car or my purse or cleaning out our bedroom closet, until I can enlist Brandon and Caleb.

The FlyLady offers suggestions for getting your kids involved. Caleb is actually a great help with cleaning—the child can really buff some woodwork—so I enlist him in de-cluttering.

"Okay, babe!" I say cheerfully and perhaps frighteningly. "We're going to pick up twenty-seven things that we don't want anymore and get rid of them. We'll fling them in this bag!" Christ Almighty. I just used "fling" in an unself-conscious manner with my *child*. "One. Two. Three. Go!"

Caleb, armed with a plastic grocery sack, races around downstairs, showing off his counting skills.

"What do we do now?" he asks.

"We just throw it in the trash!" I say. "We don't need it!"

He starts crying. "You didn't tell me I was supposed to pick up *garbage*!" It occurs to me later that Caleb finds nothing unusual in the idea of garbage lying around our house.

The FlyLady doesn't bother with tips on getting adult family members involved. I have a sneaking suspicion that, although she won't come out and say it, she thinks that the wives are subordinate to their husbands and, as such, we can only give out orders to lower-ranked members of the household: the kids.

Without any road map to enlist Brandon, I improvise. I think that maybe with the constant deluge of reminders, he might start to "FLY" as well. "So, what do you think about me signing you up for the FlyLady?" I ask him. He spends most of his day on the computer, so I feel an obligation to tell him what it involves. "It's about fifteen e-mails a day."

Brandon winces. "Fif-TEEN a day?" he asks. "Can you just tell me what I'm supposed to be doing?"

So I do, the executive summary version, but aside from one vigorous cleaning of the kitchen and an effort to keep his camera equipment put away, it has little effect; Brandon's not doing any more organizing than he did before. (That's not to say, though, he's hiding in the bedroom or "tinkering.")

I call Erin and come clean to her about the whole organizing experiment. I get reporterly. "I need to ask you some questions."

"Oh, Jen," she says. "You're either into being organized or you're not."

"What do you think of people who aren't?" I ask her.

She pauses. "I really try not to be judgmental about it. But when I'm at somebody's house, and there's a stack of papers lying around, I think, 'What's that stack of papers doing there? Don't they have a filing system?' I can't help it."

"But what about people you live with?" I ask.

In the background, I can hear that her husband is sitting right there next to her, talking to one of the dogs. "Well, since I'm home at three now," Erin says, "I just think of it as what I do."

I'm not convinced this is the right attitude for me. Actually, I feel pretty sure this is the wrong attitude for me, but I press. "But what about when you were working full-time? Did it ever bother you that Jeff didn't clean?"

"Yep," she says tersely.

I consult one last book, *Sharing a Place Without Losing Your Space*, by Regina Leeds, a professional organizer based in Los Angeles. The book is for adults moving in together—not know-you-like-the-back-of-my-hand couples like Brandon and me—but I pick it up, hoping for some crossover wisdom.

And there on page fifteen, she addresses the issue: "You can only change yourself. Trying to change another human being is folly," Leeds says, echoing Karen Kingston.

> The most powerful way to positively influence another human being is by being an example of the behavior you wish to experience in return. . . . Unless there is severe dysfunction in the family unit, everyone is going to notice that something is happening with Mom. . . . Everyone will be encouraged to get into the act and participate.

Yeah, I thought so, too. But after organizing for over two months now, I respectfully submit the following statement: This is bullshit. You either do it all by yourself because it's woman's work (Cilley) or because you're leading by example (Kingston and Leeds). In either case, it's the way that the world has wound up with widowers who don't know how to cook their own dinners or scrub their own toilets. The only thing that seems to be up with Mom, in my household members' eyes, is that she's being particularly anal about the house, borderline compulsive with the cleaning.

So, barring any sudden revelations, I have no choice but to give up on Brandon and Caleb for now.

For all of the FlyLady's cringe-worthy prose and traditional gender politics, I will say one thing: Her methods do become ingrained. Three weeks after I started, I am vigilant about keeping our hot spots clutter-free. I Swiffer every day. I try hard to clean the kitchen before bedtime. And the sink looks pretty damn good. I've added these tasks to my mental has-to-be-done list; I don't even question them anymore.

ONE SATURDAY EVENING, we have guests over for dinner, and this is the moment I have been waiting for, the platter of cheese laid out on the table next to a basket of sliced baguette, some Czech beers chilling in the refrigerator. It's way better than the night of the progressive party after using my version of feng shui methods. The throw pillows are stacked neatly on the end table, and there is even a fresh towel in the bathroom. The coffee table has three magazines on it and that's it. The floor—totally, almost obscenely, clutter-free—gleams in the summer's early evening light. That Pottery Barn moment is happening to us! I make us cosmopolitans and we sip them as we wait for the doorbell to ring. When our guests walk in, my friend says, "Your house looks great!" Thank you. Thankyouverymuch.

I think of this evening now as the apex of my organizing life, in the way King Lear must have regarded his life before he divided the kingdom. I don't realize it then, of course, but this organizing life is almost over.

The work week after our Saturday night dinner party, the perfect storm hits. Not in a literal sense, although it does rain nearly every day, soaking the yard and causing the dogs to track in muddy paw prints and dispense the smell of wet fur. I get the twisted-glove feeling. Caleb is in a high-energy phase and spends the time indoors making structures out of boxes and string. The string he also uses to make a large spiderweb across the family room. Stephanie and I have to decide content for the fall issue of the magazine and then (my least favorite part of the job) respond personally and kindly to the fifty-or-so writers whose work we liked but decided to reject. Cleo has started to refuse/throw up hot dogs and even the chicken and rice that I make for her, and I am frantic to feed her *something*. And then, on Wednesday, my eyes start to lose their ability to focus. This last one is bad. Once, in 2001, I went legally blind for a week because of my weakling focus muscles, and I can (now) recognize that this is a sign from my body. Get more sleep, lady. Relax. Slow it down.

At six o'clock, Brandon gets home from work, and there's no dinner and nothing to make for dinner. He picks up a pizza while Caleb watches TV and I lie down and try to rest my eyes. Brandon does the dishes after dinner and gives Caleb his bath. We put him to sleep and come back downstairs. The hot spots are shooting up big, five-alarm flames, and the kitchen counter bears unread mail, the remains of Caleb's bedtime snack, and God knows what else. I don't even know what I'm going to wear tomorrow. What's more, I don't care.

Instead of starting my "evening routine" late, Brandon and I assess the organizing experiment. I prop myself up on the couch, whose slipcover is laden with bits of yard that the dogs brought in on their nails. Brandon brings me a beer with a lime. "I don't think I've gotten any more happiness out of this organizing thing," I say and rub my eyes. "Did you?"

"No," he says.

"Do you think the house looks better at least?" I am not fishing for a compliment, I tell myself. I just want an objective assessment from someone familiar with Before and After.

Brandon sighs. "Better than the old house," he says. "I mean, we have more room to put stuff away here."

Do not even tell me that I am the only one who noticed.

"You haven't *noticed*?" I ask.

"Well, uh, the dining room was great for a while. The kitchen always looks nice since you've been doing this," he says. "And the bookshelves are good. We have a place to put all the books we're reading now."

"Yeah," I say. I mull this over, thinking, The bookshelves? The thing I did a hundred million years ago?

"Do you even think organizing is worth it?" I ask him, philosophically. "Are the rewards of living in an organized house worth the effort?"

"Not the way you've been doing it," he says. "It seems like you're doing a lot of work every day. I could see doing it once a week. . . . The mess isn't going anywhere."

"You're not in the house all the time like I am, living with a mess that's waiting for Daddy to come home and deal with it," I point out.

"That's true," he says.

And that's it. We finish our beers and have another. We've come to the conclusion that adults living together have been coming to for some time now: Housekeeping is work. Sometimes one person will want a higher level of work accomplished. Sometimes the other person cannot or will not do half of it.

I *can* have the organized home of my dreams. But it is a zero-sum game. Whatever happiness I gain in having an organized house, I lose in the time it takes for me—and me alone, since I'm the only one who cares about it—to accomplish it.

Worse, I realize, I have done little else but organize the house since I started FlyLady. My world shrunk to the size of my home. I didn't read books and I didn't pursue any freelance work, the small reviews and essays and op-eds that make me happy to have out there.

When Brandon and I would stay up late on Saturday nights for a little marital hanging out, I would stay up even later, taking the beer bottles to the recycling bin downstairs and wiping down the countertops before heading up to bed. This did not make me feel amorous.

When my friend Liz would e-mail to see if I could help out campaigning for the Democrats, I just didn't feel like I could spare the time.

I turned thirty-two years old during my stint with FLYing. What I had to show for that period was a clean floor I would have to clean again the next day, open countertops that had to constantly be monitored, and a routine of what to do with the day's mail. I did not deepen my relationships with my guys. I didn't even fix any of my character flaws and probably made some of them worse. The Sisyphean tasks of organizing—and their narrow, unaccomplishable scope—are not recipes for happiness after all.

IN JULY, the flylady's right-hand woman Kelly writes us, "Stop using your jobs, your comittments [sic], your home schooling, your marital status as excuses to not do this. Your life is as difficult as you make it." You said it, sister. I take myself off the Listserv.

I need something solid to build my happiness on, something that Brandon and I can accomplish together, and sitting right there on the coffee table, I think I find it.

2

The Money

AROUND THE TIME I was starting the FlyLady, Brandon was undertaking his own little project: learning enough about investing so that he might retire early. On our coffee table was David Bach's *Smart Couples Finish Rich*, a matte paperback adorned with a blond couple, their tanned backs facing the camera in a posture suggesting that their financial savvy has made them feel a little randy.

Of course I had seen the book before. In fact, it was one of the items—along with the other financial books and Brandon's investment newsletters—that I took care not to fling. Me, I had no interest in them. I regard money as something I'm lucky enough to have, like a nice piece of artwork: Fiddle with it too much and you'll certainly ruin it.

In my family, there's a little legend. We all have these stories, these anecdotes that are supposed to be signs of our character. *She was like this from way back when.* I was about seven or eight and I had been asking for something that was considered expensive, a luxury, maybe a steak instead of a burger, some exotic fruit and not a slice of cantaloupe. "Girl, you better marry money," my grandfather said. "I'm not going to *marry* money," I said. "I'm going to *be* money." The story is supposed to show my ambition or my fanciness of pants, although in hindsight, it's probably a better reflection of a certain mouthiness, or of my mother's feminism. The point is, my family, like most American families, got a kick out of this: The kid was a big dreamer. We all knew that regular hard work and talent wouldn't get you any guarantees of the high life, but *regular* wasn't going to be good enough for our little Nancy Drew addict with the smudged glasses.

Anyway, flash forward twenty-five years, and you'll see that I am indeed eating steak and exotic fruit. Sometimes I even miscalculate how much exotic fruit we can actually ingest and I overbuy; said fruit rots in the ceramic fruit bowl on our counter. But, although I've always worked hard and tried to maximize my talents, I got my money the old-fashioned way: I married into it.

I came to our marriage with credit card and student loan debt; Brandon came to it (I found out deep into the relationship) with stocks and a healthy certificate of deposit. During our engagement, Brandon worked a lot of overtime, and we both saw more money than we'd ever been responsible for. Each paycheck came faster than the last and my debt was gone before we knew it. Brandon bought a new car, a Jeep Cherokee with options above the basic model. I remember driving it one morning, my diamond engagement ring sparkling against the steering wheel. I look rich, I thought, which—considering it was a twenty-two-thousand-dollar American car and my engagement ring is less than a third of a carat—says something about where I was used to hanging out on the socioeconomic scale. Still, I thought it. Looking rich felt strange to me; I'd given up the idea that I'd "be" money long ago. I was uncomfortable but a little thrilled. A month after our wedding, we sold my $500 Chevy Citation and bought my first brand-new car. A Jeep Wrangler with vinyl seats and no CD player, it still felt incredibly decadent to me. There were children going hungry in West Virginia, and I had a convertible.

My comfort level with our money has shifted but not ever really resolved itself. The farther we get from the sort of people who base the steak-or-burger question on how much it costs, the less likely I am to even mention money to anyone except Brandon. Meanwhile, I have this hodgepodge of habits that don't match up with the reality of our checking account: I refuse to get a cell phone because the commitment of an extra monthly bill makes me queasy; I don't want to ever get used to premium cable channels because they'd be the first thing to go in a financial crisis; I cannot bring myself to buy a raincoat because, really, how many days a year do you need it? At the same time, I think nothing of buying myself a $180 cashmere sweater or dropping a hundred bucks on a nice meal for two with cocktails.

When I think about money these days, it's mostly when I'm writing out the bills, and even then, the numbers usually don't have any real-world meaning to me. But every once in a while, something about this life will strike me. I walked through our darkened bedroom last night to brush my teeth in our bathroom. When my hand hit the wall to turn on a light, it registered that we have *four* switches in the master bath: the fan, the light above the bath, the light above the shower, and the sconces above the sinks. Only Richie Riches have that much wiring in their bathrooms.

It's all completely relative, of course. Rich in Charlottesville, for example, is different from rich in L.A. (and we're not even rich by Charlottesville-area standards—people own houses with *names* around here and spend a whole lot of money just on the care of their horses), but I'm much more of a Richie Rich than I ever thought I'd be. It makes me a little nervous, all the unanswered questions surrounding money, our money. Do we have enough for retirement? Do we have too much compared to the people we love? Are we doing the right things with our money? Do we even have as much as I think we do? How fast could it all go away?

In some ways, these questions are the opposite of a clutter problem. Clutter is in your face, every day, begging to be dealt with. Finances, on the other hand, are ideas stowed away in your head or in financial institutions or in credit reports, easily ignored but never really forgotten. Clutter is the now, the messy hot spots and unkempt dining room, the magazines on the table and the laundry strewn on the bedroom floor. Money is the future, the dinner to be planned for tonight, the bill to be paid (or not) next week, the retirement to be taken at some undetermined point when you are "old," meaning "when you are a different person than you are now."

If unhappiness is linked to uncertainty, then money—tied to an uncertain future—is a good place for me to start. I regret to inform you that the learning curve will be steep.

AT A BAR ON SATURDAY NIGHT, Brandon and I drink eight-dollar cocktails. We're talking about the little projects that we've separately been worrying in the pockets of our minds, me with the self-improvement, him with the early retirement goal.

He's talking about The Market and how The Market is doing and how his investments compare to The Market, The Index, The Vocabulary Words That Make My Eyes Glaze Over. What I understand is that it would be nice to have enough money so that when we're seventy years old, we're not worrying about whether we can drink these eight-dollar cocktails.

"We should set up retirement accounts for ourselves," I say. "You know, more than what we have."

"Yeah, that's on my list," Brandon says.

I light a cigarette. "So," I say, "where do you set these things up? Can you do it at the bank? Or do you have to go to, like, a broker?" I wrinkle my nose a little. The brokers, they worry me. Who's to say that they won't lose all your money? Who's to say that they're good, scrupulous people? Who's to say they aren't getting kickbacks on the stocks they sell and are taking you for a ride? No one, that's who. This is what the suspicious part of me—that is, pretty much all of me—thinks.

"You can do it a lot of different ways," Brandon explains. "You can go to a broker—like Merrill Lynch or A. G. Edwards or whatever—or some banks have investment departments. Or you can do it online. Do it yourself." He takes a sip of his cocktail. "That's what I'm doing. I go through Ameritrade."

"But how do you know what to buy?" I ask. This is the conundrum of finances to me: You can either do it yourself (and risk not knowing what you're doing) or you can go to a broker (who may or may not screw you over).

"You do research," he says. "Like in those newsletters I get."

"Did your parents teach you how to do this?" I ask. It's one of many things I assume about people who grow up with money. Pass the cavi-ah! And have I told you my charming joke about compound interest? Not that Brandon's parents talk like this. They reuse their water bottles, for Pete's sake.

"No," Brandon says. "I didn't know any of this before I started reading about it."

"You're so smart, babe," I say. Brandon brushes the compliment off.

We order two more drinks and sit there quietly for a few minutes. At one end of the bar, a group of men laugh loudly; at the other end is a couple. The woman reminds me a little bit of myself at that age—looking a little awkward in this fancy-ish bar, slightly overdressed and over-accessorized. The difference between us is that she's sipping primly at her drink, imbibing in almost microscopic quantities, and I have always chugged whatever was put in front of me, which, come to think of it, might be how I amassed a certain amount of the credit card debt.

All this money talk, of course, leads to work talk, so I ask Brandon, "How are things at work?"

I know very well how things are. This is only a test, really, to see if we're still up against the same old issues that I've been chasing my tail over for years. Brandon likes his coworkers and *some* aspects of the work itself, but he commutes two hours each day. I mostly like my job, although I could do without the bajillion e-mails. Unfortunately, Brandon's job pays about three times what my job does and offers benefits. We got ourselves into this situation for good reasons (the baby, the local job market at the time, what happens when an engineering student sets up house with an English major, the idea that *Brain, Child* will grow and become more lucrative), none of which can easily be undone now.

It's the same old test, but there's more pressure these days. The Corporate Suits at Brandon's workplace have started downsizing in a serious, break-out-the-machete sort of way, creating an atmosphere of anxiety there: You might not be there in a few weeks; if you are, you'll get to keep both your job and someone else's. He's feeling the stress of this atmosphere—stress that's already piled on all the other stresses of providing the bacon.

He's pinning his hopes on the investing. He has a variety of strategies, none of which I fully understand. What I do understand is that work—his work, anyway—is not good for us. The job itself is do-able, but the accompaniments—the stress, the commute, the long hours—are wearing him out, and, because I make up for some of the unpaid work (child care, say, or dinner preparation) the long hours are wearing me out, too. The sooner he gets out of there, the better. But, like everyone, we need the money.

"Oh, work's the same," he says. We change the subject and order another round.

DAVID BACH, I would guess, has no money problems himself. He's the author of *Smart Women Finish Rich*, *Smart Couples Finish Rich*,

The Automatic Millionaire, Start Late, Finish Rich, and assorted workbooks—all of which are best sellers.

Bach, formerly a financial adviser, has the sort of rugged good looks that inspire trust. Although not Ken-doll handsome, he gives the impression of a vigorous man who plays racquetball, which I somehow equate with fiscal sense. (I don't know why. The confidence in smashing racquet to ball? The not minding getting sweaty? The foresight it takes to book a court?) I get started on *Smart Couples Finish Rich* one unseasonably warm afternoon while waiting for Caleb at the bus stop. Bach's writing persona is well matched to his looks. He comes across as affable, not too slick, mildly entertaining. In short, the sort of guy who will tell it to you straight while keeping the condescension to a minimum.

He starts by telling us the bill-paying fiasco that he and his new bride encountered shortly after they married—the point is, we all have the blind spots with the money. And then he relates the story of his grandmother Rose. Rose and her husband were poor, and one day she decided that poverty—well, it just wasn't for her. She saved up some money, took it to the bank, and after scuffling with The Man (who didn't want to let her invest without her husband's approval), invested her savings. The investment wasn't a good one and she lost the money—but she started over. In *Smart Couples,* Rose herself comes off a little smug ("David . . . I told you—I wanted to be rich, not poor" is a typical line of hers), but Bach's point is one of inspiration. If his people, who together made fifteen bucks a week, could become rich, so can the average reader.

Bach is concerned about the American people: He claims that 90 percent of us struggle to survive during retirement. Social Security cannot be counted on to keep us in the lifestyle we want. Money issues can ruin a marriage. Most couples "fail to plan" so they "plan to fail," when it comes to the finances. The good news is that by reading this book, I'm taking the first step toward fiscal responsibility. The other good news is our choice in the book itself. "I'd like you to think of me as your personal financial coach," Bach writes, "who can help you find your way through the obstacles and lead you quickly to the wealth and happiness you deserve."

I would like a guide to the wealth and happiness I deserve. In fact, I need one, seeing as I know almost nothing about long-term financial planning. Better yet, I won't have to convince Brandon of anything much here. He already owns the book.

So, I start with Bach's quizzes. The quizzes seem to be designed both to illuminate and to demonstrate that you are not the fiscal whiz kid that you might think you are. Brandon and I separately take the "Smart Couples Finish Rich" Financial Knowledge Quiz. We answer the true/false questions, and with each one, I think I'm doing well until I get to the last sentence. For example, I do know what our house is worth, how much of a mortgage we took out, the interest rate, how much equity we have. But—here's the kicker—do I know how much we'd have to pony up a month in order to pay off the whole thing in half the time? Damn. Got me there.

Brandon and I both score a ten out of a possible eighteen, which means that we're not complete 1950s housewives, waving our hands in ignorance about the finances, but our knowledge is spottier than it could be.

Bach apologizes for bumming us out (his words), but he promises to inspire. He knows that change is hard and some people would rather stick with mediocrity. "It's a place where your life isn't really that great, but it really isn't that bad, either. It's just so-so," he writes. Oh, yes, David Bach—I hear you. But he points out that me and my partner are not average. We can do it.

And you know what? I sit there on the couch and continue to read and I *do* feel motivated. It's true that I married money, but, with a little help from Rose's grandson, perhaps I can *be* money. Perhaps I can figure out how Brandon can get away from his soul-sucking and time-leaching job—and make it so we can drink eight-dollar cocktails way into old age. *That* would be peace of mind.

"DO YOU STILL happen to have your Value Circle?" I ask Brandon the next Saturday afternoon.

He's putting away the groceries and looks up out of the veggie drawer. "Excuse me?"

"You know, the five values that are important to you. The thing where you figure out what you want your money to do for you. The thing David Bach said."

"Oh. I think I skipped that part and went right to the real information," he says.

Which is completely flouting Bach's admonition to "please don't skip this step."

I say, "When I'm finished, I'll leave the book on the table so you can read the chapter and figure out your values, okay?"

He hoists some orange juice into the fridge and nods.

What we're going to do is tailor our plans for our money to our own selves. For some reason, this exercise is an immense relief to me. I'd assumed that these money books would reflect the values of a person who might score a 10 (Money = Most Important) on the money feelings continuum. Brandon and I know a man who's constantly on his cell phone doing business. Seriously, like, all the time. He fancies himself a grand entrepreneur; one day after hearing him talking figures and logistics for a good fifteen minutes, I turned to Brandon and hissed, "I buy and sell people like you *every day*." I was afraid that the money books would suggest I turn into this sort of person.

Luckily, David Bach wants me and Brandon to think about what our values are and how we can use money to live by these values. "Remember to stay focused on values—not goals, not things, not stuff to do," he writes. We are to arrange these values on five curved arrows that form a circle, so as not to rank any of the values over the others. Mine are:

marriage
family
fun
security
making the world better

I set out my notebook and ask Brandon to write his in it. The notebook lies on one of our hot spots for a few days until one morning when I wake up, I see that Brandon has written his values in it before he left for work.

marriage
family
freedom/peace of mind
fun
security

Our arrow circles are rather crudely drawn and Brandon has added a note: "Size of the arrow does not reflect relative importance."

Bach congratulates us on writing down the values—in essence we're writing down who we are. "Certainly, values are a lot more powerful than any sense of obligation or responsibility," he tells us. In case we didn't get it, he says, "Ultimately, your values are what motivate you and shape your life."

Now we're to take these values and create a plan to meld them with our money. The first step of this plan is to create a filing system— because you can't really plan if you don't know what you have, right? And it's not just any filing system. It's the FinishRich File Folder System. It's where you put everything financial, from information about your 401(k) to your tax returns to your mortgage statements and insurance policies. For some reason, this strikes me as risky. What if someone breaks in and finds the box that has every single piece of my financial life in it? I picture Bach, freshly showered after playing racquetball, throwing some of his no-nonsense reasoning my way. How many identity thieves actually break into people's houses? And think about the risk you take by *not* having it all together: Let's say you die and someone has to track down everything. I take his point, and remind myself that we will always have at least one dog who will rip the liver out of anyone who should try to B&E our house.

Thanks to Karen Kingston and our big dining room purge, I actually do have a filing system. It takes us about a week to track down every piece Bach wants in it—Brandon has some accounts online and I have no idea what the specifics of his benefits are—but soon we have a snazzy new system. It feels good to have everything at my fingertips.

After we put this together, we're ready to set our goals for the next year. The goals should be related to our values.

Before we start, though, Bach wants to say something. He intends it to be motivational, I'm sure, but I have to say, it pisses me off a little: Life is difficult, he says, but, "Life is totally fair." He goes on, "You get what you go for. Go for nothing and you get nothing. Go for something, and even if you miss your main goal, you might still achieve a lot of good stuff along the way." Look at Oprah, he points out, a woman who grew up super-duper poor. Look at Michael Jordan, who didn't even make varsity first go-round in high school. If they can do it, so can anyone.

I'm not trying to deny Oprah or Michael Jordan their props, but as I read Bach's pep talk, into my head pop the many people I know for whom life has *not* always been fair. I have no doubt that Brandon and I can become even richer—we can invest more, we can pay more principal on our mortgage, we can find ways to fund vacations that won't bring us into debt. In just a week, I will find out our net worth—and see that it puts us in the highest 20 percent of Americans, according to the U.S. Census Bureau's report "Net Worth and Asset Ownership of Households: 1998 and 2000." The median net worth for that group was $185,500 in 2000, and our net worth is well above that figure.

But what about the other four quintiles, whose median net worths ranged in 2000 from about $7,400 to about $78,000? How easy is Bach's advice for them? Living Example Grandma Rose would say all it takes is determination.

Is that true? It's time to bring in my people.

I E-MAIL MY THREE SISTERS and my mother the next morning.

> *Hey, ladiez,*
> *I'm wondering if any of you want to do an experiment with me. I'm starting David Bach's SMART COUPLES FINISH RICH. He also has other books like SMART WOMEN FINISH RICH and START LATE, FINISH RICH. Basically, you'd just do what I'm doing: taking his advice. I'm about halfway through the book and so far, the advice has been:*
> * *making a list of my five values (what I'd like money to do for me)*
> * *coming up with a plan to put those values into action*
> * *making a handy-dandy filing system of all things financial*
> * *learning about saving and investing*
>
> *A big goal of this book is to have you save enough (and invest well enough) to live off of when you retire. He claims that almost anyone can be a millionaire, regardless of their income.*
> *Won't cost you any money and you can stop any time you want to. Let me know if you're interested and I'll order you a book and we can get this party started.*
> *I love you!*
> *xo,*
> *J.*

Krissy's not interested, Jill is lukewarm, and Mom doesn't check her e-mail all that regularly. But Erin, who's two years younger than me, e-mails back: "I'll do it!"

On the face of it, Erin and I have pretty much identical lives. Husband? Check. Cute kid? Check. Nice house, two salaries, two cars, two dogs, annual vacations, decent Christmases and birthdays? Check, check, check, check, check, aaaaand . . . check.

The difference between our financial lives is almost imperceptible, but I'll lay it out: Brandon and I are of the old-school middle class, while Erin and her husband, Jeff, are of the new-style middle class. The old-school middle class generally involves someone holding an old-school corporate job and receiving all that comes with it: health insurance, life and disability insurance, a company-sponsored retirement plan, paid vacation days, etc. These jobs are a dying breed in the United States.

The new-style middle class, by contrast, comes about when you have a job that pays about the same as an old-school corporate one, but without the extras. Jeff owns his own drywall and plaster business, and Erin works part-time for a small print-brokering company. Unlike many in the new-style middle class, Erin and Jeff have one big advantage: no debt. Like many in the new-style middle class, though, Erin and Jeff are often stymied when they look at their tax returns—a lot of cash when you look at it!—and yet wonder why they're still juggling bills.

One answer is that they pay for all the old-school corporate frills themselves. The health insurance alone costs a pretty penny, and many people in the boat that Erin and Jeff are in—far from the lowest quintile but still living paycheck to paycheck—don't have health insurance at all. The reasons vary, but the Census Bureau reports that, in 2002, 43.6 million Americans didn't have health insurance— that's 19.5 percent of all Americans. And that doesn't even count the Americans on Medicaid.

On the other hand, Bach's Grandma Rose wasn't exactly living the high life, either, when she made her first investment. Some people would say that things are different now, people like Elizabeth Warren and Amelia Warren Tyagi, authors of *The Two-Income Trap: Why Middle-Class Mothers and Fathers Are Going Broke*. In their 2003 book, they claimed that today's parents spend a crazy amount of money on expensive but modest dwellings that are in good school districts, and that we're now also allowed to qualify for mortgages and credit cards that we can, in no way, afford.

But I'm pretty sure David Bach would consider those things excuses. *Who's making you live in a decent school district, huh? Who's signing up for those credit cards?* I can imagine him asking in the teasing way he has with his workshop participants.

But, like Bach, Erin specializes in keeping it real. So we'll see.

BRANDON AND I separately fill out our plans, then reconvene on the porch to coordinate them. Caleb and his friend Sophie are having a snack of crackers, string cheese, and melon at the table next to us.

We were supposed to come up with financial goals and specific ways to make those goals happen for us. As it turns out, our goals are pretty similar.

"So, I figured that the only way I can help you work less," I say, "is for me to increase my earnings by fifty percent." I'm figuring we'd have to make up for both the loss of Brandon's salary and the loss of the benefits. I push back on the swing. "One of my ideas is to start ancillary products for *Brain, Child*, and I'll have to talk to Stephanie about that."

"My idea," he says, "is to either start working part-time or to find another job where I'd commute less. So I could talk to someone about going part-time or start looking for more jobs in the area."

"What do you think they'll say about you going part-time?"

Brandon shakes his head. "Last time I brought it up, it was suggested that the job-sharing program is really just for women and that if the bosses think that we can afford me to only work part-time then they'll think they don't need me at all." He shrugs. "That's their reasoning, anyway."

I'm aware that there may be a slight negative vibe here, but we *are* being cautious. No one's shooting anything down just yet. Neither one of us is saying that this little dream—me increasing my earnings by more than half (I'll find out later that the ancillary product idea would up Stephanie's workload to ridiculous levels), or Brandon jumping into the great earnings unknown—seems overly ambitious. Is it? We *just don't know.* Because we haven't really even gotten to the meat of David Bach yet. It's only the beginning!

Happily, most of our other goals are more modest. Brandon would like to schedule more vacations. We'd both like to continue our Saturday nights out on the town. I'd like to invest some money so that if my mother ever needs some help after she retires, we can easily provide it, and I file this under "Family."

In the next forty-eight hours, I will write two e-mails and play with the calculator an awful lot. Brandon will read the classified ads and bring me up to speed on our savings. And I will plunge headlong once again into *Smart Couples Finish Rich.*

BRANDON HAD WARNED ME: "Every single one of those financial books—or the ones I've read anyway—will mention lattés. I'm serious." In the world of financial planning, a latté is never just a frothy little pick-me-up. It's a symbol for wasteful spending.

Bach has gone so far as to trademark his talk about lattés. It's called The Latté Factor, and it's where you'll find the ten dollars a day you'll be needing to invest to become a millionaire. "Our problem is not our income . . . It's what we spend!" he declares. Bach tells the story of Jim and Susie, participants in one of his seminars who spent ten bucks a day at Starbucks but claimed they didn't have any extra money to put away for retirement. Well, Bach pointed out that if they took that ten bucks they spent every weekday (and made coffee at home instead), it would add up to $200 a month. If they invested it under certain conditions, "by the time they were sixty-five, they'd have a nest egg of *more than $2.3 million*!" Understandably, Susie liked the sound of that.

So Brandon and I take one of Bach's challenges, which is to write down everything we spend for a whole week, without changing our spending habits a whit. Do we have an extra ten dollars a day to put aside for our retirement? Oh, probably. Excluding our regular bills and one charity donation, I spent $280.69 over the course of the week. Some of it was for necessary items, like Caleb's winter coat and a donation to cover the cost of pizza at the PTO's Read to Succeed Night, but most of it went to things like Brandon's and my Saturday night out ($129.02, including the babysitting) and my having tea and a bagel with my friends Emily and Peter, who blew into town one morning ($2.92).

Brandon spent less, but mostly on nonessential items. Lattés, for instance.

Dinner here and a bagel there doesn't seem like much, but Bach's carrot is the alternate universe where I could have invested that money, earning compound interest on it—and become a millionaire or more. Compound interest, Bach says, quoting Einstein, is a miracle.

The younger you are, the better. He presents two charts that put into real figures what can happen if you invest a given amount of money per month, starting at a given age. Brandon and I are thirty-two, and if we get a 12 percent rate of return on an investment of $200 a month, we could wind up with a million bucks. If we put in the same two hundred bucks and get the same return rate but we start at forty . . . we wouldn't even make half a mil.

Bach writes, "Are you motivated yet? How could you not be?"

"ERIN?" I call her one afternoon. "Have you and Jeff taken the challenge yet?"

"Why, yes, we have," she says.

"Well, what'd you think?"

She sighs. "We waste a lot of money. I probably spent a hundred fifty bucks a day."

"Yowsah—on what?" I ask, thinking of my Saturday night hedonism, my eight-dollar sandwich at a fancy deli, my paying the car taxes on *three* cars.

"Some of it's bills and groceries. The groceries are a lot." I can vouch for that; I spent a few days up there and Jeff (who literally needs the fuel) and Brit (a growing teenager) eat a lot of food. "But Amara and I go to the grocery store and I'll buy her a toy there, or we'll go shopping and I'll buy her sweaters and skirts. We go to Michaels and get all the crafty stuff we do after school. I got Brit an iPod because he got a really great report card. Jeff buys *four* mocha Frappuccinos every morning and those cost $2.09 each." She pauses, looking over her list. "Jeff needed jeans."

"Jeff needing jeans isn't really a luxury. It's part of his job," I point out, when what I'm really thinking is, Oh, my God—none of that is for her! Although we look identical on paper, the truth is that there are some major differences. She's effusive where I'm reserved, earnest where I'm cynical. When we were in high school and heard about a local house fire, we both donated clothes—but she donated ones still in rotation in her wardrobe.

"I know," she says. "But we could cut back and start saving."

"Are you going to?"

"Yeah, we will. I'm supposed to talk to Jeff about how much this weekend. But I don't want to feel *denied*."

"I know what you mean." By that, I mean that I know that I don't like the feeling of being denied either. But I also know Brandon and I will not have the sacrifices to make that Erin and Jeff will in order to put away ten bucks a day.

"I remember Mom having to pick food at the grocery store based on how much it cost and put things back because she couldn't afford it. I don't want to ever have to do that," Erin says.

"Oh, I hear ya," I say. *We can't afford it* was the refrain of our childhood shopping expeditions until I was—actually, until I was fifteen, old enough to work and pay for things myself. It occurs to me now what hopeful children we were (or pains in the ass, depending on how you look at it). The fact that we did not get Strawberry Shortcake figurines the first three hundred times we asked for them did not at all factor into our decision to forge ahead and ask for the three-hundred-first time. I don't remember feeling that I wanted for anything—we had plenty of toys, food, and heat, as well as Strawberry Shortcake figurines on special occasions—but sometimes I longed to be a spoiled child.

"I have a question," Erin asks. "Okay, I know that we're supposed to put money in our 'retirement basket,' our 'security basket,' and our 'dream basket.' Right?"

"Right."

"Do you know how much is supposed to go into each basket?" she asks. "Proportion-wise?"

"No, I don't," I say. Erin and I don't know it yet, but we will eventually get schooled in yet another way that life is not fair.

I QUICKLY SEE that there is no way I'll be able to report on every bit of Bach's advice. His genius is how he divvies up the complex world of finances. Take his baskets, for example. "The retirement basket safeguards your future, the security basket protects you and your family against the unexpected (such as medical emergencies, the death of a loved one, or the loss of a job), and the dream basket enables you to fulfill those deeply held desires that make life worthwhile," he explains.

Sounds good, I think, reading *Smart Couples* one afternoon while frying up some ground turkey for Cleo. She stirs at the smell of it and at the sizzle in the frying pan, but she may or may not eat it. Her food preferences are becoming shorter and shorter-lived. As a result, we have a variety of opened and half-used packages of meats in the refrigerator. It's a gigantic waste, but I cannot apply Bach to her because she'll starve if I do. "Oh, my tiny little girlfriend," I say as she lumbers into the kitchen and looks up at me. "Are you my Latté Factor?"

I turn off the burner and let the meat cool a little. So, retirement. The main point Bach makes is that you should "pay yourself first." If you don't do this, Bach warns, you're living beyond your means and you'd better develop a taste for Ramen noodles because that's what you'll be eating in old age. No eight-dollar cocktails, either.

Excellent, I think. Brandon has a retirement account and so do I. I convince Brandon to do as Bach says and max out his retirement account. His company matches a portion of it. Through the "miracle" of compound interest, we should be okay, in theory. We won't be able to touch it until he's fifty-nine and a half years old—another twenty-seven years—but this should do us well.

Twenty-seven years seems imaginable. My parents are in their fifties, and they're both healthy, attractive, and, to my mind, not old. But what about seventy? Eighty? The average life span for white women these days is about eighty years, for white men about seventy-five, according to the National Center for Health Statistics. I futz around on the Internet, looking up different investing options, and I can't help but think that I don't know what I'm planning for. My paternal grandmother died when she was in her fifties. On the other hand, my maternal great-grandmother is still alive at ninety-eight. Do I need enough money for ten years of retirement? Forty?

I'm still at the computer when Brandon asks me something about Cleo, something about whether she threw up today, what she ate, whatever. I rub my eyes and look at Brandon, a white man with, statistically, another forty-three years to live, expecting an answer from me. I wonder which one of us will die first, I think. These sorts of thoughts seem perfectly normal once you get finances on the brain.

OUT OF THE FOUR OF US taking Bach's advice—Erin, Jeff, Brandon, and me—only Brandon's employer offers a 401(k), which is the best sort of retirement account to have. Jeff and I are both self-employed, and Erin's job doesn't offer anything in the way of retirement savings.

But we all can have IRAs or Roth IRAs in addition to our other retirement accounts. The difference between the two IRAs is that in a traditional IRA, you don't pay any taxes until you take the money out, when you're between fifty-nine and a half and seventy and a half. (You square away the tax question when you file your income tax return that year.) In a Roth IRA, you put in money you already paid taxes on—and then when you take it out at age fifty-nine and a half or later, you don't pay any taxes on it at all. There are some restrictions, but you have to be pulling in quite a tidy sum of money a year to be ineligible for either the IRA or the Roth IRA. In 2004, the max you could put in was $3,000 a year, $3,500 if you're over fifty.

Erin calls me one afternoon. "Jen?" she asks. "Do you have a minute?"

I do. Caleb went home with a friend from kindergarten today. "I was looking at what we need to put away for retirement, and Jeff and I talked about it. For us, three thousand dollars a year is a lot of money—and that's just my IRA."

"So what do you think you're going to do?"

"Well, probably an IRA or a Roth IRA for me, and a SEP for Jeff. But how do you set this all up? I mean, David Bach gives a lot of good reasons why you should have it, but, like, where do you go? How do you *actually* do it? Who do you call?"

I repeat to her what Brandon said about the different options. Even Bach says that it's a crying shame that the average person doesn't know this—he advocates for financial know-how to be part of the public school curriculum.

Erin and I talk for an hour, discussing what Bach says versus what makes sense to us. We talk about what we want to invest in (i.e., whether or not retirement accounts should be CDs or mutual funds or stocks or bonds or whatever) and whether or not mutual funds seem like a good idea and how you find out which are the good ones, anyway. I've read a little more in the book than she has, so I can offer a little more information, but really, it's like the legally blind leading the blind. Soon, it's a half hour past dark, I need to pick up Caleb, and she needs to throw some dinner in the oven. We each promise to read more and reconvene when we get to the part where Bach tells us the logistics of getting money to the account and where to get the paperwork and how not to get screwed. In this post-Enron America, we are *very* interested in not getting screwed.

WE'RE MEETING SOME FRIENDS—a mix of fiscal conservatives and plain old liberals—for dinner. Brandon brings up a court case in which his employer is accused of knowing that they could kill people with a product they put on the market. Caleb and the other kids seem to be entertaining themselves with crayons and place mats, but I know he's listening.

When the conversation turns to Brandon's making a living with this particular company, the whole scene culminates in one of the fiscal conservatives' repeating, "Everything is about money," and my countering with, "No, it's not." I offer examples. Family is not about money, for instance. She counters with In Your Generation, Women *Do* Base Having Children on The Timing of Their Careers, and I just . . . stop myself. Later, we'll talk and I'll be able to see her point about consumerism being omnipresent in our culture, but right now, with David Bach's grandmother insisting that we can all control our money situations, I can't hear her.

"Everything *is* about money," she repeats.

I literally press my lips together.

That night, Caleb and I cuddle on the couch. "You know that Susan is just kidding, right? Everything isn't about money." This is my stab at raising a kid with money, a situation for which I have no good examples.

"Yeah," he says. Then a few seconds later, he says, "You know, Mama, I *didn't* know that she was kidding. She sounded serious."

Here I say something worthy of a sitcom parent, like "I bet you can think of all sorts of things that have nothing to do with money!" but really, I'm trying to decipher what I was arguing in the first place.

Mine was, I have to admit, a knee-jerk response. I resent that everything these days does seem to revolve around money, as if being rich is a moral goodness. There's no getting around the fact that you need money to live, money to raise kids, money to retire, but money is not the underlying value. Money is a means. What I eventually take Susan to be saying is that it's a very important means. Caleb turns his attention to *SpongeBob*, and I do a quick happiness check. Eh. The jury's still out on whether it's a means to happiness.

SO, THE SECURITY BASKET. Bach likens it to a financial air bag, meant to protect you against the unexpected. First, we're supposed to have a "cushion of cash," and to figure out how much, we fill out the form on page 273, "Where Does Your Money *Really* Go?" (As it turns out, a not-especially-surprising amount of our money goes to food, including dining out.) Bach suggests setting aside a multiple of our monthly expenses—he gives a range. This, we have—in our case, about nine times our monthly expenses.

We should also possess either a will or a trust. "This is not debatable," Bach writes. "This is not couple-specific." Why? Because "stuff happens" and because if Brandon and I fail to have one, the government—in the form of probate court—will figure out what to do with all our assets. "Smart Couples don't let the government decide anything this important. Smart Couples make sure they have a properly drafted will or trust."

Brandon and I are clearly not yet a Smart Couple. A will is something we always meant to get around to making up, but we haven't yet done it. Bach urges us to not attempt this at home—get an attorney who specializes in wills and trusts. I open up the phone book and start flipping through the yellow pages, but picking a name at random does not feel like something that one half of a Smart Couple would do. I shelve it until I can talk to Brandon about it.

We also need insurance policies. Luckily, here in the old-school middle class, Brandon and I have the Cadillac of health insurance, a fee-for-service plan (as opposed to managed care). Brandon's benefits also provide us with life insurance (Bach recommends term) and disability insurance (don't skimp here). For people in their sixties, Bach recommends purchasing some long-term care coverage (LTC); if you wait until your seventies or eighties, it gets crazy expensive. This coverage will pay for care, either at home or in a facility, that neither health insurance nor Medicare will cover.

Sobering stuff. I think of my mom, who's twenty-some years closer to needing all this than I am, and realize that everything in the security basket, like the retirement basket, is something of a numbers game. "This probably sounds fatalistic," she told me when I brought up the contents of this basket, "but I sort of never thought that I'd be alive to need it." Believe me, my mother lives a good distance from the edge, but I realize that I, too, can't believe that I'll be around to need a nursing home or disability insurance. Bad things will happen, I am certain, but I can't believe said bad things would include my becoming incontinent or being struck with a disease that leaves me, say, unable to type.

Next is the "dreams basket," a phrase that calls to mind Native American craftworks being exploited at head shops. Bach invites us to dream—and make those dreams come true. "Dreaming big is the key to happiness," he writes. As we did our values and financial goals, Brandon and I are to write our dreams down, being as "specific and measurable as possible."

After I finish writing e-mails to various magazine-related people one morning, I take out my pencil to record my dreams in *Smart Couples*—ones that are "totally crazy, totally fun, totally outrageous." Think like a kid, Bach suggests. Don't let your responsibilities temper your dreaming. Okay, I think. I'm ready. I love this creative stuff, and hey, it's the key to happiness!

Ten minutes later, I think: Totally impossible. I cannot think like a kid. Or, possibly, I was never the sort of kid who dreamed in a totally crazy way. I never wanted to be an astronaut or an athlete, or swim with dolphins, or get frocked out as a princess bride. I wanted to live in a big house with a big porch and be a writer. As an adult, I live in a house fitting this description and I do a fair amount of writing.

My problem, I think, is that I don't want an event. I want my dreams fulfilled in everyday ways. I want to have fun every single day. I want there to be new foods to try all the time and new books to lose myself in. I want Caleb to look forward to days at school, and I want Brandon to have the right mix of enjoyable work and enjoyable play. This seems more than enough to dream for without throwing in an expensive vacation or a kitchen remodel. I'm not suffering from what Bach calls the "I Don't Have a Dream" Trap (thankfully, no mentions of MLK, Jr., here), but my dreams are both modest and trickier to figure out.

Erin, on the other hand, has plenty of the sort of dreams Bach's looking for, another difference between the two of us. She's able to think like a (normal) kid. "I'd love to take Brit to Hawaii," she tells me on the phone. She rattles off four more dreams.

"The question now is, how are you going to pay for them?" Bach writes. His answer is that we will have a small percentage of our income automatically deducted from our checking account on a regular basis and invested in mutual funds, which are companies that buy a bunch of stocks and bonds and then sell a slice of them to individual investors, like you and me. Why mutual funds? Bach offers many reasons why mutual funds are the cat's pajamas, including that they're diverse, they're liquid, and they're "boring," meaning that the price doesn't fluctuate wildly.

A few days later, Erin and I talk. "I don't think we can do the dream basket," Erin says. "We just can't afford it. If we're supposed to have months' worth of expenses, we need to start saving for that. And then with the retirement basket . . ." She trails off, sounding defeated. This is the basket, after all, to "fulfill those deeply held desires that make life worthwhile."

"What do the percentages add up to in real dollars?" I ask her. Bach couches everything in terms of percentages and multiples—a goodly percent of your pre-tax income in the retirement basket, a particular multiple of your monthly expenses in a money market account, a certain percentage of your post-tax income in the dreams basket.

"I don't know," Erin says. "But it's more than ten bucks a day."

The truth is, their Latté Factor—which is where Bach finds everyone's savings—can only cover so much before it starts eating into the necessities and/or seriously affecting quality of life. If she and Jeff were to fully stock each of the baskets, they'd go into debt. There truly are only so many ways you can divvy up your income before it starts affecting your ability to pay bills.

Meanwhile, Brandon and I *can* do this because of one simple reason: We're not part of the new-style middle class. We don't have to pay very much for our own health insurance (just $60 a month) or other insurances. We don't have to worry about vacation or sick leave. We can take the money we save and provide ourselves with a cushion of cash. We don't have the extra expenses—like credit card interest, monthly car payments, or private mortgage insurance[1]—that come with being in the bottom four quintiles of American net worth.

How does this make me feel? Frankly, a little embarrassed. I bought this book for three people I know, possibly making *Smart Couples Finish Rich* a bit of a Latté Factor for me. In other words, I pushed these books on people who are not in the same boat as me. It's like the old Steve Martin joke. How to Make a Million Dollars: First get a million dollars . . .

I STAY HOME with Caleb on a teacher workday. As we tidy up the house, we talk about jobs. "Daddy makes medicine," he says. "And you make magazines."

"Yep," I say.

"Medicine is more important than magazines," he says.

"But making magazines is more fun than making medicine," I counter. I wonder if what I'm teaching him—that you must choose between a dull, lucrative job or an enjoyable, low-paying job—is universally true. In my experience, it is.

"I want to be the president," he says.

"Really?"

---

[1] Private mortgage insurance is basically an extra fee you pay on your mortgage if you don't have 20 percent to put down as a down payment on the house you buy. It goes away once you have 20 percent equity in your home.

"Yeah, because I want to be on money."

I wipe down the fireplace. "Not all presidents are on money. You have to be a really good president," I tell him.

"I know," he answers and squirts a little glass cleaner.

BACH PRESENTS A HUGE WEALTH of info about the stock market and other investing areas in the rest of this chapter and the next one. While *Smart Couples* is an excellent reference book, it's a whole lotta information to absorb all at once.

But here's what I do get: There are more than thirteen thousand mutual funds, and I should get to know the differences between them. I need more than one kind to make my portfolio as diverse—or least risky—as possible. Also, there are sometimes fees, or commissions, associated with certain funds. But, your financial advisor might be able to get the commission waived.

Financial adviser? Yep, he insists that you have one. "The rich almost always use financial advisers," he writes. "This is not my opinion; this is a fact." So this question that Erin and I kept lobbing back and forth at each other—but how do you actually *do* it?—it's sort of a moot point in Bach World.

Bach makes a solid case for hiring a financial adviser, including the aforementioned fact that all this investing information can make one's head full-to-bursting. But then he follows it up by pointing out that you need an *ethical* financial adviser, i.e., one who will not screw you over. He tells the tale of a lady who had an account worth $50,000—but her adviser racked up $10,000 in brokerage commissions in a single year. The point Bach wants you to walk away with is that you need to do your homework: Ask the right questions and investigate the adviser's background.

What I walk away with, though, is that this handing over my money will make me vulnerable. Still, Bach has not yet done me wrong. I move ahead with the advice, and ask around for broker referrals, but it's stressing me out.

Finally, one night I bring up the subject to Brandon. "Bach says we should have a financial adviser," I say, none too cheerily.

"Why?" Brandon asks.

"Because he thinks chances are excellent that we don't know what we're doing."

"*I* think I know what I'm doing," Brandon says.

"Yeah, but I *don't* know what *I'm* doing," I say.

Brandon points out that he didn't either a year ago. He also points out that Bach is—or at least was—a financial adviser himself. Moreover, what Bach says isn't written in stone. His "9 Steps to Creating a Rich Future for You and Your Partner" are not, after all, the ten commandments.

Bach also suggests asking for a 10 percent raise, but he's lost some of his expert sheen for me. I do talk to Stephanie about raising subscription rates and she agrees that we can do it maybe in the next year or so. But when I ask Brandon to see about a raise, he almost snorts his beer through his nose. "So, a raise *and* going part-time?"

Oh. I'd forgotten about our plans made on the porch, in which Brandon is supposed to be asking to go part-time. In a month, he'll present his employer with a plan in writing, excited to offer the Suits some thought-through figures on why part-time positions in a period of downsizing makes economic sense. But, although he works for a company that racks up award after award from *Working Mother* magazine for its "family-friendly" policies, Brandon will never hear about his proposal to go part-time again.

"YOUR FIRST MEETING with a financial adviser is like a date," David Bach writes. "And much as with dating, you typically know right away if there is a connection." These lines occur to me more than once as I do exactly what Bach fears: get overwhelmed and do nothing. So far, Erin and Jeff have done nothing, too, including not getting a financial adviser and not investing on their own. "I went to Ameritrade and Scottrade," Erin tells me. "I was completely overwhelmed by information and said, 'Screw it—I'm not doing it today.' "

In other words, although Bach (my personal financial guide, remember) was certainly a considerate and well-informed date, neither Erin nor I clicked just right with him. I make my mental apologies— *it's not you, it's me.* Although I did take much of his advice, including upping our mortgage payments (thus shortening our payoff by years), my questions about financial advisers were not answered to my satisfaction.

I start looking for someone new. I order Suze Orman's *The 9 Steps to Financial Freedom: Practical & Spiritual Steps So You Can Stop Worrying,* which was also a best seller. I'd seen Orman on TV before and found her maybe a little too intense for my taste; she seems to blink less often than the average person. But, unlike Bach, she comes from a working-class background and I hope that she'll offer a different perspective on things than Bach does.

She certainly does. While Bach talks about money as a means to live by your values, Orman goes a lot further and ties money to all sorts of big concepts like Freedom and Fear. Working through your emotions about money, she says, will "help you face the present honestly and clear the way for you to create a future you will love." What's more, she writes, "I know it works."

Orman asks me to write out my first memory of money. To get me going, she offers her stories (and many others): For instance, when Suze was thirteen years old, her father's take-out chicken shack caught on fire; he rushed back into the burning building and grabbed the cash register, which was made out of metal. Orman reports that the fire made the box so hot, when her father tossed it to the ground, skin came off his arms and chest. "That was when I learned that money is obviously more important than life itself," Orman—a former stockbroker and current Certified Financial Planner—writes. She has worked through that specific belief, but the memory shaped her actions for years to come. "Messages about money are passed down from generation to generation, worn and chipped like the family dishes," she writes. She invites readers to think very specifically about their money memories in order to illuminate how those memories affect their attitude about money today.

So, I lean back onto the couch and think hard about my memories of money. "When one money memory feels true, important, and keeps coming back, that's the one we want," she writes. Okay. I start writing. There are three:

From ages five to ten, I lived with my family in a very small town in Pennsylvania called New Galilee. One day my mother took Erin and me aside and told us that we were going to give our flower girl dresses to another family whose girls were about the same age as us, but smaller. Their mom had called our mom, and it turns out that these girls were going to be in a wedding but their parents couldn't afford special dresses for them. When they came to get the dresses, I hid in my room. I felt terrible for the girls and terrible that I had something that they needed and, to a lesser degree, terrible that I wanted to keep the dress even though I couldn't fit in it anymore and had no practical use for it.

When I was nine, the school district closed New Galilee Elementary School. We were all bussed to Koppel Elementary, a school where the kids were marginally richer than us New Galilee folk. The girls wore Jordache jeans instead of Lee jeans, and I remember being acutely aware of this. Once, a girl from Koppel came to my house to play; it would be the only time anyone from Koppel came to visit me. Ten minutes after the girl arrived, my dog bit her (which started my fifteen-year phobia of dogs, but that's another story). I remember being horrified by many things that day, including the hole Jake made in said Jordache jeans. I can still see the thin fabric, the ragged tear, and the puncture wound on her thigh.

A year and a half later, we moved to Virginia after the steel industry collapsed and my father lost his job. I was no more popular in Virginia than I had been in Koppel, but the kids in Virginia were even richer. My father made more money than he had in Pennsylvania, but we could still only afford to shop at Jamesway because the cost of living here was higher. I spent a lot of middle school crying because I had no friends (my own fault, in many ways) and one day my mother said we'd go shopping, just the two of us. Buy a new outfit to cheer me up. My heart sank because I knew that she meant well and that I would hurt her if I told her that an outfit from Jamesway was not going to help anything, not when there were girls with Guess jeans and underpants that said *bloomies* on the butt, something I found extraordinarily sophisticated. (Underwear from Bloomingdale's! Now that's classy!) We bought the outfit, which was all black and slightly itchy, and got back in the station wagon. When Caleb was a baby, I somehow found myself in the children's clothing department at Kmart and had to leave; the smell of cheap clothes literally made me cry.

My goodness! I guess Orman wasn't kidding when she used the term "floodgates." What did all this teach me? That it feels bad to be the richer one, and it feels really bad to be the poorer one. That the amount of money isn't as important as how it compares to your peers'. Also: that cheap clothes are to be avoided and that my mother is an extraordinarily kind woman who deserved a less bratty child than I was.

I look at my scrawl in the notebook and wonder how this is going to help me. Orman writes, "Each of our memories is different, but they all lead us to similar places, places that are riddled with self-doubt, unworthiness, insecurity, and fear." Yikes, I think—doesn't anyone have positive childhood associations with money? Orman would say probably not: Childhood is a place of powerlessness. "[We] don't grow up to claim our financial power until we look money directly in the eye, face our fears, and claim that power back."

On to the fear then. Again, Orman gives some examples, ranging from "I'm afraid I'm going to be a bag lady" to "I'm afraid my wife is going to make more money than I am." I'm afraid that these sorts of exercises would normally skeeve me out, but (1) they're really pretty gripping and (2) Suze has charmed me in this chapter. She tells the story of when she interviewed for a job at Merrill Lynch in 1980. She wore "red-and-white-striped Sassoon pants"—Sassoon! just a rung up from Lee!—and cowboy boots. The ensemble elicited an insult from her interviewers. Oh, girlfriend. No wonder she was scared to work there.

What I'm really afraid of is that everything will continue to be so unequal in this country and that the ramifications for making a bad decision are way too large. But I narrow my fears until it is just me and them standing there. "I'm afraid," I write, "that having a lot of money will make me an asshole." It's true. I'm afraid of throwing my weight around, of striking a patronizing tone, of adopting that weird self-importance unique to the newly rich. It's completely irrational—I know plenty of people with lots of money who are also generous and discreet and perfectly normal—but there it is.

So now I take that fear and make a financial mantra to combat it. It's my "new truth." So, I begin saying to myself, over the next few days: "I am not an asshole, and nobody sees me that way." I say it out loud in front of the computer, in the shower, at the sink rinsing off dishes. But part of me thinks this new truth may not be entirely true, so I revise it to "I am not an asshole *regarding money*, and nobody sees me that way." Because, really, I could still be one in many other ways, and I don't want to overreach here.

. . .

ALL RIGHT. Enough with the past, Orman writes. The next bit of the book is all about the future.

For the next eighty-one pages, Orman reviews what Bach called the security basket and what she calls Being Responsible to Those You Love: the will/trust, long-term-care insurance, life and disability insurance. Her advice is fairly similar to Bach's, but I take this opportunity to take the next step with the will/trust. I e-mail a professor at the law school and ask for a recommendation for a local estate-planning lawyer. Even though it's exam time, the professor e-mails me back quickly. People are kind, I think.

We are well on our way to Becoming Responsible to Those We Love, I have to say. It seems a little far-fetched to think that having a trust will make me happy, but Orman would beg to differ:

> What you need to know and believe is that when you have taken care of others, you have responded to the higher values of your existence—people first, then money . . . By taking these actions, you remind yourself of who you really are and what is important to you, what is important in this life. This knowledge is a powerful force. I think it is almighty.

"People first, then money" is a big thing of Orman's, and this is why I like her.

BRANDON, CALEB, and I are playing SpongeBob Life (like the old-school Life but set in Bikini Bottom) that Caleb got as an early Christmas present. It's late in the afternoon and I don't feel like a board game right now. None of us knows how to play so we read the instructions at each turn. We plod along, Caleb as SpongeBob, Brandon as

Patrick, me as Squidward. We've chosen careers and bought pets and homes. I read ahead in the instruction booklet and come across this: "Whoever has the highest net worth wins!"

"This is bull," I say to Brandon. "Do you realize that you win by having the highest *net worth*?" I raise my eyebrows. "Just what I want to teach the boy."

"On the plus side, he does get to learn how to count money," Brandon says.

"Yeah, that's something that he couldn't get outside of the game," I mutter. I decide to quit. Cleo barks at me, and I get her something to eat. When I come back, I hover near the game board and offer my thoughts on the difference between life and the Game of Life. "Even though the point of *this game* is to end with the most money, that's not the point of *real life*, is it?" I ask Caleb.

Caleb doesn't say anything, just looks at his play money.

"Because even though you need money in *real life*, the money isn't the *main point* of life," I say.

He nods, but it's hard to tell what he's thinking. I feel goofy, but I'm trying my best to instill some good values. I wonder what his money memory will be. I'm not a Communist, but I play one in our family dynamic.

ONE OF ORMAN'S LAWS of financial freedom is: "Respect Attracts Money—Disrespect Repels Money." And to whom am I supposed to be paying this respect? Money. "Money is a living entity, and it responds to energy exactly the same way you do," Orman writes. Whoa.

Wacky as it sounds, Orman doesn't let it drop. "When you really start respecting yourself, those you love, and your money, the result is that you start having control over your money," she writes and then instructs me to make a list of the ways in which I'm respectful and disrespectful of my money. So I take out my notebook, and under the respectful column

I note that I don't take on unnecessary bills; that when I give money away, I don't expect it back; and that I don't deny myself things in a miserly way. In the disrespect column, I jot down that sometimes we eat out just because I don't feel like cooking; that I never look at price tags when I shop; and that I have, on occasion, bought Caleb things because it was easier to buy than to deal with a tantrum.

Now Orman wants me to look over my list and think about how my respect or disrespect has brought about some either happy or unfortunate consequences. I'm at a loss here—I'm not evolved enough, fiscally speaking, that I can attribute any of my life's turns to my treatment of money. I just don't know if that's true or if it's a statement that can be filed under Amazing Coincidence. But luckily, I have another exercise right after this one: Arrange the cash in my purse neatly. It will remind me to respect the money. So I do.

There. Orman then launches into much of the same advice that Bach gives: pay yourself first, max out your retirement plan, you have to invest in order to have a decent retirement. Bach probably explains it all better, but you can get the same information in both books. But Suze Orman adds a caveat:

[Regardless] of what I say or what anyone says, you should invest only if you want to. The reason I say only if you want to is that even though investing for growth may be the right thing for you to do economically, it's not the right thing to do if it keeps you up at night worrying or makes you afraid all the time.

I put down the book and call Erin. No answer. I leave a message on her voice mail that has a note of urgency, as if a madman were lying in wait in our Roth IRAs! "Erin, it's me. Don't invest anything yet. I need to finish reading this other book, but I'll call you when I know more."

Later she calls me back. "Uh, don't worry, Jen. I was just taking Brit to the store. I haven't done anything yet."

. . .

ORMAN HAS A WHOLE SECTION on debt, which I read but can't apply to my own situation, then concludes the chapter by letting me know that "Respect for money and respect for yourself are linked." She writes: "When you can create money, you are suddenly free to live a life rich in all kinds of ways."

I have my doubts. So far, I know a ton more about money than I ever have and have actually taken some small steps to be more financially "free"—getting the money market account, upping the mortgage payments, setting the gears in motion for a trust or will—but although this feels good while I'm doing it, I wouldn't say it's made me a happier or even a more pleasant person. My life is just about as rich as it was before.

But maybe that's because I hadn't reached Chapter 6 yet, the one titled "Trusting Yourself More Than You Trust Others." Clearly, given my suspicions about financial planners, I do trust myself more than I trust others, but I don't trust myself all that much, in terms of investments. What I need to do, though, is trust the "little voice" inside me. Orman says that she believes it's "the voice of God." Whether or not my inner deity will reveal a plan to buy X amount of shares in Company Y, Orman says that it's important that I find that little voice and listen.

Orman makes a good case for not using a broker—namely, that brokers are human and stressed out and it's near impossible for them to consistently make good decisions on your behalf. The best scenario, she believes, is one where you "handle your own money and feel powerful and confident doing so." I like this vision of myself. Me, the savvy investor. Me, the girl who can work the Yahoo Finance page. (Brandon turned me on to it, and it has a nice feature that graphs out the performance of each fund or stock.) Me, the powerful and confident lady with the investments.

Orman, like Bach, recommends mutual funds. She calls them "the easiest and safest way to create your own fortune." She explains some key differences regarding funds. She recommends index funds (as opposed to managed ones); she recommends "no-load" funds, those without the fees and commissions.

Now, it's time to invest! Orman doesn't want you to jump right in. Instead, she suggests you invest a non-threatening amount each month, leaving a larger chunk in something like a CD. After the year's up, you can assess how you feel about investing and whether you want to wade deeper or jump out.

How do you actually do it? Orman, I'm happy to say, gives you more of a clue than Bach does. To figure out what funds to buy, she recommends I subscribe to the American Association of Individual Investors newsletter. Like Bach, she provides a list of some of the big families of funds, along with their websites and phone numbers. She warns that there shouldn't be transaction fees or loads.

Now we're cooking. I get on the computer and start messing around on the Yahoo Finances page.

Sitting there at my computer, I notice that the winter sky has started to darken. I get a phone call from Janet. School's letting out early. An ice storm's in the forecast.

SURE ENOUGH, by the time Caleb gets off the bus, the sky has started spitting balls of ice. I call Brandon at 12:15 to let him know that the roads are not looking so great over here, so maybe he'd like to start his commute home early?

By four o'clock, he's still not home, and I'm starting to panic.

At 4:30 he walks in the door, wet and tired-looking. I can't decide whether I'm pissed at him for endangering his life by staying so late, or ecstatic that he's home. My conflict must show on my face because he looks at me and says, "What's wrong, babe?"

"It was ridiculous that I had to worry today. The roads are *not good*. I thought you were going to come home early." I'm tripping all over my short declarative sentences. This is not how I wanted it to come out.

He explains the downside of the carpooling. "I tried to leave but I couldn't find anyone else who was leaving," he says. "This one guy's boss said that he could leave, but it would count as a vacation day."

I'm livid, not necessarily at Brandon, but the sum effect is the same. I go up to the attic to calm down. I answer e-mails. I staple submissions. I figure out how many pages each essay will take for the next issue of the magazine.

My inner voice is saying, "I told you so." This—this having to take a vacation day to drive home on steadily icing roads—is typical of corporations, the very corporations that I'm supposed to be throwing my money at.

All of this hemming and hawing about investing? It's because I have serious reservations about giving my money to corporations that have proven, time and again, that they will act amorally. I know some people would say that companies are not entities that can be moral or amoral, but I disagree. People—moral agents—run these entities. In fact, Adam Smith, the guy who came up with the idea of the invisible hand of the market gave a lot of thought to morality, human nature, and business.[2]

As I staple, I tick off the ways that The Corporate Suits have screwed over the American people in recent years: moving so many jobs overseas. Downsizing although the company is still making a tidy profit, as is the case with Brandon's employer. Allowing executives to steal money and not forcing them to repay it. Paying the average CEO

---

[2] See Nancy Folbre's *The Invisible Heart: Economics and Family Values* if you'd rather not take my word for it.

531 times what the average worker gets paid.[3] Paying wages that no one can possibly live on, as is the case with so many retail giants. And today: putting productivity above employees' safety, not to mention expecting the employees' spouses to subsidize the company vis-à-vis child care.

By the time I finish stapling, I see that the trees outside have a thick glaze of ice on them and I recognize the emotional state I've arrived at: vindictiveness. Am I going to buy shares in a corporation that screws Americans over like this? No way! I will *withhold* my bounty from them! Ha! I will reward only those who do business in a conscionable manner!

I get on my computer and find a website named socialinvest.org that maintains information about mutual funds that invest according to certain criteria—some will invest only in companies, for example, that use environmentally sound practices or are fair with union labor. If I've been hunting all these weeks for this elusive beast called the Right Mutual Fund for Me, I feel, at socialinvest.org, that I'm at the edge of the forest.

I find plenty of funds that, on the face of it, I'd feel good about investing in. Women's Equity Fund, for example, invests in companies that promote "economic and social" equity of women in the workplace.

In the coming months, though, I'll see what sort of quagmire socially responsible funds can be. I'll see, in more than one finance article, that the socially responsible funds have higher fees than traditional funds. Most of them have lower returns as well. I'll order prospectuses (the paperwork that funds have to give to potential investors) and see that many of the funds invest in companies that don't strike me as anything to get excited over. (Women's Equity Fund, for

---

[3] This is according to financial writer James Surowiecki, in a July 24, 2002, column on Slate.com. In 1980, the average CEO got paid only forty-two times what the average worker got paid.

example, invests in a credit card company that I know from firsthand experience makes it all too easy for cardholders to rack up unbelievable debt—this is a corporate decision that strikes me as amoral money-grubbing.) I'll see that the places where I really want to put my money are not places that will secure me a lovely retirement—but might, as the public service announcements say, Make a Difference. These organizations are nonprofits and lobbying groups, not investments. This last is not really a problem with socially responsible investing. It's my own deal, this confusing salad of money, vindictiveness, charity, and the sense of what's fair.

In the end, investing comes down to a decision that I'll have to make an uneasy peace with: Do I go with investing in the socially responsible funds, for all their problems? Or do I try to make as much money as I can using the corporations that trouble me, and then turn around and use *that* money to whatever means I like?

Having to think about this doesn't make me unhappy, per se, but my daily to-do list has gotten longer. Some days I think it's good that I am in charge of my own financial destiny. Other days, it doesn't feel like control as much as playing a game—a game I haven't mastered, a game I don't enjoy, a game that makes me think of my impending old age every single day.

BEING CHEAP is a terrible thing, and Orman tells her readers to give away a certain amount of money each month. "You must not give less than your inner voice tells you is the meaningful amount, for that is being cheap," she writes. You should make it a priority and it will feel good. It will improve your attitude about money, and money will flow back to you.

I already do this, but in a less systematic way. A few years ago, I signed up for our regional Planned Parenthood's Pledge-a-Picket Campaign. For every antichoice picketer that bothers the women using services at a Planned Parenthood in the region, I pay seventy-five cents. The money then goes to Planned Parenthood's Women in Need fund, which pays for gynecological and obstetric services for women who can't afford them. So, in a sense, the antichoice picketers are funding Planned Parenthood's services.

You can see why this appeals to me, no?

Planned Parenthood bills me every two months, and the amount varies depending on the amount of picketers, usually from $35 to $75. Lately, since the antichoicers know about the program, the amounts have been dwindling—so next time the bill comes, I up my commitment per picketer.

Through work, Brandon contributes a certain percentage of his paycheck to the local food bank and the local health clinic. He, too, ups his contribution.

Orman feels quite strongly that the best charitable donations are anonymous. To drive home her point, she sends me on another exercise, which is how I find myself walking through the parking lot of the mall with a dollar bill in my hand. I'm supposed to foist a dollar on a random person—"an ordinary stranger, not a panhandler"—and see how I feel.

The Christmas shopping season has just begun in earnest but it's a cloudy weekday morning. At the entrance of the mall, an elderly woman, heavyset and dressed in a worn plaid coat, moves slowly toward the door. I slow down. I don't want to give the dollar bill to her because she'll think she looks poor and I'll ruin her day. About twenty paces in front of me, a woman with a permed ponytail is pushing a double stroller. She has her hands full. I slow down even more until I'm moving at a ridiculously glacial pace.

I cross the road and now there's just one person out front, an Asian man smoking a cigarette and talking in a foreign language on a cell phone. I take a deep breath and walk closer. He doesn't seem to notice me at all. I take the dollar out of my pocket and hold it in my mittened hand. I walk closer and closer. My boots make a skitchy sound on the salted cement.

Finally I'm within range of handing off the dollar to him and he's still ignoring me in the way that people do when they're busy with their cigarettes and cell phones. I take a breath to say something, to call attention to myself.

But I hesitate in my step, then keep walking. I blow right past him, and I enter the mall. I shove my fist back into my coat pocket. I'm not going to do this.

I look around the mall. It's a small one, with the basic mall stores: Express, Sears, Chik-Fil-A, Lane Bryant. The people who shop here are not rich, and the people who shop here at one o'clock on a Tuesday afternoon have all the class markers of being working people or their spouses—they have perms, drive older cars with Redskins bumper stickers, wear sweatpants in public.

I take Orman's point. Her assignment is rhetorical. Nobody wants to feel like a charity case, and I certainly don't want to be the one who makes them feel that way. When I leave, I pass the would-be donation recipient outside. His leather jacket is fake leather, but he can afford his smokes, his cell phone, the gel in his hair. Jesus. I almost took someone's pride so I could learn a lesson I already know.

ORMAN OFFERS two more life lessons before her book is through: The first is Money Ebbs and Flows, which means I should just accept that sometimes I'll be poorer and sometimes I'll be richer, but everything works out for the best, even the bad things. She's asking me to be an optimist, and I sigh.

The second lesson? Being Financially Free Means Being Happy with Who We Are (as opposed to what we have). This reminds me of a book Caleb has called *The Richest Crocodile in the World*. The crocodile is loaded and has a ton of stuff, including a submissive giraffe butler, but the croc's not really happy until he lives out on the plains with the rest of the wild African animals. The point—both of the crocodile book and Orman's *The 9 Steps to Financial Freedom*—is that money can trap you and you must really live life.

Yeah, yeah, yeah. I sort of blow this last bit off as book-ending treacle until I take Cleo and Simon to their annual checkup, and I see their vet's face sadden when he sees Cleo.

Cleo's looking pretty rough. Her liver has grown so large that it's pressing her rib cage out, and the expression on her face can accurately be described as "perpetually bummed out." This time last year, I realize with a start, we were still feeding her regular dog food, going about our business. We didn't even know the end was coming.

GETTING MY FINANCIAL house in order was a worthy cause, I start to conclude, but it's certainly not the way to happiness. For one, it doesn't resolve any questions about the future; I still have no idea how much money we should have for retirement because I still don't know when we're going to die, much less what my return will be or what inflation will look like.

For two, the financial advice did zilch in the Improving My Daily Life department. In fact, I realize that these books are really only a start. In order to invest in a really savvy manner, I'll have to keep up with stocks and mutual funds for the rest of my life. And although this is what David Bach's Smart Couples and Suze Orman's Financially Free People do, staring down a lifetime of reading the financial page makes me tired.

Bach and Orman stand squarely in the mainstream, so I look to someone with a radical plan. Someone who, in fact, has launched a movement. Someone who will not spend much time at all on lattés. These someones are Joe Dominguez and Vicki Robin, authors of *Your Money or Your Life: Transforming Your Relationship with Money and*

Achieving Financial Independence. They are back-to-basics, simplicity-oriented, and on a mission: to give people a plan for living the lives they want to, even during working hours.

Joe Dominguez died in 1997 of lymphoma before the age of sixty. But since both he and Vicki had achieved financial independence (or FI, as they call it), he hadn't held a paying job since he was in his thirties. In fact, neither Dominguez nor Robin have taken any money from this book or for any job since achieving FI, but instead have donated their earnings.

Your Money or Your Life first came out in 1992, and a foreword by Robin reveals that she still stands by their work and has chosen not to update the book for 1999, when it was reissued. As a result, I settle in with the book and feel a little bit like I should be wearing my legwarmers and Cosby sweater. Clearly, the pair wrote the book for readers fresh out of the eighties; there are an awful lot of hot tub mentions. The book is also, I suspect, written for people who have New Age leanings and will find nothing at all funny about, say, this sentence about job-hunting on page 254: "You need to remain conscious during the journey."

Still, I'm intrigued. I decide to read this one straight through because, frankly, I'm not going to once again write out our expenses without a pretty nice reward at the end. Dominguez and Robin warn that nothing in the book will work unless you actually do it, but I want to see what I'm in for first.

The goal for the financially independent, according to this book, is not to have to perform paid work. Money, they claim, is "life energy." If you like your job, fine—you can continue to do it, or even do it on a volunteer basis. If you don't like your job, financial independence can free your time to do the things you want to spend your life doing. Dominguez and Robin provide charts that show readers just how many hours that, statistically, they have left in life, which saddens me when I realized that Joe Dominguez has already found out his specific answer to how many hours he had left and it was a good fifteen years less than he probably thought.

But the plan sounds good. I continue.

How can one achieve this financial independence? Well, if Bach and Orman offered mainstream plans with mainstream results, Dominguez and Robin offer some pretty radical plans to achieve their radical result.

Through a complex system of charting and graphing and writing down every single time you spend money, *Your Money or Your Life* serves up a plan to get your expenses down—way down. Forget the Latté Factor or Orman's simple not-budget in which you transfer funds from one column to the other. Dominguez and Robin expect their readers to question every single cent they spend—the eyes should be on the prize of achieving financial independence.

I shift in the armchair as I read this. On one hand, they offer a chart (they love themselves some charts) that shows a correlation between fulfillment and money spent. They call this the Fulfillment Curve. Our fulfillment rises, they claim, as we move from survival to comforts to luxuries. And that's where the curve peaks. (The peak is called, some-what testily I thought, "Enough.") Beyond that—from luxuries to excess—our fulfillment starts to decline and then our stuff creates "a mountain of clutter that must be stored, cleaned, moved, gotten rid of and paid for on time."

I can agree that there comes a point when there's just too much. I just don't think Brandon and I are there necessarily.

Or I didn't think so until I get to the pair's tips for saving money. Dominguez and Robin try their damnedest to make penny-pinching sound exciting:

"Frugal, man." That's the cool, groovy way to say "far out" in the nineties. Surfers will talk about frugal waves. Teenage girls will talk about frugal dudes. Designers will talk about frugal fashions. Mark our words!

Granted, I know almost no surfers, teenaged girls, or designers, but I'm pretty sure the catchphrase never caught on. And I see why when I look at their list of 101 Sure Ways to Save Money. There's the reasonable "Clip coupons." But they also present "Rent out unused space in your home." FIer Penny Yunuba, they say, moved to the basement of her house and rented out her bedroom. And my personal favorite: "Buy a piece of land and put a used mobile home on it."

All of this makes me want to cry. My people have worked very hard so we don't have to clip coupons, take in boarders, or live in trailers. The clincher comes, though, when I hear about how we can still go out to eat. Mary Yew, an FIer, takes her family out once a week to eat after they go shopping. "For lunch they buy themselves a slice of pizza or a bowl of cream of broccoli soup and then kick back in the restaurant chairs while the snow melts off their boots."

I cannot imagine living a life in which a bowl of cream of broccoli soup is considered an indulgence.

The other thing you do to achieve financial independence is take the money you're saving by living in your used mobile home and invest it. Eventually, this chart you've been making will show that your expense line and the investment income line will cross, and once that happens, voilà! You can now quit your job and live (frugally) off your investment earnings. You invest them by yourself. You invest them not in stocks or mutual funds, but in long-term U.S. treasury and U.S. agency bonds. Bonds? Say what? I'm feeling more and more as if I have to be an expert myself. Alas, I am not.

I CALL RUTH, who does the marketing and advertising for *Brain, Child*. She and her husband have not followed *Your Money or Your Life*, but they did decide that they would chuck a well-paying and high-stress job, a three-thousand-square-foot house in the Atlanta suburbs, and benefits in order to live more simply. For them, more simply meant living in a 1,500-square-foot fixer-upper and drinking the type of wine that comes in jugs. It also meant, Ruth tells me, that said husband could work from home, that their kids were learning their values, and that they all have more time together as a family—which is their biggest priority.

I think of Brandon, who would very much like to work from home, and this all sounds pretty lovely. "But, Ruth," I say, "I read some things in that book that scare me." I tell her about the trailer, the soup, the coupons.

"Hey," she says sharply. "One week I saved sixty dollars in groceries by clipping coupons."

"Nothing wrong with that," I say. "But can you simplify or downsize or whatever without having such an austere lifestyle?"

"I don't think you have to live in a trailer," she says. "But it's not easy. Do I miss the space? Oh yeah. Do I miss having reliable plumbing? And not having to share a bathroom with my adolescent daughter? Do I miss drinking good wine?" She laughs. "Yes! But these are material things. They're . . . inconveniences. We're still living a great life."

I prod. I'm embarrassed to say that even after she painted a fairly complete picture of their life now—poorer but happier, sometimes frustrated but overall pretty damn content—I still poke, trying to find a pocket of regret. *Quality of life? What do you miss? Would you do it again?* The answers: They have double the quality of life (as she defines it), she does miss some stuff, but they'd do it again in a heartbeat. I listen to my own voice and realize that I *want* her to complain. I want her to say that The American Way of Life—that is, the way Brandon and I have been working it—is completely right, and that to veer from it is folly. She's not going to. But then again, she is not conflicted. She is not me.

I stop interviewing Ruth after a while and we chat about Brandon. His job search is not going well. The money-making thing he's good at, which is making factories run more smoothly, is not needed here in factory-free Charlottesville, and we already have one business owner in the family. I'm chasing my tail again.

"So, Jennifer, you sound *really* interested in this. Is this something you're considering doing?" she asks.

"I don't know," I answer honestly. We talk a little longer and then Ruth tells me a story.

"There was a time when John Paul and I had a decision to make. We could either buy a house and start our 'grown-up' lives, or we could do something like go live in New York for a few years or go backpacking across Europe or something crazy," she says. "And we bought the house. We always regretted not living in New York or backpacking across Europe. Because that would have been a really cool experience to have!" It's both as if she's not talking to me, and as if she's trying to get me to look at this decision from all angles because, clearly, I am not quite getting it. "And I think buying the house and later regretting it, in some ways, made the decision to change our lifestyle easier. We didn't want to have anything to regret this time."

Soon we hang up, and I replay our conversation in my head for the rest of the day. I admire Ruth and John Paul and Joe Dominguez and Vicki Robin. They don't just wring their hands. They walk the walk. They're frugal, dude, and I mean that in the very best sense of the word.

IN THE END, I decide to decline doing the *Your Money or Your Life* program. It's not that I think I'm too good to take in boarders or clip coupons or restrict my eating-out to a bowl of cream of broccoli soup. It's just that maybe the Bach and the Orman—the be-sure-you-don't-starve-in-old-age stuff, the can't-touch-your-savings-till-you're-fifty-nine-and-a-half stuff—is too much on my mind. Or maybe it's that I'm simply not evolved enough to sacrifice my eight-dollar cocktails and big house with a big porch. Maybe I am materialistic, or just too much of a mainstream girl. Ruth may call it inconvenience, but I suspect I'd feel denied.

In any case, Brandon thinks he might, too, and I can't undertake this exercise without Brandon's consent. We talk, and Brandon remains unconvinced that a big change in lifestyle would be the silver bullet. We can hang in there longer. We can dream the little dream of finishing rich early and sacrificing nothing.

But something strange has happened by the time I finish reading *Your Money or Your Life*. Christmas is upon us, and I can decide all I want that I'm not doing the program, but the book has indeed affected me. I'm wandering through the stores and I find it nearly impossible to purchase anything that isn't on my shopping list. I pick up a little crafty thing for Caleb—something that makes rubber butterflies—and put it down. I hold up a striped shirt for Brandon for a minute but I see the price—$88—and I hang it back up. I see a fabulous sparkly necklace for myself but I remind myself that I have probably ten necklaces at home. Then I buy it anyway. The ghost of Joe Dominguez is powerful, but not that powerful.

It will take me a full year to really do any investing on my own. After much gnashing of teeth, I choose for my retirement account a type of mutual fund called "target retirement." You invest in a fund that has the year of your expected retirement in its title, and the holdings get progressively more conservative over the years. I find three, and on Etrade.com, I buy into T. Rowe Price Retirement 2035 (stock symbol TTRJX). I buy it with little enthusiasm, only a vague sense of relief that I'm doing what I should. It's also the day I see clearly on my computer screen that, barring unforeseen events, I will never *be* money.

I probably won't ever be comfortable with it, either. I call Erin and dutifully tell her about the mutual funds I invested in, but she's still working on the insurances and the cushion of cash. She's also planning a vacation. David Bach even says that our dreams are what make life worth living, and Erin's dreams are in the present tense.

Mine are, too, I think. I'll decide that thinking about my money, present and future, does not make me happy at all. Financial planning's just too complicated, too fraught, to build happiness on. I found some answers to my uncertainties—we probably have enough for retirement, we probably have more than we deserve, it could slide through our hands pretty fast if we joined the new-style middle class—but "certain" isn't the same as "happy."

The fund I buy owns stock in various companies. I'm neutral on most of them, but at least one—union-busting Wal-Mart—makes me feel very uneasy. On the up side, neither T. Rowe Price nor Etrade gets a commission and, in theory, I will have made a good faith effort to be financially solid in old age.

On the downside, I will become a hypocrite, a form of being an asshole. I'll have to mitigate this somehow.

On to marriage then.

3

The Marriage

S O TELL ME WHAT YOU THINK of our marriage," I demand of Brandon, who is keeping me company on the porch while Caleb examines his Yu-Gi-Oh cards inside.

"Um," he says, eyebrows raised. "Is there something you'd like to say?"

"Marriage," I explain. "It's the next experiment."

"Oh." He stretches back in the chair and considers. "It's . . . pretty good?"

"Babe, it's not a quiz," I say. "What do you wish were different?"

"To be honest, it's not really our marriage. It has to do with . . ." Brandon tilts his head toward the kitchen. A certain someone who would tether himself to his daddy if he could. "I'd like for him to get to sleep by himself. I'd like to spend more time with you alone."

Let's just say that if we were celebrities, there would be few shots of us "canoodling." It's an old, old story by now: Boy meets girl, boy and girl move in together, boy and girl have a baby. Boy and girl spend the next eighteen years gazing across the long expanse of their kid's childhood. There is research that shows that couples' satisfaction with their marriage decreases after parenthood. A study published in the August 2003 issue of the *Journal of Marriage and the Family* showed that, overall, the married-with-kids set report 10 percent less marital satisfaction than childless couples. The researchers, who analyzed data from 148 other studies from as far back as the 1950s, also found middle-class couples experience a 7 percent drop in marital satisfaction. Couples who became parents in the last decade experienced a bigger drop in marital satisfaction with parenthood—twice that of couples in the sixties and seventies.

Brandon and I try to mitigate it. We go out a few times a month to barhop, which may be the single ingenious piece of advice I picked up from a parenting magazine, back when I read them. They didn't say "barhop" specifically—I think it was some sad phrase like "date night." But if holding hands while watching a Hugh Grant movie is applauded, I figured that cocktails and beer followed by Hot Marital Action in the guest room is even better. Moderation is not my strong suit.

"Hey, not to change the subject, but I looked up what's going on this weekend," Brandon says. "Unfortunately . . . nothing."

"That's okay," I say. "There are no babysitters available anyway."

"What about Olivia?" She's a twelve-year-old girl who watches Caleb occasionally. "I think they're back from vacation. I bet after vacation, she'll need some more money."

"Yeah, because she blew it all on the slot machines," I say.

"And liquor."

"And whores."

"I'll give her a shout after—" I start when I notice Cleo starting to heave on the family room rug. I open the door and call, "Cleo! Here, sweetie!" She staggers over and throws up some bile on the porch. She walks away from it and lies on her side near the steps.

"Oh, baby," I say. I rub her distended belly and feel a lumpy scar through her thin skin. She's all liver now, gaunt face and big eyes. Her tail thumps against the wood flooring, and I do my mental calculation again, the same one I've been doing since she was diagnosed: Where is she on the road between sickness and death? Where are we on the road between accepting that she'll die someday and actually deciding that her life should be over on *this* specific day at *this* specific hour?

As usual, I don't know. I look at her—sad-seeming but still spunky, already barking for more treats—and I don't know. Sometimes when I wake up in the morning, before the day really starts, I forget all that I'm responsible for. It's startling when it hits me: family, house, the life and death decision of Cleo, legal, binding contractual obligations. When I first got my driver's license, I had this same feeling. I'm in charge of a vehicle? Something that could *kill* somebody, for God's sakes? Now, a traffic accident isn't the worst thing that could happen on my watch—I shudder to think of all the various ways I could slip up and destroy the lives of those who depend on me.

I sometimes think that we're all bluffing. Yes, this is the way you act like an adult. This is the way you handle your job, your mate, your child, your pets. This is how you hold a piece of someone's life in your hands: You work on instinct because if you stop to consider your responsibility, you will surely choke.

So WE ARE HERE at this marriage experiment, and it's a comfort to me, after landing in the foreign territories of housekeeping and financial planning, to come to marriage, a place that I feel I know pretty well.

Brandon is funny, kind, respectful, smart, fun, and even-tempered. And really quite hot, if I do say so myself. (I once told Stephanie that half the reason I married him was for his dimples, prompting her to ask what the other half was.)

There was a time when I confused drama with excitement, and I spent too much time imagining all the ways the world conspired to drive us apart. Maybe, during my teenage years, I was too taken with Camus and Sartre, too enamored with The Cure, but I didn't know how to reconcile my belief that a person can't ever fully know another with my desire to have a stable, grown-up relationship.

Somehow, I got it all squared away in my head before we had Caleb. There is nothing like year after year passing without incident to convince you that your guy is who he says he is. I still believe that you can't ever fully know another person, but I have somehow made an exception for Brandon. I have to believe that I know him, mostly. This is the good news.

The bad news is that we conduct our marriage entirely in hour-and-a-half sessions (between when Caleb goes to bed and when we go to bed) and on Saturday nights. Sometimes more, but only if I don't have work to do for the house or the magazine. And if neither of us falls asleep with Caleb. I often miss Brandon. He's right—this is the main way our marriage might be better.

I come downstairs to rest my eyes from the computer screen. Brandon follows me into the kitchen and pours a beer for himself. I stand at the sink and drink a glass of water. "Done for the night?" he asks me.

"No, just taking a break," I say, thinking of the illustrators who have to get their assignments tonight so I'll have the art by the time I start layout. "About three more e-mails to write."

He nods.

"Do I take advantage of you?" I ask him. This, possibly, might be another way that our marriage could be better.

"What do you mean?" he asks. Then he raises his eyebrows and smiles. "Do you want to take advantage of me?"

"Yes," I say. "Hubba hubba." I start slicing another handful of grapes. This conversation is not uncharted territory. The last time *Brain, Child* ran a feature on parenting and marriage, I badgered Brandon about How

He Really Felt about the co-parenting we do and about how the labor in our family is split up. It's unlike what either set of our parents did. Most of the time, I feel perfectly good about it, but once in a while, I'm seized by the idea that I've taken it too far, and that instead of co-parenting, I've become the 1950s father in the relationship, spending a lot of time holed up in the study with my metaphorical smoking jacket and memories of The Big Game. "No, really. Do you feel like you do too much?"

"No," Brandon says. "I don't want to be one of those men who works sixteen-hour days and doesn't spend any time with his kid."

Caleb calls for his milk again.

"It would be nice if you didn't have to work so much at night, but that's the way it is," he says. "If you were downstairs, I'd still be here anyway."

Which I take to mean: These are the facts of our life right now, and let's not kid ourselves into thinking we can change who we are.

BUT GUESS WHAT? I am at Barnes & Noble, and the exact thing I'm thinking is that we *can* change who we are—and perhaps our marriage will be the better for it. Sure, it *seems* like a time management issue, but I can picture myself feeling resentful of my time managed in a way that doesn't come naturally to me. But if I could become the sort of wife that wouldn't feel resentful of sacrificing some work time . . . Well, it's not going to kill me to try.

I stalk through the store, on a mission. Me and my man, you understand, deserve no less. First, I pick up an issue of *Cosmopolitan*. It has the annual sex survey and I'd like to understand what five-thousand men have revealed about their secret desires. As I grab the issue, a chubby man holding a coffee cup scuttles out of my way.

Next, I look for Dr. Laura Schlessinger's book *The Proper Care and Feeding of Husbands*. This may seem like an odd choice for me—an avowed liberal—but I'd heard from unlikely sources that Schlessinger is kind of a hoot and actually makes sense once in a while. Plus, I'm looking for something to rock my world a little, not just give me my own world back in soothing therapeutic sound bites.

I find Dr. Laura in the Relationships section. It's the first time I've picked up a book from this section and I blush. I smirk. Again, a man—this one petite and thumbing through a different book from Relationships—jumps back as I hightail it out of Relationships and into the safety of the paid book displays.

I dodge the New Fiction looky-loos, the Valentine's Day tender-hearts, the magazine gazers, all wandering the aisles with much less purpose than I. I make my way to the checkout line. It's a Tuesday night and two cashiers are available.

"—I'm pretty sure there's an FBI file on me, then," says one cashier, a mild-looking woman in her early twenties. "Can they do that to private citizens?"

"It's the *FBI*," explains the other cashier. He's a pasty guy with unfortunate eyewear, and his excitement at being able to share his knowledge of governmental institutions and their legislated domains and purposes to this woman—this wild thing, this *breaker of the law*—is palpable. "It's their *job*."

They notice me, and I slide my *Cosmo* and Dr. Laura book toward the woman cashier. "Really?" she asks the guy. "I thought it was just, you know, international suspects."

"That's CIA," he says. They continue chatting, the transaction on autopilot.

Then the atmosphere changes. Anyone could sense that the cashier has noticed exactly what I'm buying. "So, ma'am," she says slowly. "Do you have a Barnes & Noble card?"

It's not so much what she says but how she says it. Like I am perhaps the saddest person in the world, the woman who has somehow managed to reach her thirties and yet *still* failed to pick up on either old-school matron tips or the kinky stuff that men won't tell you.

"I do have a card," I say, and she instructs me—again, *slowly*—how to run it through the machine. I'm grateful when the book and magazine are tucked into the bag, as if the canonical writers illustrated on it have anything to do with my purchase.

My ears are on fire as I slide back into my car. "Damn it," I say. I buckle in. What do I care what they think? Why do I feel so ashamed?

It dawns on me why—because this is the shameful variety of self-help. While we Americans want to make ourselves better, we also love the idea of natural beauty, inherent genius, out-of-the-box charisma. Romance falls into that category of things we should just know how to do. I throw the car into drive and pull out of the lot. To make myself feel better, I think, *FBI file, my ass.*

At home, I start my reading. And I realize, almost instantly, that I'm not the right demographic for *Cosmo*. The sex survey asked men multiple-choice questions like "What can a woman do that'll make you cross the room and introduce yourself?" and "How do you react when a woman flat-out hits on you at a bar?" Nothing for me here unless Brandon falls victim to amnesia or leaves me. I'm more interested in the nitty-gritty—say, "What kind of kiss causes an immediate uprising in your pants?"

Caleb sidles up to me on the couch.

"Why, hello," I say. I shut the magazine and flip it over.

"Hi." Caleb looks down at the shampoo ad on the back. "Mama, is that woman alive?" he asks.

"Yeah," I say.

"I mean, is she real?" he presses. "Is she a living creature?"

"I'm pretty sure she is," I say, looking at the severely airbrushed model.

"Because she looks fake."

"Yeah, you know, she does, doesn't she?" I fold the magazine in half. On the front cover are the bold-faced taglines "SEX SURVEY" and "Love Being Naked!" He can sort of read now and, furthermore,

I don't really need a six-year-old who "loves" to be naked. I put the magazine on top of the refrigerator.

I CAN HEAR BRANDON snoring when I tiptoe out of the bedroom that night, so it's just Dr. Laura and me. We are, I find out, two people who should probably not be left alone together.

I can say that *The Proper Care and Feeding of Husbands* has its moments of common sense. It's made up almost entirely of anecdotes—Karen who does marriage right, Tina who does it wrong, Douglas who offers sex advice, Bruce who feels micromanaged—culled from Schlessinger's call-in radio show and from her private practice. Her premise is that men ("simple creatures") need "the three A's" from their mothers, then their wives:

Acceptance,

Approval,

Appreciation.

(These should not be confused with the other "three A's"—addictions, abuse, and affairs—that Dr. Laura says should be deal-breakers.)

If husbands are treated nicely, they'll, in turn, treat wives nicely, and the wives will then be amazed at the positive changes in their lives. "They see progress! They feel powerful! They are happier!" Schlessinger writes in her author's note. And all this can be yours after just five days of trying one "hint" from this book.

But then it gets sticky. Because the "hints"—or some might say, "threats," or "commandments from on high"—are girded with strange ideas.

For example, Dr. Laura advises women not to nag. Okeydoke. No adult outside of the BSDM community likes to be bossed around. But then she suggests that the reader, instead of nagging her husband every five minutes to take the trash out, ask him to do it once—and when he does, thank him for carrying the big, heavy bag out. She should also—*and this is very important*—French him on his way back, as a reward. "Which approach do you think will ensure that the trash is out of your kitchen every night like clockwork?"

I got distracted at this point, wondering what's going on in that house that the inhabitants fill up an entire bag of trash every night and why an able-bodied woman couldn't carry it out herself and why, for that matter, a sloppy kiss should be such a big deal between two adults in a long-term romantic relationship.

Or, in Chapter 7, Dr. Laura says that men deserve respect. Well, of course, right? We all do. But then she gets into Mars and Venus territory:

> It is more in the female nature to nest and nurture. It is more in the male nature to conquer and protect. . . . Most all of the women who call me who have reversed the traditional societal roles . . . are troubled by the fact that they seem to have less regard for their husbands as "men." Likewise, they report a diminished sense of their own femininity, and suffer ferocious guilt over not being their children's primary caretaker.

So, it's disrespectful to expect Brandon to pull his weight as a parent? And it should make me feel *girlish* to give up my job? Why, yes. Dr. Laura, offering herself up as a role model, says, "I work my career around my family—and not the other way around." (It goes without saying that her husband does not.) She adds, "As long as women disrespect what they have to offer as wives and mothers, they will continue to disrespect their men who serve as husbands and fathers. No one benefits. No one is happy." Yikes.

Brandon comes downstairs to get an aspirin, looking sleepy, his hair mussed. Looky here! A real live man unexpectedly in the family room! He sits down next to me, and Simon walks over and nuzzles his socked feet. "Hey, there," I say.

"How's the book?" he asks.

"Well, it's coming. Do you mind if I ask you some questions?"

"Go for it."

I flip to the chapter on men's feelings. The way Dr. Laura sees it, there's an epidemic of "gender abuse"—women ignoring men's feelings—and she sets out to let women know what men need.

"Okay, this is what she says men have told her," I tell Brandon. "You tell me if this is true for you or not."

He nods.

I'm careful to keep any inflection, any note of judgment out of my voice. I read:

A man needs to feel strong and needed as a protector for women—basically, to conquer the beast and rescue the fair maiden.

"Huh?" he says, now woken up. "Conquer the *beast*?"

"Do you feel like you need to protect me, in other words."

"Slay the dragon! Take out my big long sword and swing it around!" He gets up and refills his water glass. "Admire my powerful saber, woman!"

"Seriously, Bran," I say.

"Okay. I don't know," he says.

I continue:

What every man wants is for his woman to make him feel that he is strong and the head of the household. I am not talking caveman-style, dragging the woman around by her hair, but just as the leader of the family.

"That just sounds so stereotypical," Brandon says. "It sounds like something from a Jeff Foxworthy sketch."

"Hey, that's who I kept picturing, too!" I say. I did. What I don't say is that I also kept picturing my own parents, long before they divorced, raising kids in a small town. My father, who in fact had a Foxworthy-style mustache, worked as a shop teacher and machinist. My mother, one of those feminists Schlessinger deplores, stayed home with us. They arranged their marriage very much along the Schlessinger-prescribed lines, and for more than a decade at least, it was a happy marriage.

A few more questions with predictable answers from Brandon and then I come to this:

A man needs his woman to show him that she needs his strength to help her through life.

"You're a grown woman. No."

The man should be the major breadwinner in the family. Every man needs a battle or war to win to prove to himself that he is strong and capable of conquering any and all dragons that life throws his way. Taking care of his family by working and providing are his battles.

"What is *up* with this dragon stuff?" he says. "I have a mighty battle ax! Let me unsheath my sword and thrust it at you, maiden!"

"Your answer?"

"No," he says.

I laugh, but it occurs to me that it's all fun and games, until you consider all the people Dr. Laura's not addressing. I wonder what my friend Hailie and her partner Cara would make of this sort of thinking—that men and women are terribly different yet complementary creatures. This is the sort of cultural idea that, for them, has ramifications way outside their partnership—from dirty looks to legal discrimination.

I read:

A man needs enthusiastic approval, appreciation, and respect from his wife for being a competent man, husband, and father.

"It would be nice," Brandon says. "I don't know about all this 'need' though. It's an awfully strong way of putting it."

I concur but continue with a few more of Schlessinger's findings. I clear my throat.

"Last one," I say.

A man needs his wife's encouragement in order to be a man.

Brandon frowns. "Does that make any sense to you? So let's say a man's wife doesn't encourage him. He would be . . . what? A boy? A woman?"

I shrug. "A dragon?"

"He'd still be a man!"

I put down the book. We watch *The Daily Show* and head upstairs. We brush our teeth and I pull him close to me. I'm going to try one of *Cosmo*'s kissing tricks that is likely, in 39 percent of men surveyed, to cause an "uprising": I'm supposed to press my lips softly to his, pull back and smile, then kiss him some more.

I press my lips to his. Then, with what I'd like to think of as a mysterious smile, I pull back and look up into his eyes.

"What's up?" he asks.

"Nothing," I say. "I was just trying a *Cosmo* kiss."

"You're playing mind games with me," he says. Clearly, he does not like it.

I don't really have anything to say to that. I feel bad for manipulating him. Hurriedly we kiss—regular, no tricks—and lie down in bed.

Brandon falls asleep almost immediately, but I can't get comfortable. There is someone else in the bed with us. Someone other than Caleb.

It's Dr. Laura. I sense her there between us, her presence barely registering—but registering nonetheless. *I know men,* she's breathing through her gigantic white teeth. *I know* your *man.* Ten-plus years of learning to lose my suspiciousness, ten-plus years of trying to accept that maybe the other boot won't drop after all, ten-plus years of trusting that Brandon is who he says he is—and, now, in a little under four hours, Dr. Laura has weaseled in and planted doubt.

She wants to be the interpreter between husbands and wives. This whole book is her résumé for the job. *No matter what he says,* she hisses, *I know the truth and it ain't as pretty as you think it is, sister.* I turn on my side and listen to Brandon and Caleb sleeping. I know better—I do— than to let her get stuck in my head, but there she is, crafting her next anecdote. It's about Jennifer and Brandon. And we all know whose fault it will turn out to be.

I WISH I COULD REPORT that I wake up refreshed and Dr. Laura is no longer between me and my husband, but alas I cannot. I let down my guard, I tell myself. I got confused between her ideas that make sense and those that are out-and-out bizarre. After I get Caleb on the school bus, I tear off my mittens, feed Simon, put Cleo's breakfast on the stove to cook, and head for the book. I'm looking for reassurance that she is wrong and I am right.

Here, on page 32: "These days, so many young women . . . were indoctrinated by the anti-family feminists throughout their schooling . . ." Hah! What antifamily feminists? The married mothers who were my teachers, does she mean?

And on page 121: "[M]en forgive easier and are more easily corrected in their behaviors with positive feedback than women are." What kind of patronizing nonsense is that?

And on page 54: "Women have a hunger to be protected and cared for—whether they want to admit it or not." One of us does have Daddy issues, Laura, and it's not me.

I flip through and find that perhaps the most troubling thing about Dr. Laura is that she clearly does not like women as much as she likes men. Sure, she tells stories about women who are "smart" (read: they make Schlessinger-approved decisions), but in general, she's not willing to cut women any slack. They are always the real problem. Women should not gain weight or dress frumpily; meanwhile, it's insulting to a man to tell him that you'd prefer he didn't grow a beard. Men's jobs are done in the service of their families, while women's—if taken "too far"—are a selfish indulgence. "Women's groups" are poisonous to a marriage while men need time with the guys. I could go on.

Reading *The Proper Care* uncritically, you get sucked into this weird Boys vs. Girls mentality, which seems to me to be the opposite of what a marriage manual should do. Worse, because Dr. Laura herself is so abrasive, you can get sucked into rooting against Dr. Laura's team: the men. I had to remind myself that this is *Brandon* we're talking about, my best friend. This dichotomy that Schlessinger sets up is actually harmful to a marriage.

And yet. And yet. There is something that still nags at me. I think back to last night. Did I ask Brandon the Schlessinger-based male ego questions earnestly? Or, despite my best efforts, was there a touch of derision in my voice? Why did Brandon answer so jokingly? Was he telling the truth or just agreeing with me?

I flip through the book and look again at Schlessinger's second chapter, entitled "The White Rabbit Syndrome," in which women are so busy that their husbands feel that they are not priorities in their ladies' lives. For all of her bizarre proclamations, Schlessinger's genius is that she can really push some buttons. My buttons. Could I be like . . . oh, Suzanne, the real estate agent whose husband resents that she works on evenings and weekends? Does Brandon feel he's not a priority in my life?

I DECIDE TO TRY TWO HINTS for five days. One is pretty minor: I'll greet Brandon when he comes home, wearing lipstick and having recently freshened my breath.

The other one will be difficult: I will not work at night. I don't always work at night anyway, but two-thirds of the time I do, because if I didn't, the magazine would not get finished in time. Brandon, I think, is constitutionally incapable of issuing an ultimatum (as Suzanne the real estate agent's husband did) between divorce and my quitting my job. But we'll see if this making him Priority Number One—and helping out with Caleb at night—has any effect on either of us.

DAY 1. It's a Sunday and I'm a little hung over from an especially vigorous Saturday night barhopping while Caleb was with a sitter. I refrain from working, although I probably should work since we're nearing the end of production. Brandon, Caleb, and I spend the day watching movies and halfheartedly tidying up the house. It's a fortunate two-birds-with-one-stone thing: I don't feel like working and, thanks to the experiment, I can justify lying around with the fam.

DAY 2. I'm talking to my mother on the phone and searing some tuna for tonight's salad when I notice the time. "Gotta go, Mom!" I say. "I'm doing Dr. Laura and I have to go put some lipstick on!"

"Hey!" she says. "I used to do that—the lipstick—when I was married to your father!"

I hang up, race upstairs and rinse my mouth out with Listerine. I run back downstairs and flip the tuna. I hurriedly smear on some lipstick. I run back into the kitchen to drain the hard-boiled eggs. I hear Brandon's car in the driveway, run into the bathroom to check my lipstick, and discover that I know whatever happened to Baby Jane. I blot. I run into the kitchen and take the tuna out of the frying pan. Brandon opens the door. "Hello!" I call. We kiss.

After dinner, Caleb decides he wants to play a game, and he chooses the Chicken Soup for the Family Soul board game, a gag gift that Brandon bought me toward the beginning of this self-help quest. ("What?" I said. "Whoever weeps first wins?") It takes a long time to set up and then we're uncertain we're playing it right. Caleb wins by a landslide, although it should be noted that he gets to play the ridiculously easy kid cards.

Cleo, who knows exactly who butters her bread, barks at me constantly throughout the evening, but she refuses the different foods I press on her.

The three of us watch *SpongeBob*, then retire for the night.

Overall, a nice evening.

DAY 3. I master the lipstick routine by making dinner in the crockpot. When Brandon comes home, we eat our stew. It's then I start to itch to get upstairs. I have to finish going through the layout and making the proofreading changes that Debie handed in earlier that day.

It's starting to snow out. It's not sticking, but eight o'clock already looks like the dead of night. Caleb plays a game on the computer and Brandon settles down with an investment newsletter. I pick up a *New Yorker* and flop down on the couch. "So," I say. "You guys want to do anything?"

"Sure, if you want to," Brandon says.

"No!" Caleb protests. "I just started this game!"

"Okay, okay, calm yourself down," I say to Caleb. "What do you want to do?" I ask Brandon.

"I don't know," he says.

Come on now, I think. You're the priority here. "Me neither," I say.

We sit there for a minute.

"How was your day?" I ask him.

He looks up from the newsletter. "Fine. Busy," he says. "How was your day?"

"Good," I say. Jesus, this is boring. Brandon seems exactly the same amount of happy as he always does. I, on the other hand, am feeling twitchy, housebound, and unproductive.

He goes back to his newsletter, I go back to the *New Yorker*. Eventually, Caleb finishes his game and I run some water for his bath. "Sure you don't want me to do that?" Brandon asks.

"Oh, no," I say. I consider adding one of Dr. Laura's favorite phrases—*My hero*—but I'm pretty sure that Brandon would think I'm being sarcastic.

I'm having a little difficulty here, I realize, in figuring out exactly how to show Brandon that he's a priority. On one hand, Schlessinger cautions against my throwing too much of myself into child care; on the other hand, she's a big proponent of "fixed roles." In her eyes, Brandon's done his main job (of making most of the money for the household) for the day, and he probably deserves a break. But he also deserves some time with me. For someone who poo-poos the idea of "doing it all," Schlessinger's expectations of me are awfully high.

After Caleb's bath, we watch a little TV. I insist on cuddling with Caleb to give Brandon some space to relax; Caleb insists on cuddling with Brandon. We wind up all cuddling together—or, more accurately, smushed together on the love seat.

Cleo continues her barking campaign at me but still refuses food; Simon reaps the benefits. I start to wonder when the benefits of the Dr. Laura test will start kicking in. Brandon and I both fall asleep that night with Caleb.

DAY 4. Turns out, the snow did stick a little, and there's a two-hour delay at Caleb's school. Which means that all the work I didn't do last night has to be squeezed into an even more abbreviated workday today. Even under normal, non-Schlessinger circumstances, Brandon wouldn't take time off. It hits me that in our give-and-take, the unspoken rule is that I—with my flexible self-employment—take sick days and snow days, and that he—with his corporate job that will lay you off just as soon as look at you—will help me make up for lost time. This makes sense for us, I'm realizing, regardless of what the book says. Still, I'm reluctant to give up before the five-day test period is over. If I don't give it a fair shake, I won't really know who knows Brandon better: me or Dr. Laura.

By the time Caleb gets on the school bus, the snow has nearly melted and everything is wet and muddy. I bust ass to get as much work done as I can, and soon it's time to meet Caleb at the bus stop. "What was your favorite part of today?" I ask him when he gets off.

"No part," Caleb says darkly. "We missed PE."

"I'm sorry to hear that," I say.

I do the lipstick and mouthwash thing, and I order dinner in tonight, chicken and broccoli and shrimp fried rice. I greet Brandon, we eat, we retire to the living room. *Just one more day*, I tell myself. There have been no noticeable changes in my marriage. I offer at every turn to take over some of the "nurturing and nesting." *Why don't you play a game with Mama? Let's let Daddy rest a little. No, I don't like tying flies, but we can all do a puzzle! I know—let's make some banana bread!* I offer Brandon some "warm looks" (the nonverbal communication that Schlessinger proposes replace a wife's "onslaught of verbiage and emotion"). I feel a little like Kelly McGillis in *Witness*, eyeing Harrison Ford shyly from under my bonnet.

The thing is, this is just not what we *do* in our family, and I see now that there's a reason for it. Caleb wants *Brandon* during this time of the evening, and Brandon gets a chance to catch up with Caleb. It's hard to reconcile this regular father/son time with Dr. Laura's worldview. Brandon also gets to read his mail, his magazines, his newsletters. I find myself hanging around like the Ghost of Christmas Past. Meanwhile, there is a backlog of work upstairs, just waiting. Later, months later, I'll bring up this Dr. Laura experiment at a dinner party, and Brandon will reveal that he *didn't even know* I was doing an experiment.

We sit there and Cleo starts barking. I look over at her and suddenly there it is:

I have been, for eight months, living under the assumption that her barking, her begging, her wheedling for food was a sign of her spunk, her zest for life.

Now, I see that she barks and her tail does not wag. Her liver has pushed her ribs out and she's shedding flaky bits of dandruff, a sign of starvation. Those eyes of hers look desperate, not spunky. *I'm in bad shape*, they say. *Can you not see this?* Oh, God.

"Oh, Brandon," I say. "She's suffering."

He looks from Cleo to me. I know what he's thinking.

"It's time," I say. There is no consultation here. There is no pretending that Brandon can protect us from the death of our beagley girl. There is no question that I will need his strength, but that right now, it's my strength—if you will call it strength—that will lead us to do the humane thing.

"Tomorrow?" he says.

I nod, shocked that our decision has come like this, so fast.

There's no good way to explain euthanasia to a six-year-old, so tomorrow, Brandon will pretend to go to work. I will slyly encourage Caleb to give Cleo some loving before he heads off to school. I will not tell Caleb it'll be the last time he sees Cleo. Brandon will come home. I'll call the vet. Brandon and I both will cry and love on our girl dog in the hour and a half between the phone call and the appointment. I will realize that I am lucky to have Brandon, but he is lucky to have me, too. Dr. Laura is no longer between us—there's no room for her to squeeze in among Brandon, me, and the dragon that is our sadness.

THERE'S SOMETHING WRONG with me. Brandon is red-eyed and Cleo is shivering and Simon is mooning around confused, and I cannot stop the weird pop culture festival that's mushrooming in my head. I woke up this morning feeling normal until I remembered what today would hold. Dread is still what I mostly feel, but that does not stop the thoughts. *We kill more dogs before ten a.m. than most people do all day*. I lift Cleo into the backseat of the car and in my head there's Johnny Cash, crooning a cover of a Nine Inch Nails song. *I will let you down; I will make you hurt*. I am asking Brandon if I should stop for gas—we really are in danger of running out of fuel on the way there—and he's saying, "Yeah, it's probably better to do it now than later." I'm telling him okay, but the whole while I'm thinking of the Doors: *This is the end, beautiful friend. . . . No safety or surprise, the end*.

Cleo is no fool; she knows something's up and she acts odd. She roots around on the car floor for crumbs, of which there are plenty, and tries skittishly to jump up into the front seat with us. She's unwieldy, bigger than a lap dog even without the extra mass of liver, but Brandon holds her on his lap and whispers, "It's okay, it's okay." I give Brandon a sad smile. I would like to think that it *is* okay. I know intellectually that this is the best thing, but I can't shake the feeling that no matter when or how it comes, death is not okay, and, furthermore, Brandon and I should feel a little ashamed to be complicit in this death.

At the gas station, Cleo's anxiety escalates and she tries to escape. Finally, at the vet's parking lot, Brandon takes her leash and the three of us wend our way inside.

"We're here with Cleo," I tell the receptionist, and I watch her face fall as she looks at Cleo's file.

We stand there for a few minutes. Brandon takes my elbow and points out that I just stepped in a puddle of pee on the floor. I shrug. Eventually someone leads us back into the room—a regular exam room, not a special kill-your-pet room like I'd imagined, and someone else asks, "Here for a checkup today?" Neither Brandon nor I respond.

I'm happy to see that today we have Dr. Fietz, the Nicest Veterinarian in the Entire World. He usually gives the dogs little kisses when he examines them. "Hi," he says somberly to Brandon and me. He shakes my hand. "I'm sorry," he says.

"I just can't get her to eat," I say. I tear up and have a vision of myself as enacting a scene from a Lifetime: Television for Women Who Enjoy Melodramatic Television movie. I forget to introduce Brandon.

Dr. Fietz explains how this will go down: Cleo will get a sedative; we will wait ten minutes. "And then . . . ," he says, "basically, it's an overdose of anesthesia."

I nod. Brandon nods. Dr. Fietz leaves to get the drugs. Cleo sniffs around the room and hides under a wooden bench. We take turns coaxing her out, petting her, crying. It's the first time I have no idea what to say to Brandon. "Oh, Cleo Leo," I say. "Remember that time you ate a whole pizza?"

Brandon laughs. Ruefully. In fact everything we do in this room could be described as "rueful." I ruefully sit on the bench and rub her velvety ears. Brandon ruefully blows his nose. We ruefully hug each other. We ruefully tell Cleo more anecdotes about herself.

"Remember when we first saw you? Standing there like a little ballerina with your front paws turned out?"

"Remember when you ate all the shrimp out of the fridge before Caleb's birthday party?"

"Remember when you jumped up and licked my tears when I was crying?"

These anecdotes, admittedly, don't sound like much. It's the last day of the rest of her life, I think. And we're talking about what she ate and her interactions with *us*. Is that what it comes down to?

Dr. Fietz returns with the sedative and pulls Cleo out from under the bench to administer it. She becomes a bit unsteady on her feet, a sad little drunk. She eventually lies down on the floor, her head on her paws. Dr. Fietz and a technician come back in the room. The technician produces a towel, rolls it up, and puts it under Cleo's head.

"Are you ready?" Dr. Fietz asks.

Brandon and I look at each other. We nod.

We arrange ourselves on the linoleum tile around Cleo. I'll realize later that I hogged Cleo's head: I was the last person she saw before she died. Brandon—the person whose return home, even when she wouldn't budge from the couch all day, was the absolute highlight of her day—gets her tail end. We both rub her and say, "I love you, Cleo. I love you, sweet girl" over and over. *Famous last words.*

Dr. Fietz injects a pink liquid into her leg. He leans and listens to her heart with his stethoscope. After a minute or two, he nods soberly. "Take as much time as you want," he tells us. He leaves. The technician hands us a box of tissues and follows Dr. Fietz.

Cleo's dead but she doesn't look dead. I've seen her like this her whole life, dozing on the floor, eyes slightly open. "Oh, Brandon," I say.

"Oh, Jen," he says.

I pet her. Brandon pets her. We stare at her. I unlatch her collar, lift it from her neck, and put it in my purse. We get up and hug. We blow our noses. We're silent.

Finally, I ask Brandon, "Do you want to stay a little longer?"

We both look at Cleo's body on the floor.

"I guess not," he says. "We already said good-bye."

We did. I can't say good-bye any longer, but I'm not sure that I feel right leaving her just yet. But what's there to do? Carry her around with us as we go about our business? Now that she's dead, I think, we could take her to all the places she—a barker, a leash-puller, a general raiser of ruckus—couldn't go when she was alive: outdoor cafés, the playground, business meetings. "Yeah, this could turn into a *Weekend at Bernie's* type situation," I say.

We leave. I drive and we cry in the car. At home, we alternate between crying and acting normal.

We are lucky people, Brandon and I. This is the only death that we've been major players in, and she is, after all, a dog—a creature whose life span is short. We've known people who died and it was immeasurably more wrenching than this, but we had only to mourn. We didn't orchestrate it or pay for it; we didn't think about what we were going to do with the body or how we would tell people. We grieved, and that was our only job.

We drive downtown later for lunch. "I can't believe she's gone," I say. I look at Brandon across the booth; he has dark half-moons under his eyes and he's spearing a bite of meat loaf, and I think fleetingly, Together, we decided to kill a creature we loved.

"I miss her," he says.

We don't say much more. It's not that I'm afraid to, exactly. But I look at Brandon and feel shy about telling him that this morning I whispered to Cleo that she can visit me when she wants to. He doesn't believe in things like the ghostly return of spirits. I also don't tell him that when we were walking back up the porch steps, I was hit with a gigantic feeling of peace that I can only describe as the sensation you get right before falling into a really good nap, and that this feeling is somehow related to Cleo. It would be wrong to blather on about these things. Brandon contemplates; I barrel through with analysis and inappropriate thoughts and talking, talking, talking. This moment, this day, is not about me, and in a rare exercise of restraint, I keep quiet.

Later that afternoon while Brandon dozes, I meet Caleb at the school bus. He bounds down the sidewalk, backpack clanging against his butt. "Can I call Joey over?" he asks.

"Uh, no, sweetie," I say. "I have some bad news."

"What?" he asks.

"I'll tell you when we get inside," I say. I don't know how he'll react and I don't want a scene in the street.

But he notices Brandon's car in the driveway. His face registers panic as he looks from the car to me, me to the car. "Daddy's fine," I say quickly.

"Just tell me."

"Well, come on in."

"Tell me."

We head up the stairs—*just tell me, tell me, tell me, Mama.* The door clicks shut and I blurt it out: "Honey, Cleo died today."

"Is she here?"

"No."

I expect him to cry or yelp or, at minimum, consent to a hug, but instead he walks into the living room. Brandon follows him in there. "You okay, partner?" Brandon asks.

"I want to be alone," Caleb says.

A few minutes later, I go check on him. He's sitting on the couch, staring off into space. "I want to be alone, I *said*," he huffs at me.

"Okay," I say. "But you can talk to me. You know that, right? I can give you hugs." He glowers and I leave.

Fifteen uncomfortably silent minutes later, I announce loudly to Brandon, who's lying on the couch, "You know what I want to do, Brandon? I want to eat some of Cleo's favorite foods as a *snack* this afternoon!"

"Hey, that's an *awesome* idea!" he replies loudly. "I do, too!"

"And then I'd like to tell some *stories* about her!"

"That sounds like a *great* way to remember Cleo!"

We both belong in a remedial acting class, but we start trading stories about Cleo, and pretty soon, Caleb peeks his head around the corner. He contributes the tale about the time she ate the pizza. The three of us decide that we are not hungry for unseasoned ground meat and semifrozen green beans after all. But we would like to make a Cleo-themed photo album. So we do.

IT HAS BEEN winter for far too long now, and I am not in a good place. Let's call it Crankyville—you come for your dog's death, but you stay for the crankiness, the distractibility, the sense that nothing will ever change. The floors will always bear small puddles of dirty melted snow and you will always step in them in your socked feet. Children never speak in anything but a whine. All e-mails are filled with problems you must solve. Your mate—as God is your witness—will never, ever unload the dishwasher.

I cannot be especially nice for very long at a stretch. I hate myself when I'm like this, but it's as if I can't help myself. For example, Brandon and I happened to go out one evening after The Game. (We live in a college town. The Game is everpresent.) After the third grown man I see wearing bright orange pants (one of the team colors), I nudge Brandon and say, "Nice show of spirit." Brandon laughs. But as these spirited revelers start to clog our bars, I have trouble keeping my snide comments to myself. A group of women and men with strong Joisey accents sprawl out in front of the bar at Rapture, each wearing some hideous orange-and-blue ensemble. One woman in particular has the shrill, semi-hysterical voice of Edith Bunker, and I can barely concentrate on my conversation with Brandon, on the one night of the week that we get to be together alone.

"I said to my girlfriend! I said to her!" she shrieks, "you better buy that house now! The prices are going to just keeping going up! You don't want to be priced out of the market!"

Seated at the bar, I shriek to Brandon, "I says to my girlfriend! Why do I talk like a stereotype of a Joisey woman! Why, girlfriend! Why!"

Brandon gives me a look. I am unable to stop myself. If she starts talking about jewelry, I'm going to lose it, I think.

It's not jewelry. "Do you know they opened a new Nordstrom's! Five minutes from the house!" The shoes! The petites section!

"This is driving me insane," I say to Brandon. Clearly, he's not nearly as bothered as I am. He smiles tightly. I am ruining our evening out.

I can't seem to shake this on-edge mood. To try to center myself, I pull out all the stops: I play "Ice, Ice, Baby"; I take a half hour in the morning to drink tea and listen to peppy music; I pet Simon, who seems to like being the center of attention now that Cleo's gone. Nothing. There's no amount of white-boy rap, Lady Grey, or Simon-love that can change the fact that it's too dark all the time and I'm always cold and that the only thing to look forward to is more of the same: work, clean, sleep, drink, eat, caregive. I barely feel motivated enough to do the work I'm getting paid to do; there is no way I can lug myself into another experiment.

I can't blame the mood all on Dr. Laura, but she does leave a residual bitter taste. The sort of taste you get when you know you've been taken. So far, all the experts I've consulted have been genuine, meaning I really believe that they all think they're helping their readers. Dr. Laura, I come to think, has no such guiding light. I cannot believe I let someone with such clear contempt for women get in my head. Do you know that scene in *Ghost* where the dead middle-aged man jumps into Whoopi Goldberg's body and talks to his wife about her new hair dye ("Do you like it?" she asks) until Whoopi wrests him out of there? Remember the look on Whoopi's face, one of disgust and anger with a dose of the heebie-jeebies? That, I'm afraid, is the look on my face as I wrest Dr. Laura from my psyche.

I wait—weeks—for this mood to lift a little. The mornings get lighter. The weather gets warmer. The snow melts and I take a week off from work between issues of *Brain, Child*. Slowly, I feel normal enough to resume the experiments, and I turn to someone who bills himself as Mr. Direct, Mr. How's-That-Working-For-Ya: Dr. Phil McGraw.

Oprah protégé, Texan straight shooter, TV psychologist, he's the author of the best-selling tomes *Life Strategies: Doing What Works, Doing What Matters* and *Relationship Rescue: A Seven-Step Strategy for Reconnecting with Your Partner*. Dr. Laura wanted to be the interpreter between Brandon and me, but that didn't work. Now I'm looking for a program that gives us more of a reason to stay up and talk instead of hunkering down under the covers and falling asleep with Caleb. In *Relationship Rescue*, Dr. Phil claims that he, in fact, has that kind of program.

Phil, the mustachioed man of both therapy and controversy. I'm of two minds about him: On the one hand, he deeply annoys me. I suspect that there's something very wrong with a person who arranges his show to always play The Hero. I know people who know people who were on his Working Mother vs. At-Home Mother show, and these people informed me that he staged a catfight between women who really have no problems with one another—so he could swoop in and be the voice of reason.

On the other hand, I love me some swooping in—there is something deeply satisfying about seeing a problem tossed up into the air and swatted down, solved, with some McGraw-styled straight talk. It's entertainment, and it's also vaguely therapeutic—if not for the alleged patients, then for the viewing audience. Plus, Oprah likes him, and I like Oprah.

I open the book and see exactly what I'm in for: Phil promises to make you and your partner answer the hard questions. Why? Because it's the only way a person can turn back into the centered, excellent person he or she once was.

He goes on, "Tapping into your core of consciousness, rediscovering your inner strength and drive for greatness, can be the single most significant act of your life, and your greatest gift to your relationship partner."

In other words, following this program, you can be happy (and powerful and centered), and your happiness will result in a good relationship. Sounds good!

I'm reading *Relationship Rescue* one afternoon while Caleb and his friends play upstairs; Phil uses the phrase "relationship gone awry" and I'm suddenly overcome with some emotional déjà vu. I know exactly what he's talking about. You're chugging along and out of nowhere realize that things have taken a confusing turn for the worse and that you can only hang on, helpless, until the final anticlimactic breakup. It's a terrible, sinking feeling. (Only much later can you analyze what went wrong. No, I'm not your ex-girlfriend. No, I can't pretend that I enjoy your company for much longer. No, I will never be tiny and blonde and helpless-acting.)

Not that I'm there now. But does this mean Dr. Phil's book doesn't apply to me? Oh, no—it applies. Brandon and I, by my figuring, score a 6 on the Relationship Health Profile. This means that our marriage is "well above the norm"—but we "may have isolated areas in which we can improve." What's more, the fourteen-day program should be "meaningful" to us—"for [it] will reinforce those building blocks that make a relationship strong."

And plain old reading isn't going to cut it: *"You have to have a program,"* Dr. Phil writes emphatically. This program will be unlike anything else, because Dr. Phil desperately wants you to understand that *he is not like other marital therapists.* He'll have you know that he's all about the results, not so much the "insights." He is the New Millennium Marriage Guy: "real," unpretentious, bald, and Christian. (Well, Christian-ish, given his blasé attitude toward infidelity.)

As in Dr. Laura's book, most of the advice is targeted to the reader and the reader alone. In fact, you'll find that the vast majority of chapters don't even require your partner's participation. Dr. Laura would say that it's because the problem is with you, the woman. While Dr. Phil would agree that you're responsible for whatever problems you might be suffering—because, he says, you "generated and adopted a lifestyle to sustain" whatever sort of relationship you're in and because both partners are "one hundred percent accountable"—he's more pragmatic: You're the person who picked up the book. Phil issues warnings throughout that this will not be easy.

He's right. I start the book in the afternoon and am dismayed to find that by Caleb's bedtime at 8:30, I haven't made it past page 37. I'm having to stop along the way and take quizzes, fill in the blanks, and "journal" on various topics (for example, "Describe your sexual relationship with your partner . . ." or "Knowing what you now do about your relationship, would you still get involved with the same person if you had to do it all over again? Why?" This is all in the service of defining the problem in my relationship. The problem, I once thought, is that we perhaps have too much packed into our lives, which leaves us tired and with not as much time as we'd like with each other. The time that we do have, we're often sleepy. But maybe the problem—it's heavily suggested—is me. All this figuring out takes longer than you might think.

Specifically, defining the problem—and the rest of my work in "owning" the relationship—takes two entire workdays, plus a few hours in the evening each night. This is where, for those of us who have logged hours watching Oprah, Sally Jessy, Phil (Donahue), Phil (McGraw), etc., we get to put our armchair psychological skills to work; this is where we reap the rewards of watching daytime television. I didn't know it at the time, but I was developing *skills*, baby, when I sat cross-legged in my mother's living room procrastinating the completion of my social studies homework.

Dr. Phil is fond of breaking down his thoughts into ten-item lists, so I learn about the ten misconceptions of what a good relationship is, the ten "bad spirits" that can affect a relationship, the ten concepts you need to live by in order to have a strong marriage. I am also asked to ponder what my needs are in a relationship and to make an informed guess at Brandon's. To get there, I spend all afternoon answering questions like "Has your partner sometimes felt that his or her father has trespassed across personal boundaries?" (Answer: not sure.) This last section about Brandon takes much journaling; I am to let no thought, feeling, or hunch go unexamined. The point of it is to get me to see Brandon as a person, with his own history and needs.

During this segment, Dr. Phil also lets loose his secret to a happy relationship. "Please understand that this formula for relationship success doesn't work just some of the time—it works all of the time," he writes. Ready for it? Here goes:

> The quality of a relationship is a function of the extent to which it is built on a solid underlying friendship and meets the needs of two people involved.
>
> Now you may be thinking, "That's it? That's the big formula I've been waiting for?" Yes, that's it, and believe me, it is elegant in its simplicity.

Actually, what I'm thinking is: Oh, Phil. Did you not listen to your editor? *A function of the extent to which*? What kind of phrase is that to have in The Secret to a Happy Marriage? Is this supposed to be math? Do you, or do you not, want people to actually remember this sentence?

I forge on.

I do this at the kitchen table, pen in hand, Simon at my feet. My predominant feeling is that I am now officially the Distraction Welcoming Wagon. Did you call just to chat in the middle of a workday? Why, sure, I have *plenty of* time to talk! Might there be some e-mails to delete from my account? Better get those puppies off the server *tout de suite*! Are there some FlyLady hot spots to tidy up? Yes. Of course there are.

Because this is not so much emotionally wrenching as simply tedious. As Dr. Phil keeps instructing, I *am* putting down my most vulnerable, heartfelt thoughts and feelings. I *am* jotting down things like, "I need to feel, and be told, that I am loved." (Who doesn't, right?) But there truly is only so much navel-gazing that a person can stand.

I finish the work on myself, and I'm sorry to say that I don't feel different or more learned about myself or my relationship with Brandon. What I do feel is a sense that I have dodged a bullet. I can pretend all I want that Brandon was chosen as my very special one based on our mutual respect for each other, that I wouldn't have put up with someone whose treatment of me was just mediocre, *blahdee blah,* but the truth is, we got together because we each found the other hot and easy to get along with, and we stayed because we found each other fun and because we really just *liked* each other. I lucked into the mutual respect part, Brandon's easygoingness, his ability to buckle down with whatever responsibility is thrown his way. Maybe, even without Brandon, I would have grown into the sort of person who wouldn't settle for a guy who went through periods of ignoring me, or said things that would be hard to take back. Maybe one of the guys I dated before Brandon would have grown into a more mature sort of man, the kind that might score an 11 or less on the Relationship Health Profile with me. But I somehow doubt it. I have visions of myself trying this Relationship Rescue with one ex-boyfriend; I imagine he'd give all the right answers, green eyes liquid with feeling . . . and then, as always, he'd do exactly what he pleased. I imagine it with another ex-boyfriend whom I'll call David; he'd just flat-out refuse. *If you want to talk, fine. Let's talk like normal people.* Dr. Phil anticipates this and counsels the participating partner to keep trucking along. "You know from your own life experiences that it is difficult for someone to go against the flow forever. . . . If you have to, come back and reread this page every single day."

I stop reading for a minute, so blown away am I by the enormity of these McGraw balls. To tell somebody that he or she—but probably she—should keep toiling away at a program that her mate will not undertake because this is the *only* program that can save the relationship very likely crosses the line from simple confidence in the program into flat-out arrogance. I picture David, his thin-lipped mouth that turns down a little at the corners, his no-nonsense tone of voice, his disdain for the upper middle class. I've heard through the grapevine that he's married with kids. I consider David's wife, and I hope (1) they're happy, or at least that (2) she's not a Dr. Phil fan. I hope that she's not rereading page 165 every day. Unless he's had a personality transplant in the years since I knew him, he will never, ever, *ever* consent to a program like this.

After Caleb goes to sleep and Brandon and I creep back downstairs, I prepare to start the hardest day of the program: introducing Brandon to it, in ten steps.

Why is it the hardest? Because there's simply no way to tell your mate about the *Relationship Rescue* without sounding like you've joined a cult. Phil himself offers some suggestions on how to start the conversation, and I try to envision my speaking these words to Brandon with a straight face:

> "I have an offer to make, and I think that you are going to like it a lot. It has to do with our relationship."

> "I want to start fresh. I forgive myself for the foolish things I have done in this relationship, and I forgive you for the foolish things you have done in this relationship. I just didn't get it before, but now I do."

> "I am telling you that I own my own feelings, and blaming you is an insult to me."

It occurs to me that a loving husband might not be faulted for whisking his bride away to a deprogramming expert.

So. As Dr. Phil permits, I attempt this in my own words. I sit cross-legged on the couch, book in my lap. Brandon stretches and yawns in the kitchen. "Can I get you a beverage?" he asks.

"That would be great," I say. I clear my throat. "So, uh, I've been reading this book about relationships."

"I know," Brandon says. "The Dr. Phil."

"And I've been thinking about how our relationship could be *better*," I say.

No expression on Brandon's face whatsoever.

"Because it could always be better, right?" I take a swig. "The thing is, Dr. Phil says we have to be *vulnerable*. We're going to have to be 'brutally honest.' "

"Okay," Brandon says.

"There's a fourteen-day program that we have to do."

"Okay." He sits down next to me.

Step 1 ("open the reconnection dialogue"): done. It's quiet in the house and dark. We both look at Simon stretching out on the floor. Simon rolls on his side and groans. I take another swig.

Now I'm to describe my work. "So, uh . . ." I'm flailing here. I restart. "Listen, I've been reading a book by this bald-headed Texan that I think you would like. And I have to tell you, it's a plain-talk, action-oriented book that makes a lot of sense. And this guy's not into a bunch of pop-psychology, did-you-hate-your-mother kind of thinking."

"What?"

"I said, 'He's not into a bunch of pop-psychology, did-you-hate-your-mother kind of thinking.' "

"Are you reading that from the book?"

"Yes." Like he wouldn't have noticed. "Okay okay, let me start over," I say. " I'm actually not at all sure you'd like it"—see, I'm not in a cult!—"but he *is* less abrasive in print than on TV. Maybe parts of it will be good."

I continue with the ten steps, which consist of my walking him through what I just spent two days and evenings doing. When I start describing the first relationship myth—"A great relationship depends on a great meeting of the minds"—I realize that we're back in Dr. Laura territory: Men and women are intrinsically different. "He says that you can't expect men to act feminine and women to act masculine," I say.

"Can I say something here?" Brandon interrupts. "I'm beginning to think that there's something wrong with me. Is there something wrong with me, and you, that we think alike?"

"*I* don't think so," I say.

Brandon shakes his head. "Okay. Go ahead."

We continue on in the one lit room in our house, me flipping through the book, Brandon sitting quietly with a slightly pained expression on his face. It's 11:05, and Brandon's alarm will go off tomorrow morning at 5:40. We get to the personal relationship values, and Brandon interjects, "I'm going to be 'brutally honest' here. This is boring."

"Oh, just wait," I say brightly. "Soon you get to hear about my Partner Profile of you!" Dr. Phil promises that this may very well be the highlight of these steps, and that your partner will be both curious and flattered. "Let's face it, everyone likes to be the star," he writes. "Everyone likes to be the focus of attention and energy."

Well, as it turns out: No. Not everyone. Not Brandon, anyway.

I start walking him through it. "These are just my educated guesses," I say. "You correct me if I say something that isn't right, okay?"

He nods. I start talking—I supposed that Brandon likes his name just fine, I didn't imagine that he considers his age to be an "issue" (both true guesses)—and we get to the third section, about his "maternal relationship."

Shoot. I knew I shouldn't have used that line about how Dr. Phil isn't into any pop-psychology, did-you-hate-your-mother kind of thinking.

"Hey," Brandon says. "I thought we weren't going to be going into things like my mother."

"Yeah, well, we are," I say apologetically. "We're also going to be going into the sort of relationship that your parents have with each other."

"So he lied to us," Brandon says.

Probably, there are differences between the sort of Freudian analysis that Dr. Phil was referring to and the questions he asks in *Relationship*

Rescue (we are, for instance, spared having to muse about any possible Oedipal complexes), but to the laypeople—the laypeople being Brandon and me—the difference isn't particularly striking.

We carry on, though. Brandon, I notice, is failing to demonstrate any signs of curiosity or having been flattered. In fact, he seems to be shutting down. Maybe it's too late at night or maybe this is making him uncomfortable, but when I divulge the answers to questions that I've scrawled in my lined notebook, he answers with a flat "That sounds about right," or simply "okay." I wait for more elaboration. It doesn't come. Next question.

In the section about his other relationships, we come to "Has your partner ever had his or her heart broken? How did your partner respond?" and "What has been your partner's prior relationship history? What do you know about his or her relationships before the one in which you are now a part?"

In my notebook, I, the prim little editor, have written: "*Of* which, not *in* which." And, after some pondering, "Don't know."

I don't know because, frankly, I have never thought to ask. Brandon's long-term relationship, other than me, occurred in high school, where he dated the same girl from his freshman through his junior year. As a thirty-two-year-old woman, I'm not certain that contemplating the romantic life of a pair of teenagers, even if one of them was my husband, is really going to be illuminating. Moreover, I resist because I have an instinct that there are things that you don't need to know. I can't see any danger, exactly, in hearing about the teenage breakup, but there is some weirdness in knowing that you are not unique, that your husband has said to other people *I love you* in the same heartfelt way and meant it.

When Brandon's parents retired and moved to Florida, we inherited his yearbooks and a handful of unmarked videotapes. To get to the bottom of the videotape mystery, we popped one of the tapes in the VCR and watched a teenaged Brandon perform at his high school talent show. The screen turned scratchy, and then—voilà—there were Brandon and his parents wishing the smiling, dark-haired girlfriend luck in the mall-sponsored fashion show for which she was a model. On the tape, Brandon looks a little undercooked—he'd not yet become the man I would meet in a few years' time—but I recognized the expression on his face: He had adored her.

"Guess that's it!" Brandon said and hit the stop button on the VCR.

"A *fashion* show?" I joked, knowing that I would have totally called her a "bop" in high school. But mainly I was a little creeped out.

This is not as big a deal as it sounds—it's something that I haven't had cause to consider, actually, since it happened—but Dr. Phil wants us to revisit it. Tonight I say, "So I have 'don't know' here."

"Yeah," Brandon says.

"So, do you want to tell me how you dealt with your breakup?" I hate being in this position. I hate it, *hate* it. Because I truly *don't care* and I don't want to give the impression that I do.

"Sure," he says. "We broke up a couple of times, and when we broke up the last time, I felt relief more than anything."

I wait for him to elaborate and when he doesn't—he nods quickly, *continue please*—I doggedly explain the rest of the section. Is your partner liked by his or her peers? Is your partner faithful? How does your partner relate to authority?

In *Relationship Rescue* world, no question is left unasked, no emotional spot left unpoked. It's midnight before we call it quits. Brandon has to wake up in less than six hours, me in less than seven. My head is full. I don't understand how this will create a better relationship for us, but as I fall asleep, I try to have faith that the logic of Dr. Phil's plan will become clearer over the next fourteen days.

I CALL MY FRIEND MARLEE. The whole idea of past breakups has been gnawing at me. Brandon and I were barely old enough to vote when we met, and my experience in grown-up, committed relationships, I'm afraid, is scanty. It's possible, I think, that Dr. Phil is using some sort of shorthand for people who have had more romances than I and that those people would be better able to see the value in talking about past breakups. Marlee is ten years older than me; she's in a happy egalitarian marriage, and I know that, amazingly enough, she's in touch with her ex-boyfriends. How do other people break or put back together the Humpty Dumpty that is the long-term committed relationship?

When she gets on the line, I tell her, "I want to talk about marriage."

"Really!" she says.

"I know it's soon . . ."

"I'm already spoken for," she says. I hear her get up and walk with the phone. "No, go ahead and ask me."

So I ask her to tell me about relationships she's had that have been troubled, and what she did to try to make them less troubled. "Nothing with John," she says of her husband. "But there was this period when I was seeing Ted and Eli at the same time. I saw a therapist. I really felt like I didn't know my own mind at this point, and this therapist asked me to make a 'family chart.' It's sort of like a family tree, but you draw out all your relatives and what kind of relationships they had. I don't know if the therapist didn't explain well enough what the point was or what, but I didn't see its value and I never went back." Ah, the marital therapists that are so unlike Dr. Phil, according to Dr. Phil.

"So how did you decide what to do?" I ask her.

"I moved out of Ted's and into this horrible apartment—no, it was a hotel, really. A horrible hotel. It smelled like smoke—it was the sort of place that junkies go on a bender. I just thought I needed some time alone to figure out what I wanted. I spent about a week there, and I decided that I just needed to walk away from both of them. Get a clean break."

"Why?" I ask. I love this about Marlee; you meet me and know my whole life story in about five minutes, but she has these surprising dramas tucked away back in her earlier chapters. "Why didn't you just pick one?"

"I thought that even if I forgave them—and I really am a pretty forgiving person—they wouldn't be able to forgive me and it would be hanging over our heads for the rest of our lives," she says. "And it was ultimately good for me. When I met John, I thought, 'Okay, here's this great guy, and I know how to not screw it up.' I *did* change."

So, I think, maybe this is what Phil was getting at—lessons learned from all the people you/your partner have loved before. "Do you know people who have been on the brink of divorce or breaking up, though, and were able to pull it back together?" I ask her. "You know, people who have changed and stayed with the same person?"

"Hmm," she says. I wait while she ponders. I don't often have epiphanies, but talking with Marlee, I do feel a little enlightened. This is how mature people think: They take part of the responsibility for the end but know when the relationship is beyond repair. There are only so many blows a relationship can take before it's damaged. It occurs to me how much more wrenching that would be if you had kids.

Finally, she says, "I don't know. It's a good question: Can you change somebody? Or can you change yourself and stay in that relationship?"

"Dr. Phil says"—here I go, sounding like a cult member again—"that you can't change anybody else, but if you change yourself, your partner will be inspired to change, too. He won't feel like his back is against the wall, and he'll treat you nicer."

I imagine that both of us are flipping through our Big Mental Rolodexes of Couples in our heads, plucking out the couples whose marriages are composed of one nice person and one jerk. "What if someone keeps treating her partner better and better and he still doesn't change? Are you then changing to just *accept* that this is the way he acts?"

"I don't know," I say. "I haven't finished the book." I pause. "I'll let you know."

I SET THE TIMER. Two minutes. Brandon and I stare into each other's eyes. It's Day 5, and we've gotten over our impulse to act like it's a staring contest. Brandon stifles a yawn. I try to grab at my drink without breaking eye contact. The timer goes off.

I set the timer for three minutes. "Agreements that I have made with you and then broken or failed to live up to are . . ." I begin. "Well, the filtered water dispenser in the fridge. I said I'd call Sears to get that repaired, and I haven't. It's been, what, three months?" I look down at the timer. "And sometimes you probably think I'm going to make dinner, and then you come home and I haven't. Right?"

He's not allowed to say anything.

I continue to blather on until, blessedly, the timer rings.

"Thank you for caring enough to share, and I promise to weigh it carefully," Brandon says. That's the only thing that the program allows him to say after I finish speaking.

Timer on again. "Agreements that I have made with *you* and then broken or failed to live up to are . . ." Brandon starts. He repeats it again. "Hmm. Hopefully nothing big." He nods. "Yep, nothing big." He pauses. "I guess I used to sometimes not call when I had to work late—but I call now! Yep! . . . Agreements that I have *broken* or *failed* to live up to . . . Hmm . . ."

We sit there for the remaining two minutes until I can blurt out my scripted, "Thank you for caring enough to share, and I promise to weigh it carefully."

Dr. Phil's plan, I'm sorry to report, is not becoming clearer to me. Unless Phil's plan was, in fact, to get me to actively dislike Phil. In the mornings, I've been doing my assignments, which basically means ful-filling my checklist of ways I can meet Brandon's needs and rereading sections of the book. We've been sitting down for five evenings now, expounding on things like:

"My greatest fear in opening up to you has been . . ."

"I feel that my greatest contributions to this relationship are . . ."

"The negatives I took away from my mother and father's relationship are . . ."

I'm trying. Brandon's trying. But I have not learned a single new thing about Brandon or his needs. We talk, as it is. Phil says that these exercises are "designed to stretch you and to require you to be vulnerable. If something is easy, then that means you already know how to do it." This is all easy for me, but easy in the way that waiting for a delayed flight at the airport is easy.

What I *have* learned is that these exercises—and the whole program, for that matter—seem to reward a certain kind of person. A person like one Dr. Phil McGraw. The journaling is great if you enjoy analyzing feelings and actions—perhaps as someone with a Ph.D. in psychology might enjoy. The three minutes of talking off the cuff? A talk show host would pull that one off beautifully. Like to be the center of attention? You would indeed be very curious about the Partner Profile.

I probably have more Dr. Phil in me than I'd care to admit, but the exercises, they're not so easy on Brandon. One night, I'm reminded of a game I played with my sisters and Brandon called Catchphrase. The idea was to say something so your partner could guess what the phrase is. So, for example, if the word was "pigs," your partner might say, "The three little . . ." But playing it with Brandon, you're treated to a float down the stream of his consciousness. If the word is *pigs* and if Brandon is your partner, you get something like "So you're on a farm and there are these animals . . ." He'll sit back and dream up the next bit of the clue, all the while the timer is ticking. One night, we get a question about the barriers in our relationship, and, after about one minute of serious answers, I hear something like So, if you see these barriers—these hurdles—you'll jump them. And you'll look back and think, Whew! I cleared that one. But you don't want to keep looking back! Oh, no! Because you'll slam right into the next one. Hurdles . . . hurdles . . .

We answer the next two questions and stand for a thirty-second hug, which is the best part of the exercises. We write our "thoughts and feelings" in our journals for five minutes, minimum. They have nothing to do with the problem I thought I had identified in the beginning, which is that we don't have enough good, non-sleepy time together. They actually have nothing to do with the newer problem Phil suggests, which is that Brandon and I are Brandon and I. The irony that we're spending a half hour every night doing this—time that we could be spending talking about topics of our own choosing, or even time up in the guest room—is not lost on me.

DAY 8. Brandon finishes writing in his journal, leaning against the kitchen counter. He says, "I feel like my journal is becoming like Jack Handey's 'Deep Thoughts.' "

DAY 9. After my morning exercises, I call a friend of mine, who's in her fifties and divorced. We talk about getting help in one's marriage and she tells me about her sixteen-year marriage to a resolutely unromantic man. "We went to see a marriage counselor at one point," she tells me. "So we're there and the counselor asks us to describe our parents' marriages. And he just starts lying! 'Oh, they had a great relationship,' he told the counselor. 'They adored each other.' My jaw just dropped. They did *not* adore each other at all. His father adored his mother, and she adored herself."

"Did you ask him about it later?" I ask her, pouring myself a cup of tea.

"Well, no," she says. "When you're trying to hold your marriage together, you don't call your husband a liar."

That night, Brandon's answers to the questions regarding his "fixed beliefs" about men, women, and relationships sound uncannily like things I would say. After our thirty-second hug, I ask, "Did you say what you actually think, or what you think *I* think you should think?"

"Think think? What?"

"Are you just telling me what I want to hear?"

He laughs. "You're getting paranoid, Jen."

DAY 11. We are to choose among five character types to find the one that best describes ourselves and our partners. "For the sake of imagery," Dr. Phil assigns an animal to each type (since the book lacks footnotes, I assume these are based simply on McGraw's authorial license). Brandon has characteristics of the dog and the owl; I pronounce him a "dowlg." Me, I'm a mix of the lion, the dog, and the beaver—a "be-ion-og." We are perhaps not mature enough to undertake tonight's exercise. We spend much time making sexual innuendos regarding the beaver and, to a lesser extent, the dog ("anything goes").

After we finish and are ensconced in front of *E.R.*, Brandon says, "It seems like he doesn't really expect anyone to make it this far in the book. He's just making stuff up at this point."

"Yeah," I say. "Day thirteen: Just sit there and twiddle your nipples for three minutes."

WE'RE CLOSING IN on the end of the fourteen-day program, and I flip ahead to see what's next. In the chapter titled "Relationships Are Managed, Not Cured," Phil lays out the variety of ways Brandon and I will have to manage our relationship. I get to the part about "difference management" and it occurs to me that this is sounding a *leetle* bit familiar. "God didn't design us to be the same; he designed us to be different," Phil writes. "I've told you the price you pay for resisting the natural order of things." He goes on to catalog how men and women differ: Women like the process while men like solutions. Women are extravagant with details while men are concise. Women are emotional while men are logical (although I'm afraid that *Relationship Rescue* does not make a very good case for men's—or at least Dr. Phil's—strength in logic).

These gender stereotypes are age-old ideas, and Phil and Laura did not invent them. Neither, for that matter, did John Gray, Ph.D., author of the best-selling *Men Are from Mars, Women Are from Venus*— although Gray did bring about a renaissance of the idea that men and women are intrinsically different. Gray's specific theories are based on, from what I could tell, little more than a vivid imagination and a penchant for simple narratives inspired by episodes of *Star Trek*. ("Then they decided to fly to Earth. In the beginning everything was wonderful and beautiful. But then the effects of Earth's atmosphere took hold . . .") In fact, both McGraw and Schlessinger owe a debt of gratitude to Gray.

In some ways their books are also reactions against his. The basic idea is the same—men and women are different, and couples have to deal with that—but the solutions vary. *Mars/Venus* came out in the I-feel-your-pain nineties, and a lot of Gray's balms for a troubled marriage are about gaining insights and writing letters. Now, in the first decade of the millennium, the zeitgeist has changed, and the new experts want results. To hell with the letters. Let's put on some lipstick, sit down with a timer and a script, and knock this motherfucker out.

You can debate among yourselves whether these ideas of inherent gender difference have any validity. I was struck, though, by the distance between the prescriptions for my life and my actual life. Brandon and I can communicate with each other perfectly well. I'm not a histrionic mess and he's not an uncommunicative jerk. Gray points out that this is perfectly reasonable that I feel this way: "Generally speaking, about 10 percent of women will relate more to being from Mars. This is often simply a result of being born with higher testosterone levels than most other women." No big deal, he's saying—if you don't agree with me, it's only because you're a little mannish.

Like Gray, Phil tamps down any debate about his methods. In the section where he anticipates reader questions (called "The Doctor Is 'In' "), he addresses whether you should ever call it quits. He knows that some Christian leaders would say no, but he allows that you can walk away from a bad relationship—when you've earned the right to quit. "Arrogant as it may sound," he writes, "until you have done everything I outline in this book, then I don't think you have earned the right to quit." Four pages later, in a letter to his women readers, he reveals that, as a husband, he's been something of a prick, but his wife made the marriage work. In case you didn't pick up on the idea that long-suffering Robin is supposed to be your role model, he makes it clearer. "And she did it without my help and active participation. So can you."

By now, it's become clear to me that *Relationship Rescue* is not going to make me any happier, or my marriage any better. I can make a guess that the fourteen-day program is designed to simply acclimate us to talking about deep feelings; the last two days get at things like when a partner is proud of the other one and what a partner finds sensual in his or her mate. There may be some value there for other couples, but simply figuring out each other's needs is neither Brandon's problem nor mine.

I put down the book on the kitchen table, pick up the phone, and dial my sister Krissy's cell. She and her husband have a very different sort of marriage than Brandon and I do. I don't think John has ever once cooked dinner; he, a devotee of Ayn Rand, works late and Krissy knows that most likely he always will. Krissy, in many ways, fits the Venus model better than I do—she loves to shop, for example, and I don't know anyone better at comforting than her. She and John both acknowledge that there are things that they can't get from each other; as a result they rely on their friends. Still, they love each other.

They've had rocky times, but they say their marriage basically works, and they're the ones who would know.

"Hey, Kris," I say. "Got a minute?"

"Yep," she says. "Hang on—I have to merge."

While she drives, I tell her about the Dr. Phil, the experiments, the idea that men and women are different, the question of whether people can change. "I'm trying to figure out whether this program would work for other people," I say. "So let me ask, first of all, if you came to John and said, 'Let's do this Dr. Phil program,' would he do it?"

Krissy laughs. "He'd be like, 'What the hell are you talking about? Dr. Phil's a nut.' "

"Okay," I say, jotting that down. "It seems like the program is to get couples talking. Do you know what John's answers would be to some of these questions?" I flip through the book and rattle off a few that seem the most down-to-earth—the greatest pain ever experienced, what's going well or badly in one's life, traits one partner admires in the other. "And do you think John would know how you'd answer?"

For some of the questions, Krissy reports, she could make a pretty good guess at what he'd say. And she thinks he'd know what she'd say. "I think that, actually, he'd know what I'd say better because I'm the one who talks about my feelings more," she adds. "It's not like he's this big mystery, but he doesn't talk about things like this." She pauses. "Men and women are so different."

"That's funny you should say that," I say. "Because you and John *are* so different, but Brandon and I aren't really very much at all."

"True," she says. "And John and I might be extreme examples. Mr. Macho. Miss Emotional."

I tell her about the idea that you can change yourself and your mate will start treating you better. "Do you think that's true?"

"No," she says. She pauses. "It depends on the person. Some people will continue being assholes no matter what. Some people need to have that relationship taken away before they change." The phone cuts out for a second. "And some people might change on their own. I don't know—people are different."

I could thunk myself on the forehead. "People *are* different!" I exclaim. She's brilliant, my sister Krissy.

BRANDON AND I make it through Day 14, and we draft a "mission statement" for our relationship. "Wait—weren't our marriage vows our mission statement?" Brandon asks.

"I guess this is a supplement," I say. At the kitchen table, we read the passage about the mission statement, and I suggest, "We are united against Dr. Phil. We pledge to never, ever time our conversations again. We will never use the phrase 'Thank you for caring enough to share, and I promise to weigh it carefully.' We will use our time in the best way we see fit." We sign our names with a flourish.

IN LATE SPRING, I'm online at ParentCenter.com, taking a break from thinking up cartoon ideas by looking up the work of Catherine Newman, who writes a funny column for the site. On a whim I type "marriage" into the search field on the screen. There is a question about whether or not a mother and her mate should take a vacation without their five-month-old baby. I don't even read the answers. My baby is six years old and I know that I need a vacation. We haven't taken one since Cleo was diagnosed, and we've never taken one without Caleb.

It's a sign. Everywhere I look, it seems, the experts are urging me to vacation alone with Brandon. In the mail, I get a review copy of the book *We Should Do This More Often: A Parents' Guide to Romance, Passion, and Other Pre-Child Activities You Vaguely Recall*, and I flip through for confirmation that people *do* this, vacation without the kiddo. On pages 61 and 62, author Lorilee Craker writes, "Consider taking a longer trip together. . . . Remember: *Anything that's good for your marriage is good for your kids!*"

That's been the undercurrent of all the marital advice, really—save the kids, plus save the economic unit—but when Brandon's parents suggest they take Caleb to Sea World while we travel to another destination, I'm on it.

In June, Brandon and I fly to Key West. We fall into a routine almost immediately. In the mornings, Brandon and I compromise on which tourist-y things we do (I drag him to the historic fort tour, he drags me snorkeling); we eat lunch, then swim in the pool; we go out to dinner, not knowing or caring if the food will be too spicy for Caleb. At night, we watch a woman named Dawn Michelle sing at a bar, with pretaped music and a microphone. She has a small dog on stage with her and if you give the dog a dollar, she'll sing what you request. The music is perfect for the slightly drunk: songs that make you wistful, or songs that make you want to press up against your partner, his lips on your neck, both of you damp with the Florida night humidity. We drink copious amounts of beer. We talk and talk and talk. We shower, we fall into the canopied bed, we kiss on the balcony, we sleep late, soundly, and undisturbed.

When we fly back to retrieve Caleb, I feel a little sad that the vacation is over, but truthfully, I was yearning to get back home by the end of our stay. Traveling—the airports, the living out of suitcases, the labored efforts just to find a good cup of tea—exhausts me. I missed my boy. I was curious about what was going on at the magazine. Strangely enough, I was pining for Virginia, the big deciduous trees, the dark blacktops, the orderliness of daily life.

The evening we get back, I'm unpacking my suitcase and I realize that I forgot that this vacation was supposed to be a little bit of a marriage experiment. I just went about my business as if everything were hunky-dory. Hmm, I think, as I throw the dirty laundry in the hamper. *Did vacationing without Caleb make my marriage stronger?*

I hear Caleb in the shower, calling for a towel, and Brandon running down the attic stairs to bring him one. I gather up my toiletries and stick them in the hall closet. I don't know the answer. The vacation—all that unstructured time together—certainly didn't *hurt* my marriage. And I surely enjoyed it. But it occurs to me that maybe everything in the marriage department *is* just hunky-dory, that it doesn't need fixing. Out of all the elements in my life, my relationship with Brandon might be my strong suit.

While Caleb's getting dressed in his pajamas, Brandon comes in and flops down on the bed. "Hey there," he says.

I flop down next to him. "Hey back atcha." I wiggle closer. I kiss him on the neck.

The door opens wider and Caleb climbs up onto the bed between us. "Mama!" he says. "You're in my space!"

I almost forgot. The sleeping in Key West—just the two of us, side by side, nobody's heel in my back—was *excellent*. I make a mental note to work on that.

{4}
The Kid

IT HAS BEEN DARK and quiet for five minutes now. The three of us are in bed. "Mama," Caleb whispers. "I want a drink of water."

"No," I whisper back. "It's time for sleeping, babe."

Silence for a moment.

"A sip tinier than a peanut," he whispers.

I don't say anything. I am faking my own sleep.

"A sip tinier than a peanut," he repeats.

Silently, I will him to please forget the water and fall sleep so Brandon and I can indulge in a little marital hanging out.

"Tinier than a peanut. Tinier than a peanut. Tinier than a peanut."

I sigh. I sit up and hand him the glass.

He lies down again. Part of the trick of getting him unconscious is knowing the nuances of his wiggling. Crazy, over-the-top wiggling gets him a stern warning to "be quiet, be still, and just relax." There is another kind of wiggling that gets him the same warning but in a softer tone. Somewhere down the wiggling food chain, there is normal shifting: If I say something during this period, it'll just prolong the getting to sleep. Later there is stillness; the hard part is figuring out whether the stillness means he's asleep or just almost asleep. Right now, Caleb shifts normally. I hear him scratching his legs. The sheets scritch; he bonks into Brandon and Brandon softly says, "Ow."

I almost never fall asleep when Caleb does. I'm a grown-up after all, and it hardly seems fair that I'd have to call it a day by nine o'clock at night. I lie there waiting. In body, I'm the picture of stillness, but mentally I'm busy with my thoughts, a litter of sharp-teethed puppies in need of constant monitoring. Somebody should go to the grocery store. I wonder if the city is going to fix the sewage system problem. I need to e-mail and make sure Debie got that review copy. Breathe in. Did I deposit my paycheck in the savings or checking? I wonder how big the magazine circulation can actually get. Breathe out. I should call Grandma and Grandpap tomorrow. Breathe in. I should make an appointment for a physical. I have a mole on my face—I never used to have a mole on my face. Is it possible that I always have had a mole on face but never noticed it?

Caleb is finally still. I count to sixty. I get out of bed, and quickly—but not *too* quickly—flee the bedroom.

Downstairs, I wait for Brandon, but he never makes it down. I read a magazine. I watch *The Daily Show*, and I go to bed. The next morning the clock radio goes off—why, hello back at you, Lionel Richie!—and my first thought is, as always, *Maybe I'll take a nap today*. The nap rarely happens, but there's no denying that if I allowed myself to, I could fall asleep pretty easily at any given minute.

I DID NOT intend to be in this situation. Funnily enough, we started this thing—called the Family Bed, or Co-Sleeping, or Bed Sharing, or Sleep Sharing, or the Chronic Experience of Waking Up to a

Child's Feet Pressed to the Small of Your Back—in an effort for me to get more sleep. I love the sleep: sleeping in, falling asleep, dreaming, cozying down under the blankets, pushing the pillows so they're just so, relaxing, each muscle limp, each thought drifting out of the waking mind.

It will come as no surprise then, that Caleb's springing onto the nighttime scene in 1998 cramped my sleeping style. I became cranky. I looked terrible. But, worst, I was afraid that I—a natural non-athlete, a stumbler, an oftentimes breaker of precious objects—would drop him in my sleep-deprived haze. I remember once nodding off in the armchair and startling awake with him in my arms. He probably wasn't falling, but I clutched him quick and tight—*whoamygod!*—and woke him up.

Luckily, I discovered that I could nurse while I dozed on my side in bed, a practice that's promoted by pediatrician William "Attachment Parenting" Sears. I slept, Caleb ate, Brandon did what he could to be a good helper. That's what we did pretty much until Caleb was thirteen months old and I took back possession of the breasts.

Many parenting experts warn that once you let your child start sleeping in your bed, you're asking for a world of trouble: The children simply will not leave. In my case, these experts are right. We've tried, with varying degrees of success, to get Caleb to conk out in his own bed. But, like mercury spilled from a broken thermometer, our family may diverge but will always meld back together in one bed. Our attempts to kick him out have been earnest but fairly short-lived. In hindsight, the situation never warranted an all-out mission. That is, perhaps, until now.

In addition to the daytime tiredness, there have been some night-time disturbances. I have a hunch that it may be connected to the co-sleeping. Parenting is next on The List, and I will aim where sleep and parenting intersect.

. . .

BY THE END OF SUMMER, the people have started making noises for a new dog. The loudest voice is, surprisingly, mine. Our family without Cleo feels flimsy, unsubstantial. I start trolling the Internet and wind up on Petfinder.com, a website that lists all the pets currently in the custody of shelters or rescue groups. Homeless mutts mostly, although you can find some pure breeds if that's the sort of thing that floats your boat. My boat likes a mutt. My boat does some research and decides that, given Simon's age and sex and our family's desire for canine compatibility, my boat would like a young girl dog, not a puppy but not set in her ways either. My boat would like a certain Boston terrier mix named Luna who lives in foster care a county away from us.

She was rescued, I learn from her foster mother Amy, from an over-crowded shelter in southern Virginia. We're all hanging out in front of a grocery store where passing shoppers can ogle the dogs. In person, Luna is just as cute as she is on the Internet. She wags her tail, greets people, sniffs the sidewalk.

Still, I'm guarded. I don't want to get all goopy and make a bad decision with a decade's worth of ramifications. Simplifying expert Elaine St. James, in her book *Simplify Your Life with Kids*, straight up informs her readers: "The most demanding pet to have is a dog." She follows up by claiming that the simplest pet is a cat. It's what the cartoon cat Garfield has been arguing for years, and not a debate I want to step into here, but I take her point: A pet can require more or less work, depending. Brandon and I chose Cleo solely on the basis of her cuteness, but we found that sometimes cuteness gets you snapping, vindictive peeing in the house, incessant barking. I loved her, but I might be forgiven for not wanting a clone.

I give Amy the third degree. "I see she requires a fence," I say. "Does she dig under or jump over?"

"Neither, really," Amy says. "We just thought that given her energy level, it would be easier on whoever gets her."

"How is she with other dogs?"

"Good," Amy says, stooping to pet Luna, who clearly loves her Amy. "I've only ever seen her growl at one other dog and it was a dominant female who wanted to eat Luna's food."

It's always the dominant female that's the pain in the ass, isn't it? I press on: She seems to be fine with the house training, she likes to play with tennis balls, she's nuts about kids, she's crate-trained. She sounds perfect.

Luna herself, a lean smushy-faced dog with the eyes of Bernie Mac and the smile of Al Franken, has a certain unconventional appeal. She licks people on the chin by way of saying hello. She's more than a little goofy, as a dog should be. I like her.

I drag the family up to meet her, including Simon, who tries to make a break for Bed Bath & Beyond. (Perhaps it's the "beyond" that appeals?) Brandon likes her. Simon likes her. Caleb loves her. "Oh, my little Luna," he coos, rubbing her head. "Does your name have to be 'Luna' or can I change it?"

One application and a home visit later, Luna becomes part of the clan. We call her Luna, Luna Tuna, Lulu, Looney Tunes, Miss Tuna Our Girl Dog. She's a runner, a cuddler, a lap dog, a humper, an obsessive who chews her own feet. She fits in just fine. She's work but not as much work as Cleo. I can come up with no rational reason for wanting another dependent, but I'm glad she's here. We're five again.

"DO YOU HAPPEN to know when I left the bed last night?" I ask Brandon one evening as we clean up after dinner.

"No," he says. "Why? Don't you remember?"

Nope. I remember falling asleep in our bedroom, and the next thing I know, Brandon's standing in the door of the guest room, telling me that it's time to wake up. Last week, after falling asleep in the usual spot, I awoke on the couch downstairs with Simon balled up in the crook behind my knees. The week before, in the wee hours, I caught myself about to go into our walk-in closet and shut the door. The guest bedroom and closet excursions don't bother me that much; they're on the same floor as our bedroom. The trip downstairs, though, takes me through some perilous terrain: I had to travel down a flight of wooden stairs, hop over the dog-blockade gate at the bottom of the stairs, and wend my way to the family room couch.

I've been a sleepwalker for most of my adult life. (I've asked my mother if I did it as a kid, and she said, "No, I don't remember you sleepwalking." She paused. "Although maybe there were so many people in the house that I just didn't notice.") Given the aforementioned clutziness, I've been lucky. The scariest sleepwalking episode I've had was the night after my first day of an internship at an alternative newsweekly. Unconscious, I'd walked from my bedroom to the window-less bathroom, shut the door, got in the shower, and pulled the shower curtain closed. Then I woke up in pitch black. In my confusion and growing panic, I thought that somehow I was in the paper's basement office. "Margaret?" I called tentatively. "Eric?" No answer. "Hawes?" Surprisingly, the people who worked at the newspaper were not in the bathroom with me. I stood there frozen for a few minutes before I worked up the courage to extricate myself.

In the past, I've sleepwalked intermittently; a year, a good six months, might pass between episodes. But starting fairly recently—sometime back in February when I was doing the Dr. Laura—it's ramped up, and I'm getting concerned. I don't know how sleepwalking works: Is it like, say, an allergic reaction, where each time the experience gets more intense? I certainly hope not, but I'm haunted by something Stephanie told me a few years ago. A woman she knew—a perfectly nice middle-aged entrepreneur who lived a quiet life with her partner—was found dead in her yard one morning. It was determined that the woman sleepwalked out onto her roof and fell. Notwithstanding my fear of dying in such a way that might cause people to shake their heads and mumble, *God, that's weird*, this story plain freaks me out. There but for the grace of God go I out onto my own steeply pitched roof.

One afternoon in the early fall, I turn to the Internet for a Very Special Lesson on sleepwalking. Google brings me to MedLine Plus, a website by the U.S. National Library of Medicine and The National Institutes of Health, and its page full of sleep disorders. I also find the National Sleep Foundation. I had no idea there was this much information out there. For years, I'd been operating under the assumption that sleepwalking was just some strange personal characteristic, like the ability to roll your tongue or the tendency to pick up regional accents, but as it turns out, there are reasons that people sleepwalk.

At the National Sleep Foundation's website (on its "Sleeptionary"), I learn that it's not uncommon for adults to walk in their sleep and that sleepwalking—or somnambulism, as the M.D.s say—is not usually a tip-off to psychiatric problems (although it can be associated with them). Sleepwalking also tends to run in families.

I could have told you that. My sister Jill recently burst into my mother's bedroom, barked "Move over!" and fell right back asleep next to a startled Mom. Another time, my sister Krissy went to bed early; a few hours later and to the surprise of those of us watching TV, she marched out and flung open the front door, setting off the alarm system.

There's not a simple way to cure sleepwalking, although treatments can include hypnosis, drugs, or "simply improving sleep hygiene." (Sleep hygiene is not explained, leaving me to muse about the cleanliness of my sheets.) Both the NSF and the sleepwalking entry on Medline Plus's Medical Encyclopedia (disappointingly, no one thought to name it the En-*sleep*-lopedia) agree that sleepwalking can be caused by:

fatigue or sleep deprivation
drinking or using drugs
stress

I can't rule any of them out—yet—but there's a theory called Occam's Razor that says the simplest explanation is usually the likeliest. Given my general sleepiness during the day, the likeliest explanation seems to be sleep deprivation, so I latch onto it. Dr. Phil exercises notwithstanding, I usually get about seven or eight hours of sleep a night, which should be plenty, quantity-wise. It's the quality that I wonder about, which brings us back to the co-sleeping conundrum.

According to the National Heart, Lungs, and Blood Institute (the federal research organization charged with studying sleep), large gaps exist in science's understanding of sleep—not a huge surprise given the difficulties in conducting good controlled experiments of it. In the plan for future study, the institute hopes to figure out the effects of co-sleeping, among other real-world conditions.

But it makes sense to me that co-sleeping with a wiggly fifty-pound kid can't be helping my sleep. So far in my experiments, the experts have warned me time and again that you should never try to change another person. But now I'm boldly going into parenting advice— where the experts encourage you to do just that.

I'm going to get Caleb to try to sleep in his own bed.

AFTER SCHOOL ONE DAY, Caleb and I hunker down over some books in the living room. For him: his journal and a stack of Brandon's old comic books. For me: a pile of parenting advice books I bought when he was a baby, either for actual advice or for nefarious purposes in *Brain, Child.*

I went to Barnes & Noble this morning and confirmed what I'd suspected: In the world of parenting advice, there are a ton of books from pregnancy through toddlerhood and then again for the teen and "tween" years, but experts offer precious little for the parent of an almost-seven-year-old (unless the seven-year-old happens to have special needs). I never took these books to heart the first time I cracked them open—most of them suffer from an unfortunate double whammy of bad prose and alarmist attitude—but this time, from the safe remove of seven years, I'm taking a tour through Parenting Expert Land.

I have to confess something here: I've built a modest career on being an anti–parenting expert, in a way. The philosophy of *Brain, Child* is that mothers know their kids better than experts. Generally, we mothers have the common sense to take care of business. It's not as if every issue of the magazine is devoted to bashing an expert (we hardly mention them at all), but Stephanie and I have little interest in hearing what mothers "should" do. Stephanie has good, solid principles motivating her. Me, I think I just have a bad attitude regarding authority and, as a young mother, did not like to be told what to do.

So, sitting here, I pry my heart open to receive, as the religious would say.

Caleb adds a little flourish to one of his pages. "Do you want to read my journal?" he asks me.

"You know, you don't *have* to show me it," I tell him. "It can be private."

"It *is*," he says. "Only you and Daddy can look at it."

"In that case, I'd love to read it," I say. He hands me the journal. I'm not at liberty to divulge what I saw, but I can tell you that, although it made me smile, reading Caleb's journal gives me absolutely no insight into what he's thinking. Which, come to think of it, might be how these books can proliferate like they do. Look up "parent" on Amazon, and you find over thirty-five hundred books offering you insight into the mystery that is your child.

The books in front of me span the whole philosophical spectrum. For kicks, I leaf through *On Becoming Baby Wise: Book Two*, part of a series of child care manuals penned by Christian-conservative civilian Gary Ezzo and Christian-conservative doctor Robert Bucknam. They hail from the heart of spare-the-rod-spoil-the-child country, and they're very big on the "dangers" of child-centered parenting. The Babywise sleep advice? Ezzo and Bucknam don't even mention co-sleeping. It's not surprising given that the book is about "moral training," which includes things like teaching a five-month-old "high chair manners" and self-control.

Most of the books on the stack in front of me fall somewhere in the middle of the parenting philosophy spectrum.[1] You have your American Academy of Pediatrics (AAP), your authors of the *What to Expect* series, your T. Berry Brazelton. Dr. Richard Ferber of *Solve Your Child's Sleep Problems* (a book so popular "Ferberizing" became a modern parents' verb) also falls into this category. The AAP is the most authoritative, and the others here are well respected although all have their own quirks—the *What to Expect* authors show a certain fussiness regarding diet, for example, and Brazelton has become known for his laissez-faire attitude toward potty training (and shilling for a diaper company). Ultimately, what these experts offer is mainstream, Main Street advice.

The AAP on sleep arrangements: "Once the [bedtime] story is over and you've said your goodnights, don't let him stall further, and don't let him talk you into staying with him until he falls asleep. He needs to get used to doing this on his own."

---

[1] For a good look at the history of the mainstream experts, check out Ann Hulbert's *Raising America* or, for the more academically inclined, Steven Mintz's *Huck's Raft*.

Finally, I get to Dr. William Sears, who writes with his registered-nurse wife, Martha. I sigh and steel myself. I come to Sears with some baggage, yet I'm also pinning my hopes on him.

While Ezzo and Bucknam feel that no parent should have to kow-tow to a baby's whims (it "attacks" the marital relationship), Sears is all about the kowtowing because, he says, it makes for an "attached" parent and child—and attachment is what you really want. So he's all for nursing on demand, wearing the baby in a sling, co-sleeping. In the evolution of parenting advice, Sears sprung up as an alternative to the mainstream doctors, who were then preaching formula feeding and letting babies cry it out, practices that felt counterintuitive to some mothers. (Incidentally, these mothers include women of all political stripes.) But by the time Caleb was born, Sears's program, also called "attachment parenting," had become just as dogma-hardened as the mainstream parenting advice, particularly among the well-educated crowd. (The Babywise people remain fringe, although recent years have brought us faux-hip, tough-love experts like Muffy Mead-Ferro, who in her book *Confessions of a Slacker Mom* preaches hard work and no coddling for the kids.)

A big part of me wants to like Bill and Martha Sears—many of their methods dovetail nicely with my inclinations anyway—but I just can't. As if his own sanctimoniousness isn't bad enough, he's infected his many devotees with it. They're a cranky bunch, as devotees generally are. They're twice as convinced as mainstream types that their favored parenting style isn't just as good as whatever the mainstream's doing—it's *better*. They write letters to *Brain, Child* with alarming frequency, letters that are passive-aggressive in tone: *I feel sorry for you and your child* . . . To which I think, Don't cry for me, A.P.-dogma people. The truth is, my mothering decisions aren't your business.

Anyway, I open *The Baby Book* and find that Sears not only says that sleep sharing is okay but provides (anecdotal) evidence that sleep sharing helps babies sleep better and longer, generally makes them "thrive," and even prevents sudden infant death syndrome (aka SIDS, the acronym that strikes fear in the heart of every parent with an infant).[2] Sears makes a gesture at reassuring parents who choose not to co-sleep, but it's clear that he thinks it's the cat's pajamas of sleeping arrangements. Looking for a solution here, I'm vulnerable and I find it difficult not to pat myself on the back.

Which is why, when I get to page 316, I let out an audible gasp, so noisy that Caleb looks up from his journal and asks me if I'm okay. I am. It's just that I never noticed this before: "When the time comes, your baby will wean from your bed just like all the other weanings."

Why, Dr. Sears—that's just not true.

The editors have placed an illustration of an empty queen-sized bed with a smaller mattress at the foot of the bed. In the smaller bed lie a boy toddler and a female person—whether that person is a girl child (the toddler's sister?) or simply a girlish-looking woman, I can't tell you. But they are sleep-weaning. I cannot believe I went all this time and never even heard the phrase.

I shut the book and place it on the stack of all the other parenting books. I'm thrown. I'd planned to pore through and find at least a mention of our situation. But no mentions lie in this particular stack of books. I'll have to figure something else out. I lean back and rub my eyes.

"Are you *crying?*" Caleb asks.

"No," I say. "Hey . . . do you know what I was just reading?"

"No," he says.

---

[2] As I write this, there's a controversy a'roiling over some new AAP recommendations regarding the prevention of SIDS. The AAP recommends that babies be in close proximity to parents at night to facilitate breastfeeding, but not in the same bed because babies have died of SIDS in their parents' beds. The co-sleeping camp points out that babies die of SIDS in cribs, too. We might all do well to listen to British pediatrician Penelope Leach, who writes in *Your Baby and Child*: "It's unlikely that any of these findings are simply right or simply wrong. . . . Deaths due to SIDS are, by definition, inexplicable. . . . Crib deaths are so dreadful that health authorities understandably prefer to play it safe and stay simple in the advice they give to parents."

"I was reading this book that says that parents can teach their kids how to sleep in their own beds." Not altogether true, but maybe a good introduction to the idea?

Caleb frowns. "That's mean," he says.

"What's mean?"

"Those writers are mean. You're not supposed to tell people what to do!" He falls against the couch dramatically.

Under other circumstances, I'd totally agree.

THE NEXT DAY I find myself at AskDrSears.com, a website for all things attachment parenting: lots of co-sleeping, breastfeeding, wearing the baby, something called "father nursing," a practice of extended cuddling that Sears himself took up after the birth of his sixth child (he has eight altogether) and that he chronicles with fairly drippy prose.

Finally I find what I'm looking for in a Q&A. Someone out there has a six-year-old and a two-year-old who sleep in the bed with her and her mate. Sears replies that while bed-sharing is a godsend for those parents who need to "reconnect" with their infants (i.e., employed parents), it can be tough, especially if there's more than one kid.

The idea is that eventually, you move the futon into the child's own room. As the picture suggested, you put a mattress in your room as a temporary measure to get the kid out of your bed—but still within whispering distance.

I e-mail the page to Brandon with the note: *So . . . want to try a "special bed" for Caleb.*

Within three minutes, I get back: *Yes.*

THIS SCREWING AROUND with the nighttime routine cannot be taken lightly. One afternoon, I evaluate the bedrooms, going so far as to whip out a tape measure. There's not a whole lot of space at the foot of our bed or anywhere else in our bedroom, but I can move the laundry baskets off to the side by the bathroom, or maybe in the closet. I'll drag Caleb's mattress into our bedroom. Maybe, I think, I'll buy some snazzy new sheets and a fleece blanket for him. He loves a fleece blanket.

I let Brandon in on the blueprints for getting Caleb into his own bed.

Then one night after we read a chapter from *Teen Titans: Cyborg, Come Home!*, I say to Caleb in an excited voice, "How would you like to start sleeping by yourself?" I expect grumbling, but I plan to counter with all the wonderful things that await him: new bed! A headboard! Heck, maybe some fresh paint!

"I am never ever going to sleep in my own room," he says flatly. He stretches out on our bed.

Brandon and I look at each other. Uh-oh. "Why?" I ask.

"It's boring there," Caleb says.

I straighten the covers. "How can it be boring in there? We're *sleeping*. Sleeping means that you're not even awake. Sleeping isn't supposed to be exciting."

"If I was in my room by myself, there wouldn't be anyone to cuddle with." Caleb rolls over and buries his face in the pillow.

Well. I don't know what to say. I stand there poised to click off the lamp, and I look at this almost-seven-year-old boy, slightly embarrassed that he verbalized how much he likes to fall asleep cuddling with his parents, splayed facedown in the middle of my bed. His dark blond hair needs cut, his limbs are tanned, his hands lightly callused. This is the body of a big boy. I don't have very much little-kid time left with him at all.

I have become, I realize, the proverbial old woman in the grocery store who instructs new mothers—tired, frazzled, cranky new mothers—to *enjoy* it, but I can't help it. I feel like I have finally reached that part of Caleb's childhood where I *can* enjoy it. The embarrassment, the face in the pillow, is my warning: This will not last much longer. Two, three years maybe.

Just like that, I abort my sleeping-alone plans. I can't do it. I don't want to do it. I can hack it a little longer, I think, sleepy days and pitched roof be damned.

I switch off the light and slide in next to Caleb. "Good night, family," I say.

"Good night," Brandon says.

"Good night," Caleb says. Downstairs, we hear Luna rattle her crate.

"I like cuddling with you, too," I whisper to Caleb.

"Do you know what ten and ten and ten is?" he whispers back.

"Thirty. Now go to sleep."

"Okay," he says. We are a people who like to have the last word.

AM I A SUCKER? It depends on what you think children are.

The Babywise people operate under the impression that kids are inherently self-centered, manipulative, and amoral. "The ultimate objective of parenting in a free society is a moral one," Ezzo and Bucknam write. "When you rightly train the heart of a child, you lay down a solid foundation for the other disciplines of life." In other words, every parent faces the challenge of taking a wild creature and molding her into a rational, disciplined, moral person. By Babywise standards, I'm pretty much the stupid girl who got taken in by some bad poetry and a bottle of cheap red. Cuddling, I imagine them scoffing behind their aviator-style glasses (because—for real, now—all the crazy Christian conservative types wear the aviator-style glasses). That's the oldest trick in the book.

The mainstream experts—the folks at the AAP, the delicious-sounding T. Berry, the *What to Expect* crowd—like the idea of independence. In that sense, they're the quintessential American advice-givers:

Like all Americans, Caleb should be preparing to get on his horse and go it alone, Lone Ranger–style. Certain allowances can be made for his age and it doesn't happen naturally, but parental eyes should be on the prize of getting a functioning member of society out the door. By all means, attach, bond with the kid—but, you know, not in a *weird* way. So by mainstream standards, I've also failed. I should have made like Cher and simply told him that we all sleep alone.

And Sears. To him, children are these natural wonderful creatures, not unlike a coral reef. My job was simply not to mess Caleb up and to foster enough attachment to me that the boy would *want* to go to bed by himself. He'd feel *that* secure. "Between two and three years, most children accept weaning from your bed," Sears writes. "[A] child's needs that are filled early will eventually go away; a child's needs that are not filled leave an empty space that can come back later as anxieties." Caleb doesn't feel secure enough to sleep alone, apparently. So, yes. I've failed again.

If Sears had been the first person to tell me about co-sleeping, I might feel bad about failing. But the truth is, I did not get this co-sleeping idea from him, or any of the academics studying ethnopediatrics, a field that looks to anthropology, sociology, and evolutionary biology for evidence of the validity of non-Western types of parenting. I got it from Steel City, baby: home of the Terrible Towel, the pronoun *yoons*, and, at least in my family history, the sort of wages that couldn't afford everyone their own bed. My sisters and I grew up middle class (kind of, mostly), but there were some generational holdovers in the parenting. The co-sleeping being one of them.

"What's up with me?" I ask my mother on the phone the next night. "Why would I give up so easily?"

"Maybe you don't think that Caleb being in your bed is so bad," she says. "I don't think it is. Jill slept with me until she was nine."

And Jill, age twenty-two, can sleep by herself just fine, I think.

"Kathy [my aunt] and I shared a bed. We lived in the foundation"—meaning, the cinderblock foundation of my grandparents' current ranch-style home, a foundation that's incredibly small by any standards, much less for a family of six—"and there wasn't any other choice."

My mother, a first-grade teacher, is no stranger to theories regarding children, but on this issue, I can hear her impatience with the hand-wringing. What she means when she brings up the foundation and Jill is that this is a nonissue. You want your kid in the bed, fine. You don't, fine. The sleep issue has no psychological ramifications at this point. For Caleb anyway.

"Yeah, but what about the sleepwalking?" I ask. Someone broke into a few houses in my neighborhood recently, and, given my night-time rambling, my first thought was that maybe *I* did it. Maybe the sleeping me likes to burgle. Maybe the sleeping me was jonesing for some cash, iPods, and camcorders.

"I don't know," she says. "Are you sure the sleepwalking is related to Caleb being in your bed? Why would you start sleepwalking now and not any other time during the seven years he's been there?"

"I'm not sure," I say. "I don't know."

The problem with the self-help, I'm beginning to see, is that although I call what I'm doing "experiments," my life is a big unscientific jumble. I can't separate out the co-sleeping from everything else that may or may not be causing happiness. There are no controls.

So for now, I shelve it. Maybe I'll revisit the sleep issue when I get to the health experiments. Debie dropped off some review copies this week, and I saw a promising book titled *The No-Cry Sleep Solution*, whose author, Elizabeth Pantley, seems to have the sort of whatever-works attitude that I appreciate.

Besides, I see another parenting issue on the horizon, and for the first time since I started this whole program of bettering myself, I know for certain that this situation is indeed causing me stress.

. . .

A WORD PROBLEM FOR YOU: Twenty-three children live in your neighborhood, not counting the two babies due in less than three months. Five of these children—two girls and three boys—are roughly the same age. How many games of tag, kickball, indoor imaginative play, and miscellaneous interpersonal interactions can occur before the parents (a qualitatively nice bunch of people) become aware of some weird dynamic between two of the kids?

Answer: About two months' worth.

Parker and his family moved in down the street in July. Brandon and I like his parents, young professors of the unpretentious sort. We get a kick out of Parker's little brother Martin, a gravelly-voiced two-year-old who will tell you, with the insouciance of someone who knows his facts to be straight, that he's five. Parker himself is a cute, likeable kid. At our first meeting, he wore a man's tie over his summer ensemble, and he talked very very fast. He and Caleb and Joey, another neighborhood child, kicked a ball around while the adults Got to Know One Another.

Parker and Caleb went to the same summer camp, and we parents carpooled. Driving the boys home, I had the invisibility of a chauffeur, and of course I listened.

"You're my best friend, you know," Caleb told Parker.

"I thought Sophie was your best friend," Parker said (very very fast).

"Well, she was—but now she's not," Caleb said. "You are."

My ears perked up. Please say something nice back, Parker. Don't leave the boy hanging. Parker simply changed the subject, but apparently I was the only one who noticed. They continued chattering in their booster seats, slurping on their freezer pops, making plans to play after we got back home. They were two smart little guys who agreed that Parker's castle set was cooler than Caleb's but that Caleb had better dragons.

Slowly, things started going wrong, and try as I might, I can't pinpoint when it started. I know that Caleb was outraged when Parker came up and rang the doorbell without calling first. ("*You're never supposed to invite yourself over!*" he cried.) I know he was similarly outraged when Parker, afraid of the dogs, rang the doorbell and fled when Simon and Luna started barking. I was never one to micromanage their conversations, but I can imagine that they could have come up against an issue that they could not agree upon, and given their similar personalities—a little headstrong, more than a little dismissive of ideas they deem wrong—there could have been some words exchanged. Strong words. Fighting words.

However it started, though, it came to a head the evening Parker's family threw together a potluck with Sophie's family and us. Brandon and I, we had a delightful time. But in the parallel universe—the potluck the kids experienced—the gathering was not such a success. Sophie was struck in the head, she reported, at least twice. Martin was not treated kindly and burst into tears. Parker was "told what to do" and he did not appreciate it. Caleb, we were informed later, was asked when he was going home. It was implied that his departure could not come soon enough.

"I'm not going to play with Parker anymore," Caleb told us.

He kept his vow. School started, and in the warm afternoons after the bus dropped the kids off, what I now think of as the playdate wars began. Caleb and Parker wouldn't play nicely together—but they both wanted to play with Joey. Or Sophie or Eva. Caleb and Parker vied for the available kids, and from our separate ends of the war, Parker's parents and I independently decided it best to leave the playdates up to the luck of the draw.

Clearly, we could not get the once lovely friendship back. But just as clearly, we couldn't have this ongoing feud either. Neither family plans on moving anytime soon, and what's more, this social smoothing is part of life. It was exhausting being on guard whenever we spotted Parker and his family (which was pretty often). I started trying to convince Caleb to stay inside. I was getting grumpy and stressed out.

Finally I thought, I can't manage their interactions, but maybe I can teach Caleb a more sophisticated way of dealing with his irritation.

"Caleb," I said over dinner one night. "You don't have to be friends with Parker but you do have to get along with him."

Caleb dipped a forkful of potato in ketchup.

"You know, there are people I don't like, but I get along with them."

He looks up. "Like who?"

"Neil," I say. Neil, a man in our social circle, is certainly not all bad. More like a mystery wrapped in a conundrum wrapped in a thick layer of interpersonal irritants.

"*Neil!*" Caleb says. "You don't like *Neil!* How come? He's great!"

"See, you might think so, but I don't like him. He talks down to people—" I cut myself off before the lesson I impart is Why Neil Sucks. "I don't like him, but I get along with him."

Caleb scoots his zucchini around with a fork. "There's nothing wrong with Neil," he says.

"To me, there is," I say. I clear my plate from the table. "But I get along with him. And you can get along with Parker."

Caleb grumbles. I scrape my plate. I should have picked a different person, I think. Neil has partially redeemed himself in recent months, but once someone pisses me off, that's about it for me. I can see that this . . . this whatever I'm about to teach Caleb may not be exactly intuitive for me. I'm not known for my ability to conceal irritation, and these sophisticated methods I'm so eager to apply might be a foreign concept.

IN TERMS OF HAPPINESS, parenting is a weird thing. Because my son is not me, not even necessarily a definite reflection of me, and yet our happinesses are tied pretty well together at this stage of the game, that stage being seven years old.

Like any decent mother, I want the boy to be happy—that's the big goal. I want him to be happy, but he can't scarf down another bowl of ice cream. I want him to be happy, but there is no way I'm eating dinner at that nauseating children's pizza place. I want him to be happy, but he can't hurt Parker's feelings. It's this constant negotiation between his happiness, his well-being, my happiness, and The Rules. And it's up for debate how much parenting even matters in the scheme of things. I'm not 100 percent liable for his happiness, but I'm not 0 percent liable, either. Who knows what a job well done looks like? Mostly, I err on the side of putting forth my best effort to teach him. Mostly, it seems to be working out okay. Mostly, I feel satisfied that I'm doing my best.

But then I come to this mundane little dilemma with Parker, and my best may not be cutting it. The situation stresses me out, and it stresses Caleb out. Since I'm the parent here, it's my burden to share, as unwieldy and dicey and possibly unsolvable as it may be.

THERE ARE NO BOOKS called *How to Make It So Your Kid Gets Along with Other Kids in Your Admittedly Commune-Like Neighborhood*, so don't bother looking. The situation, though, falls into the broad category of social graces, and I come home from the bookstore with *How to Raise a Child with a High E.Q.: A Parents' Guide to Emotional Intelligence*, by Lawrence E. Shapiro, Ph.D. The big, bring-it-to-the-people book on emotional intelligence—which is basically an aptitude for dealing with feelings, both your own and other people's—was Daniel Goleman's 1995 best-seller *Emotional Intelligence*. Shapiro's book came out in 1998, the year Caleb was born. So these aren't exactly hot new ideas I'm reading about here, but they are the sort of theories that get trotted out cyclically. Every time there's a national news story about children being shockingly brutal, emotional intelligence pops back up in the media. *Good God*, the people say about the mean girls/ the teenaged killers/the boy bullies. *Don't our children know anything about how to treat one another?*

I tend to agree that a little kindness goes a long way so I'm looking forward to spending much time nodding at Shapiro's wisdom. Lay it on me, brother. But when I crack open the book while Caleb spends the afternoon with Brandon's parents, I'm a little disappointed to find that *How to Raise a Child with High E. Q.* doesn't read like such a grand departure from most other parenting manuals. There's that certain tone, the frightening consequences, the oversimplification of studies. I'm going to have to overlook these flaws, though, if this book is going to be of any use to me.

But I'm up to the task because Shapiro's view on what children are—and really, what adults are—is not so out of sync with cultural ideas. Basically, he thinks they're living chemistry sets. Hey, I've heard of Prozac—this is not a novel idea to me. What Shapiro says is that it's up to us parents to make sure the right chemicals are engaged in our kids' heads.

Literally. Shapiro spends a few pages relating how findings in neuroanatomy and neurochemistry relate to emotional intelligence: "Perhaps what is most interesting about taking a role in your children's emotional education is that you are literally changing your children's brain chemistry, or more accurately, teaching them ways to control their brain functioning themselves," he writes.

Shapiro offers a wide range of emotional lessons parents can teach their kids, from basic manners to nonverbal communication to optimism. Much of it makes sense to me. In "Encouraging Empathy and Compassion," Shapiro advises parents to "raise the bar on your expectations," which means no allowances for chores—the kids should know that's just what we *do* to be part of a family. In "The Pleasures and Significance of Humor," he makes the claim that funnier and more entertaining people are more well liked (than, I suppose, their dour and humorless class-mates). In "The Negative Moral Emotions," he points out that shame and guilt actually have very useful functions in our society.

Shapiro also unpacks the fun fact every once in a while, and what reader doesn't like that? In "Communication Beyond Words," he quotes psychologists Stephen Nowicki and Marshall Duke, who find that when a person makes a verbal mistake, others assume that the mistake-maker is uneducated or unintelligent; but when a person makes a body-language error (facing the back of the elevator, say), others assume the mistake-maker is weird, strange, dangerous.

Another nugget: He claims that when you smile, your brain gets the message to make more seratonin, the neurological chemical that got famous when Prozac hit it big. "When we tell our children to 'just smile' and things will seem better, we are absolutely right. Little things make a difference."[3]

Behind all the fun facts, though, I see that this will be some serious work. With the clutter and finances, I could do it myself, more or less. With the marriage experiments, I had the willing and good-humored Brandon to work with. With the parenting advice about physical needs—sleeping, feeding, health—the advice is fairly straightforward. But I wonder how willing Caleb will be this go-round. He's my kid but he's also his own person. Even the sleep thing didn't fly with him. He's a child who panics if we leave for the bus stop one minute late. I can't imagine he'll be any more welcoming of someone screwing around with his brain chemistry.

SHAPIRO'S WORDS are running through my head. I'm driving on the interstate at sixty-five miles per hour, and on my face I wear a perfectly

---

[3] On a related note: In the spring of 2006, one dermatological study found that injecting Botox—the drug that makes it impossible for people to frown—helped alleviate major clinical depression in many of the study's subjects.

ridiculous-looking rictus of a grin. I'm having, or at least I think I'm having, an unprovoked panic attack. I've had one in my life: on the day Brandon went back to work after paternity leave, leaving me alone with defenseless newborn Caleb. I've been making this trip to get my hair done every month for the past two years, but somehow this particular trip includes a bonus freak-out.

My heart is doing strange things and I feel *not right*. I grip the steering wheel and try to remember this feeling to describe it later, but *not right* is the best I can come up with, a sad state for an editor to be in. Trembly, maybe, something a little off with the vision, although it's not blurred or blocked.

I blast up the air-conditioning even though it's a cool, damp fall day. I turn down the music. *I am doing the best that I can* is the last phrase that I heard from the CD player, and I repeat it in my head. I continue smiling. I feel like a complete nutcase. After a mile or so, the symptoms abate, but still I smile, afraid that they'll happen again. I'm using the smile as a talisman, something to ward off the panic attack. Thank you, Lawrence Shapiro, Ph.D. Thank you, big seratonin-inducing smile.

As I get closer to home, I imagine people passing me in their cars. *What the hell is she so happy about?* I grin, I grin, I grin. I'm not unintelligent or uneducated. I'm just a little strange, weird, dangerous.

SHAPIRO ENCOURAGES his readers to take a little here and there from his book to tailor emotional intelligence tactics to their own children's needs, so I decide to focus on two chapters, including "Manners Matter." I have to admit that, thus far, I haven't been really stringent on the manners; I'm all about the spirit and not so much about the letter of Caleb's behavior. But manners, I figure, can only help in his dealing with Parker because manners dovetail with The Rules.

Choosing another chapter presents me with an advice crisis. What I'm really trying to eliminate is Caleb's tendency to get fired up and eventually scream, "Leave me alone!" to whoever pisses him off, following up with a crying jag. (This, however unpleasant, is an improvement over his preschool technique that sometimes culminated in a note home to us: *Your child bit one of his friends today*. . . .)

Shapiro discusses how this sort of reaction comes from the emotional brain, not the logical one. In one chapter, he claims that you can teach your child to stop reacting from the emotional brain. Yet in another chapter, he claims you can't. So, which is it?

In the end, after puzzling through the two chapters and reading between the lines, I decide on "Solutions Training," the chapter that promises that we'll be able to create pathways between the two parts of Caleb's brain, short-circuiting the emotional reaction. As I read, I have a vision of myself as someone who doesn't work on intuition, but a gentle mother in a lab coat. I've done my homework, and I can tell you just what's right for any given situation. Now, kids, we're going to forge a pathway.

I COME DOWNSTAIRS one evening with five copies of a questionnaire regarding Caleb's manners. It's intended to be distributed to at least five people, including Brandon, me, and Caleb himself.

"What's that you have in your hands?" Caleb asks.

"It's a little quiz that I thought might be fun to do," I say. I'm supposed to average the scores. Fifty is a perfect score; under 35 "should raise a red flag."

"I want to do it!" Caleb says cheerfully.

I hand him one sheet of paper. He's to rate himself on various areas of politesse. For example, "_____ is punctual." I explain how to do it.

"Okay," he exhales. " 'Caleb is polite,' " he reads. "Five. Always."

Brandon and I look at each other. "Really?" I say. "You're *always* polite?"

"Well . . . yeah," he says.

"Okay," I say. When all is said and done, Caleb—or Mr. Emily Post, if you will—has racked up an impressive 41 (out of 50) points on his Manners Test.

"I want to do more," he says, surprising me. We take the next step, which is to come up with three rules for Caleb to follow.

Shapiro gives an example: "If introduced to an adult whom you do not know, or whom you rarely see, shake her hand as part of your greeting." As much as I like the novelty of having a child who shakes hands (and I do like it—it reminds me of the time I trained the two-year-old Caleb to call Brandon "Daddums" for my own amusement), I think our rules have to be more basic. Soon we have a list, of pleases and thank-yous, no interrupting.

Shapiro claims that the kids love playing these games, and I see he's not kidding as Caleb asks for more to do.

We settle back down and embark on the "Brainstorming Game," which is supposed to make children "generate as many solutions to a problem as possible and then [pick] the best ones." This is the thing that, in theory, will forge those connections between Caleb's emotions and his logic and permit him to shrug it off when Parker (or anyone else) does something he doesn't like.

Shapiro says to start out with something simple. He once asked a classroom of kindergartners what they could do with a bucket before moving on to more real-life scenarios. I hold up a crumpled paper bag left on the coffee table. "I need you to tell me all the different things you could do with this bag. It doesn't matter if they're good ideas or silly ones," I tell Caleb. "Just tell me all of them."

"All right," Caleb says. "A mask." He stops. "A paper ball." When he's done, we have a list of seven alternatives should Caleb ever encounter a paper bag that needs to be put to immediate use.

"Now, we're going to do something different. Let's say there's a kid whose friend keeps irritating him. What should he do?"

"Say, 'Stop it,' " Caleb says immediately.

"What else?"

"Tell a grown-up."

I write it down. "Okay, what else?"

Caleb is silent. "I don't know." He sits on the child-sized chair we've pulled up to the coffee table, his lips twisted in concentration. "I can't think of any more."

It occurs to me how helpless, how powerless kids are. Because, really, what other acceptable options are there? When I was a kid, we weren't allowed to take the first punch, but we had our parents' blessing to fight anyone who physically threatened us or one of our sisters. This sort of thing doesn't fly today, which has its good sides and bad, in my opinion. "You know, Caleb, they don't have to be *good* ideas. They can be silly," I pause. "I have one."

"What is it?"

"Punch him," I say softly, and we both laugh.

"Kick him," he says, getting into the spirit. "Hit him."

I'm writing furiously.

"Hit him with a fork," he says rapid-fire. "Poke him with a straw."

Poke him with a straw? Oh, this is not good. Shapiro gives me an E.Q.-building game and I turn it into a revenge-fantasy session. Coming up with the bad options is way more fun than finding good solutions. "Okay, okay—don't forget to think of some good solutions, too."

I can see by the look on his face that I've harshed his mellow. "Walk away," he offers after a few minutes. "Say, 'I don't want to play with you anymore.' "

"How about 'Take a deep breath and get calm'?" I ask. He shrugs. I write it down.

Caleb reads over the list and finds that we have four good solutions for the child whose friend is irritating him: *Say "Stop it," tell a grownup, walk away, and take a deep breath and get calm.* I have no idea what effect this has on Caleb, but it saddens me. It's a pretty meager toolbox.

We do one more scenario—a girl is experiencing meanness at school at the hands of some classmates—and Caleb comes up with the exact same good solutions (although he riffs on some more bad solutions, including "Take away their backpacks" and "Say mean things to them"). He gets 4 points. He draws a picture of a brain that looks slightly tornadic in nature and labels it "Brain Storm game!" It's time for bed.

I'M DRIVING on the windy road between the Indian restaurant where we just ate and home. It's seven o'clock and dark already. My headlights hit the gray pavement and the trees that form a canopy over the road. I'm fiddling with the CD player when the panic hits me again. My heart goes nuts and my vision gets strange. "God *damn* it," I say loudly, then panic harder because swearing, I feel, can only make things worse. Not *God damn it*. Calm. Calm. I take deep breaths and assume the anxiety grin.

PARKER AND CALEB are at it again. After what seemed to be a truce, with Caleb, Parker, and Joey playing tag nicely for five minutes, Parker has disappeared, ending the game and ticking my boy off. Immensely.

I don't know what to do here. What brain am I dealing with? The logical one? Well, it's true that it defies logic that a child would leave a seemingly fun game five minutes into it. Or is it the emotional one? Clearly, Caleb's seething.

Joey stands patiently by our porch. "Aughhhhhh!" Caleb screams, filled with a sense of injustice.

"Hey," I say sharply. "That's enough screaming. There are babies in this neighborhood who might be sleeping." He glowers at me. I walk down the stairs. "So, are you just going to stand there and act like a nut over something you can't control, or are you going to play with Joey? Let's brainstorm what you can do."

I thought working "brainstorm" into this lecture was more than a little clever, but Caleb continues. "It's not fair! Parker said he wanted to play outside and he just leaves! He can't JUST LEAVE!"

"No," I say. "It's not fair." I pause. "Do you have any ideas what you and Joey could do?"

"We want to play chase with Parker," Joey says.

"I know, but you can't. Any other ideas?" The boys stand there, Caleb still huffing, Joey looking a little confused. For a distraction as much as anything else, I grab some chalk and bring it to the sidewalk. I write *Fat Babies*—an inside joke between me and Caleb—in lavender chalk. Caleb and Joey start writing numbers on the sidewalk. Parker doesn't reemerge, and I know that this incident will be filed in Caleb's ledger of grievances (which is now, thankfully, a metaphor—last year, it was an actual ledger with people's initials and check marks representing infractions). When Joey and Caleb are done writing out their numbers and Joey's sister comes to chase him home for dinner, the sidewalk is filled with what looks like a complicated equation, the sort of thing that keeps you up at night.

I SIT ON THE PORCH and read a magazine, enjoying one of the last warm nights this fall. Brandon will be out in a minute, as soon as he gets Caleb settled with his half hour of computer games. It's getting dark and I hear three neighbor women. "I have room for one more in my car!" one of them calls to the others. They're dressed up. There's apparently some sort of girls' night out in the neighborhood, to which I am not invited. They don't see me on the porch. I read. Chances are excellent that, invited along, I would have demurred anyway, but still. It's been a long time since I've been the unpopular girl. I don't watch them walk down the street. It stings, a little.

. . .

I DIDN'T LIKE being a kid; for me, childhood was something to be suffered through until I could enter the adult world of freedom. Being a child meant being helpless, being bossed, being taken less than seriously.

It's no surprise then, that the way I mother reflects my own experience as a kid. What do I think children are? In some sense, I think they're just undercooked adults. As such, I don't really have a parenting philosophy at all. I just have faith that he'll be shaped by our treating him nicely, our examples of how to act like good people, the few rules we've erected, and his experiences.

I call Brandon at work. "This is Brandon," he answers.

"Hey there," I say. "What do you do when someone annoys you?"

"Poke them with a straw," he says.

I laugh. "No, really?"

"Hmm. Somebody annoyed me this morning, and I tried to see where he was coming from and figured out what questions I had to answer. Kept it short. I don't get annoyed that much, really. What do you do?"

"I avoid them, and if I have to deal with them, then I try to keep the conversation as short as possible," I say. "And then I go home and make fun of them to you for an hour."

Uh-oh. Shapiro devotes an entire chapter to "teaching by example"—but it seemed irrelevant to our issues at the time. "Do you demonstrate to your child how to solve problems through your day-to-day words and actions?" he asked. I answered yes, but now I'm not so sure. Is mocking Neil's know-it-all attitude behind his back really that much different from Caleb's getting enraged that Parker flouted the rules of chase? "Brandon," I ask. "Did we teach him to be this way or was it something he was born with?"

"There's not a smart-ass gene, if that's what you're saying," Brandon says, which leads me to imagine a study: In it, Caleb has an identical twin we gave up at birth to a family outside Western culture. In my mind's eye, this not-Caleb, he's getting pissed because some other kid didn't skin his antelope right. He's irritated because another child monk is meditating too close to him. This not-Caleb knows how to say, "Leave me alone" in languages I've never even heard spoken.

Alas, there is no study. I wonder if Brandon had stayed home with Caleb when he was little whether Caleb might have picked up Brandon's way of dealing. If he would have been a calmer, less easily provoked child. Who knows. Nature or nuture—it's a moot point by now, I think.

WE'RE DRIVING HOME from a restaurant. Brandon is making a left-hand turn and a family—a man pushing a stroller and a woman—are in the crosswalk. The man trots quickly across the street, but the woman halts in the middle of street, false starting and false stopping.

Caleb calls from the backseat in a dopey voice, "*I don't know what to do! Do I go? Do I want to get hit by a car? I can't decide!*"

"Caleb!" Brandon says, but he's stifling a laugh.

"Oh my God," I say. I'm not laughing. There's a definite shift in someone's brain chemistry right now. It's my brain, and it's the chemical you get when you realize that you're spoiling pristine nature, your child, the coral reef.

THIS IS NOT FUNNY: Through pretty much serendipity, I feel like evidence is accruing: the Parker trouble, the lack of invite, the dawning realization that Caleb is more like me than I'd ever noticed, and it's all leading me to some nasty ideas. I spend four days feeling terrible about myself. I speak hesitantly to people; all my actions feel tamped. Is this what regular people do? I ask myself before speaking, before waving to a neighbor, before making any offhand comment. Reading Dear Abby in the newspaper one morning, I burst into tears. At least "In Separate Beds for Now" knows what his problem is. Me, on the other hand, I have this defective personality. Something unspecified is wrong with the very core of me, I feel. I try, but I cannot talk myself out of this feeling. In Shapiro terms, my emotional brain has bypassed my logical one.

TO THE BOOKSTORE AGAIN. As I walk in from the parking lot, I know full well that I'm of two minds. One of my minds—the one that edits *Brain, Child* and knows that mothers get blamed for every damn thing—is telling me that I need to just stop the self-help for a while and get my confidence back. I was overconfident before, with my parents-know-best schtick! I could have just a smidgen of that confidence back and have plenty! But the other mind—the one who has been taking self-help advice for a year—is beefed up and boisterous. She's been fed, fueled, doped up like a solutions junkie.

She is the one who marches to the parenting magazine section, a fire in her belly. She grabs *Child* magazine and quickly flips through it. There, in the table of contents: "controlling poor behavior." On page 72, one Ms. Christiane Lavin, mother of four from Fairfax County, writes: "When a child has serious behavior issues, therapy may be in order—for Mom and Dad, that is. Researchers at the University of Washington in Seattle studied 514 children ages 3 to 8 and discovered that conduct problems improved more when the parents—not the kids—sought help for themselves."

This sucker punch—it's all my fault, I'm messing my kid up—feels about right for the masochistic self-help me.

I take the magazine to the clerk up front who stifles a yawn, nostrils flaring prettily out. Compared to this person, I feel frumpy and sad, no makeup, wearing jeans that lost their Spandex hold hours ago. A thought flutters up—I can get a book on how to look better!—but for once the old me comes to the rescue and quashes it dead before it takes wing.

CALEB, PARKER, SOPHIE, and Joey are playing outside Parker's house. Caleb runs ahead of me. By the time I catch up, I hear Caleb telling Parker that he needs to apologize to Sophie. "Not your job!" I say to my boy, the justice squad.

Parker's mother is on the porch, minding Martin. "He's right, though," she mouths to me. She puts Parker in a time-out and sends Sophie, who's seeming cranky, home.

Caleb and Joey run back up the street to our house. Parker's mother and I chat. Inconsequential things. She seems distant somehow, and I try to think of what I did wrong.

It's only later, as I'm throwing together some stew for dinner, that I realize that I have become a person who thinks everything is about me. Part of me is relieved that I might not have pissed Parker's mother off, and an equal part is disgusted at my newly heightened self-absorption.

YOU KNOW WHAT? I can't really stand to tell you about that night after Caleb fell asleep. I ranted and raged and punched the couch. There was a dramatic monologue of dubious quality that featured the word *craaaaazy* followed by a choked little weeping noise. After months of free-falling with the sleepwalking, the panic attacks, the crisis of faith in myself, I landed hard.

The parenting experiments ended that night. It wasn't Sears or Shapiro or *Child* in particular, although it's true I'll never be the mother those experts envision. It was the six months of questioning every move I made with my family. That night, after the performance,

Brandon suggested I needed a break. I agreed, and ding dong, the Self-Help Me was, if not dead, weakened for the time being.

AT THE BUS STOP a week later, Parker shakes a sapling in Caleb's direction. It stormed the night before and droplets of water splash all over Caleb. Caleb starts to cry and jogs toward me for comfort. On his way, he shoves Parker a little. "Apologize to Caleb," Parker's father says. I don't suggest that Caleb apologize for the shove. In my book, you spray rainwater down on a person who's dressed for school, you deserve what you get.

Later, explaining to Sophie's mother why Parker wouldn't hug him before he got on the bus, Parker's father says, "He shook water on Caleb. Caleb pushed him. And I made Parker apologize."

Is it implied that I should have done the same? I can't tell.

I raise my eyebrows but I don't say anything. I've been distancing myself from the neighborhood, and it feels good to not appease. If the choice is between my happiness, Caleb's happiness, and The Rules, I'm going to choose my happiness and Caleb's happiness. To hell with The Rules. It feels good not to care if Caleb and Parker ever speak to each other again. I say good-bye and turn heel back to my house.

THE LOGICAL THING TO DO would be to stop here with the experts. They got me into this emotional mess, and I'd be a nut to think they could heal me.

And stopping here is *exactly* what I'd do, if it weren't for two things: One is that this whole episode with the parenting experts is, frankly, embarrassing. I, of all people, should have been immune to reacting so strongly to parenting advice. And if we couldn't follow simple steps to get Caleb to fall asleep in his own bed, what made me think that I could follow more complicated steps to change his brain chemistry?

(It goes without saying that the real me should have questioned the wisdom of mucking around with his brain in the first place.)

Months later, I'll look back at this period and wonder what the hell was wrong with me. I'll also feel immense gratitude that the advice didn't work. I like the boy how he is. If I had a child who defused fighting words and shook the hands of adults, would that child still be my Caleb? Would he stick up for himself? Would he be a cuddler? Would he flop down on my lap and demand that I tickle him? I am—and should be—ashamed at how lightly I took who he is, how cavalierly I thought I could change us, how arrogantly I approached the whole messy business of sending the kid off into the world, as if I could control any aspect of it, as if it had anything to do with me.

So I won't stop here because I want to redeem myself. I suspended my disbelief about the parenting experts, when I should have hung on to it. Disbelief is a lovely thing. I plan to wear it loud and wear it proud into the next experiments.

The other reason I'm not stopping here is the existence of one man: Martin Seligman, former president of the American Psychological Association and a man quoted in more self-help books than you can shake a motivational paragraph at. If anyone can get me back on track, it's him. Just remembering that someone with his research and credentials is out there lifts my spirits.

The Attempt to Screw My Head on Straight

I REALIZE TOO LATE that the title of Martin Seligman's book I ordered online has the same effect in public as the marriage manuals I bought at the bookstore. The effect being that people will look at you as if you are a sad sack. I popped *Authentic Happiness: Using the New Positive Psychology to Realize Your Potential for Lasting Fulfillment*, its cover a brilliant blue, in my purse, thinking I'd read while I ate a slice of pizza downtown.

If you have any doubts that there's a cultural disdain for a certain type of woman, here's what you do: Go out to lunch by yourself. While you eat, read your book whose title betrays a bald yearning for happiness. Time everything so that no one's done laundry in a while and you have to wear a pair of faded black "yoga pants." Time it so that your hair is simultaneously frizzy and flat and in need of a good dye job. Time it so that the only available seat at the pizza place is right in the window. Sit there. Read. Eat your slice of pizza. Drink some iced tea. Notice that you're pretty much invisible. Read more. Accidentally slop a little cheese on your bosom. When you look up to grab a napkin, catch the eye of a twentysomething preppy boy. He looks from your face, to your sauced-up chest, to your book. Notice him wince.

I'm open to the explanation that the wince could be attributed to my own self-consciousness. Or—who knows—the guy could have just had dental work done. But my first response to him is the evil eye. I put on my figurative babushka and mutter a curse: *May Saint Oprah smite you and all who would judge the soft-bellied women who read self-help.*

MARTIN E. P. SELIGMAN, PH.D., opens *Authentic Happiness*, like all rousing stories, with some quotes from nuns.

In 1932, researchers asked 180 new nuns to write an autobiographical sketch; they then kept track of the nuns throughout their lives, noting the women's health and mortality rates. The nuns' lifestyle is pretty uniform across the board, Seligman notes; among other similarities, they eat the same sort of food and they neither smoke, drink, nor fool around, which makes them a pretty good control group. As it turns out, the researchers found that the young nuns who used more positive emotion in their autobiographical sketches lived longer and were healthier than those who weren't as ebullient, even when they factored in other variables. This, Seligman writes, was "the most remarkable study of happiness and longevity ever done."

Some years ago, Seligman, a professor of psychology at the University of Pennsylvania, became increasingly disturbed that his field was limited to the study of mental illness. Certainly a worthy cause, he thought, but hardly all-encompassing of the human mind. "Psychologists now can measure once-fuzzy concepts as depression, schizophrenia, and alcoholism with considerable precision. We now know a good deal about how these troubles develop across the life span, and about their genetics, their biochemistry, and their psychological causes," he writes. "Best of all, we have learned how to relieve these disorders."

But alas, he points out that this sheds no light on how to live a good life, a meaningful life, a happy life—which is what most of us want. Positive emotions, Seligman says (and with some data to back him up), are more than just the absence of negative emotions. They're the reason for living.

Sometime in the 1990s, Seligman and some colleagues sought to end this hiding of positive psychology under a bushel; Positive Psychology (in the title case) was born. There are three branches of it—positive emotion, positive traits, and positive institutions—but for the purposes of this book, he's only concerned with the first two. Seligman thinks Positive Psychology is the key to happiness. "Positive Psychology takes seriously the bright hope that if you find yourself stuck in the parking lot of life, with few and only ephemeral pleasures, with minimal gratifications, and without meaning, there is a road out."

Right about here I start to get nervous. Given my troubles lately, the very last thing I need is a cheerleader with a Ph.D. I fear that I might hate Martin Seligman and that hatred would then shatter my hopes for getting back on track.

But luckily, it does not. In fact, I like Martin Seligman very much. He confesses that he's a dyed-in-the-wool pessimist. He's given to glumness. He holds his breath when he asks people to jump onboard with any given project of his because he doubts that they'll do it. And, he writes: "I have to confess that even though I have written a book and many articles about children, I'm actually not very good with them. I am goal-oriented and time-urgent and when I'm weeding in the garden, I'm weeding." Hey, me, too! I thought. Except for the weeding bit, which I don't do.

On that day in his garden, his young daughter Nikki was goofing off and he snapped at her. What she told him, he claims, was an epiphany for him: She remembered that she whined every day from age three until age five. Then she decided she didn't want to be a whiner anymore. "That was the hardest thing I've ever done," she told him. "And if I can stop whining, you can stop being such a grouch." He realized that he was indeed a grouch and resolved to change his Oscarly ways. He also realized that the tools for him—and others—to do it were in the toolbox of Positive Psychology, and it was time to start building a better Martin Seligman.

I HAVE NOT QUITE given up on trying to resolve the Caleb/Parker fracas, but I seriously don't know what to do. As it turns out, I will have to do nothing.

One weekend, Brandon decides that he'll remind Caleb every single time before they see Parker that he is mature enough to just let things go. If Parker gets in his face, let it go. If he does something that irritates Caleb, let it go. To me, this sounds like the exact same thing as *walk away*, but for some reason, it works.

I run into Parker's mother, who tells me that she overheard Caleb telling Sophie, "Let it go, Sophie," when Parker was doing something a little goofy to get the other kids' attention.

"Yeah, that was Brandon's doing," I tell her. "I think it helped Caleb to be reminded."

"You know, maybe we should try that with Parker," she says. "I'm not sure what's going on with him lately."

By the next week, both boys are clamoring to play with each other. At first it only works when it's just the two of them, but soon Caleb and Parker run around in a pack with the other five- to seven-year-olds. I'm embarrassed to say exactly how much relief this elicits in me. The problem between the kids isn't solved forever, but it's solved for now, and that's good enough.

THE FIRST THING I learn from *Authentic Happiness* is that I'm maybe a little bit of a snot. I'm really very excited about this book—way more than I was about the other experts. Is it Seligman's credentials? Maybe. All I know is, the less I know about a subject—whether it's how retirement accounts work or why optimists have better lives—the more enthusiastic I am about the advice. Don't get me wrong—I'm trying *all* this stuff in earnest, but my inner Lewis & Clark loves some completely uncharted territory.

The second thing I learn is that I'll have to take many tests and do many exercises to get the full benefit of Seligman's program. (You can either do them in the book or online at authentichappiness.org, but you need the book to really understand the results.) The first test I take is the Fordyce Emotions Questionnaire (named for its creator, Michael W. Fordyce), in which you rate your "average" happiness." I rate myself as 6—"Slightly happy (just a bit above normal)." The average score for American adults, Seligman reports, is 6.92—somewhere between slightly happy and mildly happy ("feeling fairly good and somewhat cheerful"). It would be nice, I think, to be at an 8, aka "pretty happy" in which my spirits are "high" and I'm feeling "good."

Next I take a test in which I figure out my "affectivity" of positive and negative emotions. What it measures is how strongly a person feels a given emotion. This is just the temperament—"giggler or grouch," as Seligman puts it—that you're born with. The possible scores range between 10 and 50. Perched on the couch between Caleb and the dogs (who are, to my irritation, wrestling), I take the quiz. I'm supposed to rate, on a scale of 1 to 5, how I feel right this minute. Right this minute I am not in the best mood, I have to say. The weather has been nasty and wet and the dependents fairly high-maintenance. I score a 29 on positive affectivity and a 20 on negative affectivity, which means that I don't often feel huge bursts of joy *or* crushing waves of sadness.

I retake the test two weeks later in my office, in a better mood, alone on a warm, sunny day and find that my scores are 28 for positive affectivity and 18 for negative affectivity. Taking the tests online, you get the extra benefit—or self-consciousness–making factor, I suppose—of seeing how your scores compare with other test-takers in general and ones of your gender, occupation, age group, etc. My positive affectivity was pretty standard, but my negative affectivity was lower than about 75 percent of the other test-takers, across the board. In other words, I may not be ebullient, but I'm statistically more resistant to deeply felt negative emotions than many other people.

Still, as Seligman says, "not depressed" does not happy make. And happy's what we want. He debunks the idea that happy people may be cheery but out of touch with reality. He points out that it's all situational, and happy people can better adapt their tasks to whatever level of reality is needed. Need to be critical? Happy people can do it; they just don't *have* to. They can turn it off. Seligman suggests, for any given task, that you set your mood up to accommodate the task. If, for instance, I need to be proofreading the pages of the magazine so we don't run a ton of typos and look like dumb-asses, I should do it "on rainy days, in straight-backed chairs, and in silent, institutionally painted rooms," he writes. "Being uptight, sad or out of sorts will not impede [me]; it may even make [my] decisions more acute." On the other hand, if I need to write some headlines, dream up a good Valentine's Day present, or any other creative task, I should make my surrounding as good-mood–inducing as possible.

It's not just my realism that will benefit from my happiness. Among other benefits, Seligman points out that being happy makes you more energetic (thus healthier and longer lived), more productive, better at coping with adversity, and more popular. Except for the more popular bit, these all intuitively strike me as worthy goals. He's preaching to the choir here.

CALEB TROMPS UP the front porch stairs and crumples over onto the porch swing. His face is red and smeared with tears. He's howling.

I open the front door. "What's wrong, baby?" I ask. "What happened?" He went with Sophie and her father to play at the nearby soccer field.

He rushes inside. "They just sent me *home!*" he sobs. "I didn't *want TO COME HOME!*" He kicks off his shoes hard and they hit the wall, leaving a mark.

"Hey!" I say. "There is *no* need to ruin the house." Which ticks him off even more and he fumes. Somehow, slowly, he comes out of his funk, but we can't get him to divulge the events that took place at the soccer field.

Until Parker's father comes to the house a few hours later. His arrival is heralded by Simon and Luna flinging themselves at the door and barking madly. Brandon steps out front to talk with Parker's father, and somehow I know that this is related to the behavior of another member of the household.

Apparently, Parker and his father joined Sophie et al. at the soccer field. The three kids were playing a game of keep-away with a ball. Parker was the monkey in the middle, and everyone was cool with this until Sophie fell. Caleb insisted that Parker tripped her, and in retaliation, he hit Parker. The fathers decided that this little excursion was over for all three kids. Exeunt.

Brandon relates this to me as he cooks and I huddle next to him. We're getting our story straight before we talk to Caleb. Brandon whispers the story, then pauses to put the meat in the skillet.

"So, what?" I whisper back. "What was the point of telling us?" This whole situation is bringing out some snippiness in me. I thought this was resolved, and I'm back at my default setting of Let The Children Work It Out. "He came over to *tell* on Caleb?"

"Oh, no, not at all," Brandon whispers. "He said that they sent Caleb home and wanted to know if *we* thought that was the right thing to do, or if he should have put him in time-out or something."

Oh.

We talk to Caleb and he immediately bursts into tears. He knows that it's not right to hit people. We say, "Caleb, you know that it's not right to hit people." We say, "Hey, we expect better behavior from you." He cries a little, but he gets it. He's harder on himself than we usually are. We drop it. We eat dinner, and then we play a board game.

Later, as we lie in bed and wait for him to drift off, it occurs to me—and not for the first time—that I assume the worst about people.

Before I had any experts on the subject, I did an experiment on our way to Key West last summer. Brandon and I had a six-hour layover and once we exhausted all the regular time-killing activities—a leisurely lunch, browsing in the various retail shops, even playing air hockey in the arcade—there was nothing to do but people-watch. I kicked back in an armchair and watched the travelers go past. I am a very important business executive, I thought about a gray-haired man barreling through while talking on his cell phone. I told my hairdresser, just give me the most frumpy look possible, I thought about a woman with a youthful face but the hair and clothes of someone much older. Why do I have to be so nasty? I thought about myself.

So I tried to inject a little kindness into my people-watching. His mother loves him—his phone calls are the highlight of her week, I thought of a total dweeb of a man meandering down the walkway, scratching himself. She volunteers with sick babies, I thought of a Latina woman with bleached hair and four-inch roots. She has a heart of gold.

But even I could tell that this was not kindness so much as pitying thoughts, the likes of which I'd hate for someone to direct at me. I told myself to think of them as adults I respect.

A sunburned man leading three sunburned children and a sun-burned wife came traipsing down the hallway toward the food court, each dragging a rolling suitcase. He's a tiger in the sack, I thought of the father. And *her*. Mm. Mm. Mm. Stop. Stop. How did this get pornographic? And "tiger in the sack"? Who am I? Mr. Furley?

I look at the glass of water on my nightstand and sigh, which causes Caleb to shift. The unspoken criticism of strangers, that's a victimless crime. But Parker's father—a neighbor, a friend—that's something else altogether. He's a perfectly nice man with good intentions. Why was my first response to assume he came over to scold?

Dr. Seligman, I need more than a quiz.

THE NEXT MORNING, I get an equation:

$$H = S + C + V$$

where H is your enduring level of happiness [as opposed to "momentary happiness"], S is your set range, C is the circumstances of your life, and V represents factors under your voluntary control.

All right. Now we're cooking. Seligman goes on to break down the symbols.

My S, as Seligman describes it, is my happiness thermostat. Humans adapt to almost any change and, after some adjustment time, we absorb a big change for the better (like winning the lottery) or the worse (like becoming quadriplegic), and the change doesn't really affect our happiness. In fact, Seligman asserts that there is such a thing as the "hedonic treadmill," which is what happens when life gets better but you don't get lastingly happier. The treadmill "causes you to rapidly and inevitably adapt to good things by taking them for granted." Rich people are only marginally happier than poor people and the gorgeous are not happier than the plain. Even physical health "barely correlates" with happiness.[1]

---

[1] Seligman notes that there are exceptions, of course, to the adaption idea. People who have lost a child or spouse in a car accident, for example, family caregivers of Alzheimer's patients, and people dealing with the sort of poverty you can find in countries like India and Nigeria are much less happy.

Seligman points out that misconceptions abound when it comes to people's *C*, the circumstances of our lives. As the saying goes, money really *can't* buy happiness. And education level, race (in the U.S.), and climate don't affect happiness, either. Gender, Seligman says, has a "fascinating relation to mood." He points out, "In average emotional tone, women and men don't differ, but this strangely is because women are both happier *and* sadder than men."

He parses out all sorts of variables, but it comes down to this:

[I]f you want to lastingly raise your level of happiness by changing the external circumstances of your life, you should do the following:

1. Live in a wealthy democracy, not in an impoverished dictatorship (a strong effect)
2. Get married (a robust effect, but perhaps not causal)
3. Avoid negative events and negative emotion (only a moderate effect)
4. Acquire a rich social network (a robust effect, but perhaps not causal)
5. Get religion (a moderate effect)

My Dr. Seligman is no nut, and he points out that all these variables aren't exactly easy to change, and even if you could change them—you know, maybe an impoverished dictatorship just isn't a good *match* for me—it would only make a difference in between 8 and 15 percent of the variance in your happiness. (No word on what percentage your *S* and *V* account for.)

Most of *Authentic Happiness* is about *V*: the stuff that we can, with effort, voluntarily change. Not to brag, but I do feel that I've become pretty good at putting in the effort. I'm looking forward to achieving results.

. . .

WITH POSITIVE EMOTIONS, like everything else, you got yer past, yer present, and yer future. Ideally, Seligman says, you'll be able to achieve all three kinds of happiness, but he points out that they're not "tightly linked." For example, he points out, "It is possible to be proud and satisfied about the past . . . but to be sour in the present and pessimistic about the future." Or, the other way(s) around—the three kinds of happiness are pretty much like a flip book. Mixy and matchy.

He starts with the past. I take another test in which I rank my satisfaction with my life. I come out in the second highest category—"Very satisfied, above average." According to the website, I scored higher than 79 percent of all test-takers. And if what follows in the book is any indication, this is because I'm not a dweller in the past.

Seligman has some harsh words for the experts who would lead you to believe that your childhood traumas have anything to do with the happiness you have as an adult. He clearly loathes the concept of one's "inner child" and loathes even more the studies that try to link childhood woes with adult troubles. "There is no justification in these studies for blaming your adult depression, anxiety, bad marriage, drug use, sexual problems, unemployment, aggression against your children, alcoholism, or anger on what happened to you as a child."

He intends this to be "liberating," and as a person who may or may not be inflicting childhood traumas on her own child, I find it liberating indeed. Unlinking childhood events from adult troubles is a great step in the dismantling of mom blame.

On the other hand, Seligman tosses off a paragraph that I find troubling:

This attitude [of feeling imprisoned by past events] is also the philosophical infrastructure underneath the victimology that has swept America since the glorious beginnings of the civil rights movement, and which threatens to overtake the rugged individualism and sense of individual responsibility that used to be this nation's hallmark.

Whoa. Marty! Did you just set up a dichotomy between "victimology" and "rugged individualism" and place the civil rights movement on the "victimology" side? No, you didn't.

Oh, but he did. And this is like tin foil on a filling to me because I know very well what end of the dichotomy I'd be staring down if just one detail of my life had been different, like the year I was born or the ambition of my parents. He might as well have written, "Rich white guys are the best things about the United States!"

What rankles more, though, is the dismissive tone he strikes. I mean, nobody likes a whiner, but does Seligman claim to know what separates the true victims from the practitioners of "victimology"? I think about my great-grandfather. His name was William Crawford. He worked as a coal miner, and when he first went into the mines, miners were expected to pay for their own headlamps, among other things, which drove them into debt to the company store, seriously affecting their quality of life. To the larger culture, this seemed okay—or at least okay to ignore. But William Crawford and a group of other men formed a union, and eventually demanded to be treated fairly. Still, almost a century later, Henry Clay Frick, the owner of the mine, is remembered as a captain of industry, a rugged individual. I sit back in my armchair and I get worked up because it sure *sounds* like Seligman is not rooting for the William Crawfords of this world, but for the H. C. Fricks.

I sure wish Seligman would address this disconnect head-on. I really need to like this book. I need to want to hold hands with it. I need for my heart to go pitter-patter when I think about it, but what I get instead is some prose that looks as if it were lifted from a welfare reform bill.

But since Seligman doesn't address it for me, I read between the lines and see what I can come up with. And, giving Seligman the benefit of the doubt, here's how I reconcile it: What Seligman wants readers to do is not become *immobilized* by feeling like a victim. In other words, don't say, "I'm a victim and there's nothing I can do about it." That just spawns some personal unhappiness and changes nothing.

Second, Seligman calls the civil rights movement itself "glorious," so we can assume he *does* think agitating for social change is a good thing. As long as an individual doesn't let the injustice define who she is. Seligman's interest here is in *personal* happiness, and that's (in theory) a whole different ball of wax from improving living conditions for people on a larger scale. What's good for the individual psyche isn't always what's good for Making a Difference.

Or something like that. Seligman, of course, doesn't untangle what he means here. It seems to me that he's saying that personal happiness and Making a Difference are two unrelated things. This would make sense, given all he has already said about the circumstances in one's life—the *C*—not affecting happiness very much. And in that case, issues related to Making a Difference would veer off topic for his book.

Still, why bring up civil rights? Why plant a trip wire in his prose, setting off alarm bells in my head? Alert! Man armed with conservative agenda in Sector B! And, in a larger sense, if one can be perfectly happy living in unjust circumstances, then why even have something like a civil rights movement?

I sigh. In order to continue with *Authentic Happiness*, I'm going to have to take this—that Making a Difference and personal happiness are not related in this way—on faith.

I need to meet the school bus, so I put down the book and pull on my coat. I'm beginning to see that, in some ways, seeking personal happiness is a deeply conservative quest. It's about changing your attitude, but making do with the status quo.

. . .

STRANGELY, this little imaginary blowout I have with Seligman energizes me, and I dig back in the next morning. I take a gratitude test—the other positive emotion connected with the past—and discover that I score a measly 33, placing me in the bottom quarter of test-takers. I am an ingrate.

In my defense, I was rating the applicability of statements like: "I am grateful to a wide variety of people." Which is a surprisingly hard statement to unpack. What do you mean by "grateful"? What do you mean by "wide variety"? Should I feel gratitude toward just the people who intentionally enrich my life? Or should my gratitude extend to, say, the trash collectors, who aren't doing me in particular any favors but who make my life a lot more pleasant, whisking away our old chicken bones and dirty tissues every Thursday. (I answer this question with "4," meaning neutral.)

To up my gratitude, I am to do two things. The first is something that Seligman does with his psychology students, something that he calls a "real world assignment" that's "meaningful and even life-changing." I am to write a one-page letter to someone in my life I've never thanked properly, laminate it, meet him or her in person, and read it to him or her. Seligman warns that, almost without fail, people cry.

My low test score aside, I realize that I have a bounty of people to whom I'm grateful. Brandon, for one; my parents, particularly my mother; my sisters, all of whom I admire in different ways; my grandparents, who have shaped me in more ways than they probably know; various friends for various reasons. But the person I've been most lax in thanking is one Ms. Stephanie Wilkinson, my pal and my business partner, who has been picking up the slack on the magazine while I dedicate some time to these experiments.

Seligman suggests I take about a week and write the thing in my spare time. I pride myself on being a fast-ish writer so I thought I could whip that baby out in an hour or two. I was wrong. I'd type and erase, type and erase. Getting the tone of the letter right is crazy hard. I realize that I have absolutely no experience in writing a letter of gratitude. Because I don't want to go all Hallmark on her, my first try doesn't sound grateful at all. My next two tries sound as if I have Stephanie alone to thank for every good thing that has ever happened to me; they sound very much like I was wondering if she ever knew she was my hero.

Finally, I get it. I print it out and laminate to the best of my ability, which is not very good at all. I call her one Friday afternoon and, per Seligman's suggestion, tell her that I'd like to see her. I suggest we meet the next Monday, Martin Luther King Jr. Day, for a lunch of Mexican food. I put the letter in a bag and wait until Monday when I will undertake this meaningful exercise.

WE'RE SPREAD AROUND a corner booth at the restaurant, Stephanie, her two kids, Caleb, and me. We've finished our meals, and our dirty dishes lie among the tortilla chip crumbs and straw wrappers. We've opened belated Christmas gifts and discussed with the children whether or not a certain gift has a strong enough magnet to stick to the refrigerator. We've debated with them the merits of the old *Charlie and the Chocolate Factory* movie versus the new. On top of these conversations, Stephanie and I are making a good effort to talk about the Seligman book. I say, "Speaking of that . . ."

I reach into my shopping bag and pull out the laminated letter. "I want to read you something."

"Is that *laminated?*" Steph asks.

"Yep," I say. "That's what Seligman says to do."

"Is this going to make me cry?" she asks.

"I hope not," I say.

We hush the children and I start. My voice, I can tell, is already a little wavery, and I'm mindful of the warning about crying, so I read my testimonial to Stephanie as if it were a bedtime story, but more slowly and with (I hope) more feeling.

"Stephanie," I read. "When I was reading *Charlotte's Web* to Caleb, we came to this passage: 'It is not often that someone comes along who is a true friend and a good writer. Charlotte was both.' And I thought, *Hey, so is Stephanie!*"

I can feel everyone at our table staring at me. I look up so as to "read . . . with eye contact," as I was advised. Stephanie smiles. I continue, "You've had such an influence on me. I remember sitting there in the *C-Ville* offices and reading your column, wishing I could write like you." Years ago, I was on staff at an alternative newsweekly for which Stephanie wrote a freelance book column. "I was a little scared to meet you because I admired your writing so much. But you were just as great in person—funny, smart, engaging. I was planning my wedding some months later—"

"Who did you marry?" Stephanie's five-year-old son asks.

"Brandon," I say quickly, then continue, "—and thinking that I wanted to keep my last name, and somehow the fact that you did it cemented it for me."

"Wait," Caleb says. "Did Daddy write this?"

"No, I did," I tell him. I read, "Now, a hundred years later, my admiration for you has only gotten deeper. *Brain, Child* would not be what it is without your insistence on quality, your hard work, your immense talent. I'm incredibly lucky that you're so generous with your time and analysis."

At this point the kids are getting bored and starting to chat loudly among themselves. Stephanie shushes them.

"But even outside the magazine work, I'm always learning something from you. You know how to be a good friend. When you were telling me what you did when your friend got sucked into the pyramid scheme stuff, I thought, Man, that takes guts. [This is a long story not really germane to the letter but take my word for it—you'd be lucky to have a friend like her.] I can totally see why you're invited to so many dinner parties—you make people feel interesting and important. You're just an excellent person to be around. You have, as the New Agers say, 'good energy.' This is all to say thank you. On so many levels, you've made such a difference in my life."

I gulp. Although Stephanie is one of my best friends and we have the sort of unique relationship that two people in a creative partnership often do, I feel naked here in the restaurant telling her this. This unguarded outpouring of positive emotion . . . it's unlike us. We are, after all, the founders of a magazine that purports to be keeping motherhood real, one quarterly issue at a time. This medical-grade gratitude, uncut by conflicting emotions or ambivalence, is certainly sincere but a little intense. For me anyway. It takes some effort to keep my shit together.

Stephanie looks slightly choked up herself. I pass the laminated sheet across the table.

"I'm glad that this is laminated!" she says and looks it over. "Thank you. This was the best present."

If I were doing this exercise totally by the book without the complication of children who have the day off from school, I would "[n]ext let the other person react unhurriedly." We'd "[r]eminisce together about the concrete events that make this person so important." As it is, Stephanie is supposed to be back at her house to watch another friend's kids in half an hour. Caleb is getting a little antsy and so are Stephanie's kids. We pay the check and leave.

THE OTHER THING I can do to increase my feelings of gratitude is to keep a running list of up to five daily things I have to feel grateful for. On the first day, in addition to making my list, I take two tests. For the next thirteen days, I set aside five minutes to reflect and jot down those things in my life that I can give thanks for. On the fourteenth day, I retake the tests to see if I'm any more grateful. In other word, it's like Thanksgiving at my mom's house every day, except without the binge eating and with some pencil pushing.

The list of things for which I'm grateful contains no surprises. Seligman offers up examples like "waking up this morning," but I'm not that far gone. I'm grateful that my husband rocks, that my mother can be counted on for incredible support, that Caleb is fun, that dinner was delicious, that my sister Erin left a very nice compliment for me on our answering machine. By the fourteenth day, I'm starting to repeat things—twice I've noted that I'm grateful the dogs are healthy—and when I retake the tests, I get the same results. Which is kind of a relief for me since, if it worked, I'd have to "incorporate it into [my] nightly routine."

My routines are becoming longer and longer, the more self-help I undertake. It's not that any of them are burdensome all by themselves, but they do add up. Once a day, I make like the FlyLady and put out my hot spots, although I'm not as maniacal about it as I once was. Like Karen Kingston, David Bach, and Suze Orman, I file or destroy every financial scrap of paper that comes into the house. I've added an exercise routine in the morning and started eating breakfast. And then there's the gratitude list. Five minutes here, a quarter of an hour there means that instead of starting work at 8:15, I start closer to nine o'clock. Instead of starting my nightly relaxation—the time that I can crack open a beer, hang out with Brandon, watch TV, read, or otherwise veg—at 9:30 P.M., I'm often futzing around with the checkbook or the hot spots or some such until 10 or even 10:30. My workday is getting squeezed and my weekends are getting more structure to them. At this rate, improving myself will become a full-time job.

. . .

MARTIN SELIGMAN BELIEVES so strongly in the power of optimism, he wrote a book about it—*Learned Optimism*—which I haven't read, but I do read chapter six in *Authentic Happiness*, and take the quiz. It's one where I'm supposed to imagine a given situation occurring and how I'd respond. For example:

You get a flower from a secret admirer.
A. I am attractive to him/her.
B. I am a popular person.

Or

You fall down a great deal while skiing.
A. Skiing is difficult.
B. The trails were icy.

I answer what seem to me to be the only reasonable answers: A. Should I receive an anonymously given flower or fall down skiing, I would assume that I'm attractive to the secret admirer, or that skiing is difficult. If I got, say, *ten* flowers from secret admirers, I might be able to extrapolate some sort of popularity. (Or, more realistically, I would worry that I'm putting out a come-and-get-it-fellas vibe.) And if I were already an ace skier, I might be able to blame the trails and not my own skiing ability or lack thereof. But these don't seem to be very realistic answers to me.

And, apparently, they're not very optimistic answers either. The scoring of this test is a bit complicated, but Seligman notes that you can separate the optimists from the pessimists by having a look at how each view "permanence" and "pervasiveness." When something bad or just irritating happens to a pessimist, she thinks that this sort of thing is always going to happen. Typical, she'll think. Or, she'll take a good event and consider it an isolated occurrence. An optimist will do the opposite; she'll take a bad event and think of it as an isolated occurrence, or take a good event and think that it has a "permanent cause."

What's more, a pessimist will make up a "universal" explanation for bad events. She'll "catastrophize," as Seligman puts it. An optimist, on the other hand, will keep the explanation specific to the situation. Seligman offers the examples of Kevin and Nora, who were both pretty pessimistic in regards to permanence, but when they got laid off from their jobs in accounting, Nora bounced back because she saw that, although the job situation was bad, other aspects in her life were going swimmingly. Kevin, on the other hand, took the layoff and catastrophized—his whole life, as he saw it, sucked.

There's one more dimension to optimism and that dimension is hope. In fact, Seligman says, "Perhaps the most important scores from your test are your Hope . . . scores." Hope—formerly "the province of television preachers, politicians and hucksters"—can be scientifically scored using the permanence and pervasiveness totals.

I tally. I am, with a score of –2, "moderately hopeless." Which would be a good name for a Goth band, but is, according to Seligman, a recipe for unhappiness.

THIS IS THE FIRST time I've ever scored a negative number on a test, and I don't know if this offends my overachiever-ish sensibilities or what, but I become a little obsessed with being moderately hopeless. What Seligman doesn't address, I think to myself, is luck. I've said it before, but in case you were skimming, I'll say it again: Bad things will happen, and probably to you; your job is to have a nice life anyway.

The ancillary to this is a discussion of Why Bad Things Happen to Good People, Why Good Things Happen to Bad People, and—the stickiest issue for me—Why Very Good Things Happen to Some Regular People, Yet at the Same Time Very *Bad* Things Happen to Some Other Regular People. I am one of the regular people to whom very good things have happened, across the board. The husband, the child, the network of friends and relatives, decent health, the money, the job, and the opportunities for fun. My life *looks* practically perfect in every way. And this has happened despite my pessimism, despite my many flaws. Meanwhile, I know other regular people who have filed for bankruptcy, whose mates make their lives worse, who are simply trying to survive either financially or emotionally, who have battled cancer, who have other serious and ongoing health problems, who have no realistic way out of soul-deadening jobs, and/or who have few opportunities for ordinary fun. I know regular people whose children have died.

The best explanation I have for this—the disparity between my good fortune and other people's misfortune—is luck. Not in the sense that I'm an overall lucky person or other people can be summed up as unlucky, but in the sense that luck, good and bad, strikes indiscriminately and the good things that have happened to me aren't due to some virtue on my part. Conversely, the bad things that happen aren't due to some moral failing.

I say as much to Brandon one night while we're lounging on the couch with the dogs, waiting for our TV show to come on. He listens and cocks his head. "But isn't it a depressing thought that you don't have control over *anything?*" he asks.

"No, I'm not saying that people shouldn't *try* to fix things," I say.

"But if everything is luck, then why bother?" Brandon says.

I'm getting frustrated with my inability to communicate what I mean. "It's complicated . . ." I start. "Not *everything* is luck. But some things are and you don't know what is or what isn't." I'm not making sense. I have a background in neither philosophy nor religion, and it's showing. "Okay," I say. "Here's an example. Take me. I am not a great person. I'm not a terrible person, either. But because I was lucky enough to marry you—who makes a good living with benefits—and because we're lucky enough to set our lives up with some flexibility and I can do things like meet Caleb at the bus after school and volunteer for the PTO and—I don't know—pay all of our *bills* on time, I'm seen by some people as a good person. But take, oh, that woman I used to waitress with. She and her husband had a decent life, then both of their children were born with health problems and because of all the medical bills and no insurance, they wound up living in their car. It wasn't her attitude that made that happen to her, and she wasn't a bad or lazy person."

Brandon nods.

"And I didn't do anything to deserve all this." I gesture around the living room, which at this moment doesn't look all that grand, what with the Teen Titan toys and empty beer bottles and big dust bunnies, but we understand what I mean: It *is* comparatively grand.

What I also mean, I guess, is that it's complicated. There's bad luck, bad choices, and the snowball effect of the two. "I just hate that people think that your life, the material things in your life, is a direct reflection of your attitude or your inner character. It's easy to say, 'I made my life great, and everyone else should be able to, too. So let's cut all the social programs!' It's so arrogant."

"But that's politics," Brandon points out. "They're two different issues."

So we're back to where I was the last time I was questioning Seligman: the distinction between personal happiness and Making a Difference. *Medium* comes on the TV and I'm glad to turn my attention to the pickle Patricia Arquette find herself in when the ghost of her father-in-law appears in her bathroom.

SO THIS IS THE PARADOX: While I'm busy worrying about what implications Seligman's theories have in government and social policy, my panic attacks go away. At night, I stay put in bed. (I still talk, which is technically a variation on somnambulism—Brandon reports that one night I sat bolt upright and said, "Okay, then, I'll have to try it *another* way"—but I can live with that.) I read about my own personal happiness and think about what this means to other people. This allows me to think of myself as a better person, a person who can get outside her own head, a person who is not *that* self-absorbed. It allows me to escape the self-image that the marriage and parenting experts have nurtured: that I'm selfish, immature, inconsistent, and a terrible role model.

Is it true that I'm not self-absorbed? Maybe yes, maybe no. After all, no one at all was helped by my stewing about civil rights, "victimology," and rugged individualism. No one was helped by my conversation with Brandon about luck. But I somehow convince myself that because I am *thinking* about this, I'm not self-absorbed. In other words, no one was helped by my supposed lack of self-absorption . . . except me.

I'm not exactly happy yet, I think as I get in the car to buy some lunch, but I'm at least back to where I was, hovering around neutral. If I'm of two minds, at least now they're not the crazed, self-conscious self-help me with gaping emotional wounds and the real me. They're the real me and the ideal me. The real me is the flawed one. The ideal me is the one who is capable of writing, laminating, and reading aloud a letter of gratitude; the one who cares about the implications of self-help in the larger culture; the one who has compassion for the underdog (at a distance, at least). This ideal me may not Make a Difference in the end, but she has the potential to, and that may be my version of hope.

THANK GOD, because the real me is still petty. I may be reading Authentic Happiness with my ideal self, but the real me still lives in the real world, and is still getting fired up, one real annoyance at a time.

My next assignment from Martin Seligman, in the fight against pessimism, is to learn how to argue with myself. The idea is, if someone else said to me that I was a crappy mother or a bad editor or whatever, I'd protest. But if my own inner voice says it, I accept it as true—and that's just crazy talk.

I'll apply Seligman's "ABCDE model" to the next five events that cause me adversity—and they don't have to be major traumas, just incidents that bug me.

Not surprisingly, it doesn't take long to find the sort of adversity that gets my ire up. At the grocery store one Saturday, the clerk asks me for my "discount" card, and I reach into my purse and hand it over. The card is still embedded in the large sheet of plastic it came in. I like it that way because I can easily find it in my purse. (I know, they offer the smaller version that you can put on your keychain, but that, to me, is the equivalent in ugliness of keeping your warranty taped to the door of your microwave.) The clerk, who's young, blond, and efficient, promptly pops the card out of its large plastic sheet.

"I—I didn't want you to do that!" I say. I know I'm speaking a little loudly, but it's better than what's running through my head, which is: *For goddamn Christ's sakes, you stupid fucking bitch.*

What arguing with yourself means, in my case anyway, is talking myself off the ledge:

Adversity: The checkout clerk at the grocery store ripped my card from the larger piece of plastic—this is the second time it's happened.

Beliefs: What an idiot! The audacity to think you can just take someone's personal property and destroy it. She may "mean well," but people don't have any boundaries anymore. Did she really think that I didn't know how to remove it myself?

Consequences: My blood pressure rose and I couldn't even look her in the face. I told Brandon about it that night. Thinking about it *still* pisses me off.

Disputation: Her actions don't really reflect on me at all—it's perfectly understandable to want the card in the large plastic sheet and *not at all weird*—and, while she probably does mean well, it's not that big a deal. So next time I go, I'll just sign up for a new card.

Energization: So, I'll sign up for the new card and reinforce it with tape so as to prevent "well meaning" clerks from doing it in the future.

You may note that the quotes around "well meaning" betray the fact that I'm still hanging on to this, uh, adversity, but truly, the ABCDE model does help.

And I get better at it:

Adversity: I just couldn't write the damn scene today. I screwed around all day on the Internet and took a nap and thought a great deal about getting a different hairstyle because I couldn't focus on the *single* thing I had to do.

Beliefs: I'm lazy. I'm not committed enough to this self-improvement project, and as a result both I and this book are going to suck. Big time.

Consequences: I just gave up for the day. I took a nap. Didn't let Caleb have any friends over after school. Tried to make up for it in some strange way by going to a PTO fundraising dinner at an awful pizza place.

Disputation: Yeah, I had an unproductive day. I just finished half of the manuscript, and am waiting to hear the verdict from my editor. I also spent the last two days writing for *Brain, Child*. I don't have to work so hard all the time. I met my first deadline, even though I didn't write every single day. Energy levels are cyclical, and I can afford to cut myself some slack.

Energization: Okay, one bad day. But I finished the scene this morning, and I called Steph to read it over. I *am* doing the best that I can at any given moment. I'll finish on time.

The beauty of this ABCDE model is that it transforms balls-out whining into something useful. You might notice that the whole internal struggle over being productive and the conclusions (or "energization") I reached was done and done better by Billy Joel in "Vienna Waits for You"[2] on his *The Stranger* album and, for that matter, was also promoted by my mother, who let us occasionally play hooky, but both Billy Joel's song and my mother's "mental health" days happened decades ago, and I'd forgotten Mom's and Mr. Joel's wisdom. The ABCDE method *helped*, a fact that would inspire me to write Martin Seligman down in my daily gratitude list, if I were still doing it.

The only downside is, I'm unable to apply the ABCDE model as the adversity is happening. I can only do it in hindsight.

FINALLY, seligman gets to happiness in the present, which, to my mind, is the most important of the happinesses.

He starts out with a distinction: There is a difference between pleasures and gratifications. Pleasures, he says, "are delights that have clear sensory and strong emotional components . . .: ecstasy, thrills, orgasm, delight, mirth, exuberance, and comfort." Gratifications, on the other hand, don't elicit any "raw feelings." They're things that we enjoy doing—like reading a book, cooking, skating, etc.—that we can lose ourselves in. "Gratifications last longer than the pleasures," he writes, "they involve quite a lot of thinking and interpretation, they do not habituate easily, and they are undergirded by our strengths and virtues."

---

[2] In which he advises an ambitious "crazy child" to take it easy on herself.

Embarrassingly, this is all news to me. I realize that what I've been doing is trying to cram as many minutes of pleasure into my life as I can, thinking that more pleasure minutes equals more happiness. Seligman explains that that's not the way it works. Pleasures are momentary, and you get used to them pretty quickly.

Not that he's against pleasure. In fact, he offers several ways to enhance pleasure in his section "Enhancing the Pleasures." For one, "Rapidly repeated indulgence in the same pleasure does not work," he writes and backs that up with biological evidence.[3] The key is to spread your pleasures out and stop when they cease to give you pleasure. If you can't, he suggests, you might wonder if you're addicted.

Also, the element of surprise enhances pleasure because it helps you to not take the pleasure for granted. Seligman suggests trying to take yourself by surprise, or taking loved ones by surprise—even small gestures that take up little time, like an "unexpected cup of coffee." So I do whip up some surprises, with mixed results. I send Brandon a love e-mail at work, and he responds that I made his day. On the other hand, while Caleb's at school, I make plans to spend a lovely mother-son afternoon with him, getting hot chocolate and visiting the hair salon, but when I unveil my plans, Caleb's reaction shows me that it's not exactly a good surprise (much like I'd react to "an unexpected cup of coffee") and I wind up ditching the afternoon's plans and letting him run around with his friends.

Anyway, savoring things and remaining "mindful" are two other ways to Enhance the Pleasures, and Seligman invites me, as he does his students, to "have a beautiful day." That is, plan a day of doing things that bring me pleasure.

This is the best experiment in my entire quest so far.

I plan my Beautiful Day for a Friday. Since I have a child, there are,

---

[3] "Neurons are wired to respond to novel events, and not to fire if the events do not provide new information," he writes. In other words, your brain really only likes that first sip of beer, forkful of cheesecake, etc.

of course, parameters. I can't savor Bloody Marys all day, for example. But I set my sights on small pleasures and keep my expectations flexible so as not be disappointed.

When I wake up that Friday, I feel . . . happy. In fact, how I feel that Friday makes me realize the attitude I normally wake up with must be one of mild dread of all the things I have to do.

I get Caleb on the bus, come home, and brew a cup of tea. The morning is sunny and cold, although it warms up later. I do my exercises. I plop down in the recliner under a blanket and read *Dope*, a very good mystery, which has nothing to do with self-improvement or motherhood. My grandma calls, and I talk to her and my grandfather for an hour, unhurriedly. Finally I get dressed and pick up a shrimp BLT and a cup of hot chocolate at a fancy market. I eat slowly. After school, Caleb plays outside with his friends, and I chat with Janet and Kathleen in the warm afternoon on Janet's porch glider. Brandon comes home, and we all go out to dinner at a brew pub we like. After Caleb falls asleep, there is activity in the guest room and pale ales with my guy. This may not sound like much, but in my book, it was an extraordinarily beautiful day.

I'm being mindful to live in the moment, which is harder than I thought it would be. My impulse, pleasure-seeking hedonist that I am, is to try to have a beautiful day once a week. But then I'll become accustomed to it. I lie in bed next to my sleeping boy and close my eyes. I vow to surprise myself with a beautiful day every once in a while.

Months will pass, though, and I won't do it. I'm afraid of the beautiful day losing its power. Eventually, I come to think of the beautiful day as something I should keep behind glass, to be used in an emergency of bad mood.

THAT'S JUST AS WELL, because as far as Martin Seligman is concerned, gratification is where it's at. Although, strangely, most people can't really describe what gratification feels like.

It is the total absorption, the suspension of consciousness, and the flow that gratifications produce that defines liking these activities—not the presence of pleasure. Total immersion, in fact, blocks consciousness, and emotions are completely absent.

This is why people who don't have the capacity to experience emotions very strongly—the folks with low positive affectivity—can have a good life, Seligman says.

One key component of gratification is something called flow. Seligman points to the research of his colleague Mike Csikzentmahilyi, who is the big kahuna of the flow concept. Csikzentmahilyi interviewed thousands of people, a diverse sample, and asked them about the thing that gratifies them. Whether it's studying minerals under a microscope (an intellectual thing), riding motorcycles with a group of fellow enthusiasts (a social thing), or performing ballet (a physical thing), Seligman says that the activity, to qualify for flow status, has to have the following components:

- The task is challenging and requires skill
- We concentrate
- There are clear goals
- We have deep, effortless involvement
- There is a sense of control
- Our sense of self vanishes
- Time stops

Granted, even when you do the activity, you don't get flow all the time. And some people get it more than others. But one of Csikzentmahilyi's studies suggests that the more flow you have, the better off you are.

Seligman doesn't offer a handy online quiz to test how much flow a person has in her life, but I know what he's talking about. I read an awful lot, and my favorite books are the ones that I get lost in—ones that foster flow. Every once in a while, I'll get some flow from writing. For a period in late high school/early college, I got flow from playing a Nintendo game called Tetris, although I still wonder where the line between flow and addiction was in that case.

Seligman, whose earlier work related to the prevention of depression, points out that life is set up so that people have a choice: Do I do the pleasurable thing, like watching TV? Or do I do the more gratifying one, like reading a book? His theory: The reason so many people are experiencing unipolar depression these days (as opposed to bipolar disorder, what used to be called manic depression) is that we're choosing the pleasures over the gratifications. He calls this "an over-reliance on shortcuts to happiness" and claims it's a sickness of wealthy nations. We're picking the activities that produce momentary positive emotions and giving the cold shoulder to those that require skill and effort and, not to put too fine a point on it, getting out of our own head. "One of the major symptoms of depression is self-absorption," he writes. "The depressed person thinks about how she feels a great deal, excessively so." In the margin of my book, I write, "Ha!" Which means, in this context: "Hello, last year of my life!"

I don't think I'm depressed, and I wonder briefly whether or not someone in the depths of depression can work themselves out of it, armed only with gratifications, but Seligman moves on briskly. The question that we should be asking, he says, isn't "How can I be happy?" Instead, Seligman writes: "When an entire lifetime is taken up in the pursuit of the positive emotions . . . authenticity and meaning are nowhere to be found."

In other words, you can have one giant orgasm for seventy years straight, but you're not going to be living the good life. Seligman tells his readers that he will give us some advice now: Get ye some gratifications.

OF THE WOMEN I know well enough to know what's in their medicine cabinet, about half are on some sort of psychiatric drug, either for depression or an anxiety disorder or some combination of the two. According to a *Mother Jones* article I read, between 1990 and 2000, prescriptions for these drugs increased eightfold.

Plenty of books have been written that try to pin down why Americans are so depressed, and this here is not one of those books. But the general consensus seems to be that something is wrong in our culture. For example Judith Warner, in her 2005 book, *Perfect Madness*, makes the argument that American culture is set up so that mothers drive themselves crazy. Gregg Easterbrook, in his 2003 book, *The Progress Paradox*, finds something very strange in the fact that, although life has gotten better for most Americans, we haven't gotten any happier, and he asserts that our very success may be causing these feelings of depression. These writers and others—like Richard Layard and Martin Seligman, for instance—tend to fall into two camps, though, when they try to figure out how to fix what's ailing us: Some, like Judith Warner, would argue that the culture needs to be fixed. Others, like Martin Seligman, argue that people need to fix their coping devices.

On the face of it, the Seligman camp's suggestion sounds, well, easier. Is it? I called some of these women I know. One friend described feeling "crazy" while not on medication; another just couldn't summon up whatever it takes to actually care about anything. There were a lot of descriptions of tears and lethargy and frustration. And these are not women I'd describe as victims—in fact, they all thought they were doing the responsible thing by taking action and visiting a doctor.

I also got the feeling that getting your depression treated with medication was hardly a shortcut to happiness. Not every medicine works for every person, and most people have to try different medications until they find the one—and the dosage of that one—that works. And then the dosage or the medication can stop working, forcing the depressed person to start anew. To be honest, the whole process sounds pretty demoralizing.

After talking with these friends, I think I can say with some certainty that I'm not depressed—another item I'd write down on my gratitude list.

HOW DOES A person get some more gratification in life? A good start, Seligman claims, is to look at your character.

He knows that the concept of character has gotten a bad rep, what with "Victorian moralizing" that encouraged people to equate bad character with the poor, back in the day. He posits that social science was an antidote to the idea of character: Instead of blaming a person's character, we could blame his environment for whatever bad behavior was going down. In some ways, that was a good thing. "[S]ocial science lets us escape from the value-laden, blame-accruing, religiously inspired, class-oppressing notion of character, and get on with the monumental task of building a healthier 'nurturing' environment," he writes.

But not so fast, wise guy. Even though, as Seligman sees it, social science was more in step with American egalitarianism, the idea of character is woven so tightly into our culture that "[a]ny science that does not use character as a basic idea (or at least explain character and choice away successfully) will never be accepted as a useful account of human action."

So he and some colleagues set out to study culturally ubiquitous virtues and strengths, which would be less laden with judgment than just their own opinions about what strength and virtue means. (They use the word "ubiquitous" because they wanted to find values that *almost* every culture prizes—there will always be some smart-ass anthropologist who points out that Tribe X doesn't value Virtue Z.) They studied about two hundred religious and philosophical tracts and figured out a list of six virtues that (almost) everyone values.

And then there are the strengths, which are subsets of the virtues. The researchers identified twenty-four strengths. Strengths are distinct from talents—they're choices a person makes and feels good about. For example, you might be talented at running long distances, which is all well and good, but a strength would be if you ran a very long distance to bring medicine to a stranger who was sick and unable to get it for himself.

Everyone has personal strengths—those parts of their personality that are admirable and inspiring. The idea is that by using those strengths, we can get more gratifications in our life and make it meaningful.

This all sounds just dandy, but I'm itching to get to the quiz where my strengths will be revealed. I remove Luna from the chair where I want to sit and place the laptop on my lap. It'll take about twenty-five minutes to finish the two-hundred-plus question quiz, so I start plugging away.

Dr. Seligman wants to know how much these statements sound like me (on a scale of 1 to 7, 1 being "very much unlike me," 7 being "very much like me"). I start plugging in answers to statements like these: *I always admit when I am wrong*, or *It is very important to me that I live in a world of beauty*, or *I always look on the bright side*.

I'm kind of excited about this, although I can't really explain why. Other questionnaires—from *Cosmo* quizzes to the corporate-friendly Briggs-Myers personality test—I take with a whole shakerful of salt. As my friend Liz points out, it's the questionnaires themselves that make you skeptical because, given different circumstances (at work, at home, with a group of strangers, with a small group of friends), each question could have many answers. And I tend to agree with her that this it-depends aspect is the Achilles' heel of many questionnaires. But

I've been with Seligman for so long now that I think I know which me he's talking about.

Twenty-five minutes later, my strengths are revealed. They are, in order from strongest to less strong:

Love of Learning
Creativity/Ingenuity/Originality/Street Smarts
Humor and Playfulness
Capacity to Love and Be Loved
Industry/Diligence/Perseverance

Seligman notes that if one of them just doesn't feel like the real you, ditch it. If they meet certain criteria (like "invigoration rather than exhaustion while using the strength"), the rest of them are your "signature strengths." Mine all feel pretty real, so I keep all five.

You also get your signature weaknesses, and mine are, in order of weakest to less weak:

Forgiveness and Mercy
Modesty and Humility
Spirituality/Sense of Purpose/Faith
Self-control
Hope/Optimism

Looking at the list of my weaknesses calls to mind what was hot in Puritan culture. And let's just say that if Goody Niesslein were around in Salem circa 1692, she might have had some troubles.

Only the weakest attribute—forgiveness and mercy—is a surprise to me. I scored in the 1 percentile across the board in forgiveness and mercy, meaning that 99 percent of all test-takers scored higher than me. It is an odd feeling, seeing statistical evidence of your mean streak there on the computer screen.

I'll leave it at that. Like other people's dreams, the results of the Strengths Questionnaire are really only of interest to the people who experience it. You can find out your own strengths at authentic happiness.org.

NOW, I'M SUPPOSED TO BE "polishing and deploying [my] strengths" and "using them to buffer against [my] weaknesses and the trials that weaknesses bring."

Seligman names the third section of his book "In the Mansions of Life," and in it he offers some ways to apply your signature strengths to the big parts of life: work, your love life, your parenting, and finding meaning in your life.

I like his work section. (That is, I find it not exactly pleasurable, but it's gratifying in that it appeals to my Love of Learning.) Basically, he says that to be happiest in your job, you need to find some way to use your signature strengths to make it a "calling"—you need to see what you do as "contributing to the greater good."

He tells the story of an orderly at a hospital where his friend was dying. The orderly took it upon himself to decorate the patients' rooms with art in order to give a little beauty to people who were in decidedly unbeautiful situations, and it elevated his job from basic grunt-work to something bigger. Seligman also points out how lawyers—who suffer disproportionately from depression, alcoholism, and illegal drug use, and have a higher divorce rate than the rest of employed people—can use their signature strengths to combat the pessimistic, let's-look-on-the-dark-side nature of the job. The message I walked away with is that, most of the time, using your signature strengths at your job will create additional work for you, but it'll pay off (in gratification) in the long run.

I like my job just fine. I've made a temporary peace with how entertainment can also be helpful toward the greater good, and I do view it as a calling. But I think of Brandon, particularly when I came to this passage:

> Decision latitude refers to the number of choices one has—or, as it turns out, the number of choices one *believes* one has—on the job. . . . There is one combination particularly inimical to health and morale: high job demands coupled with low decision latitude. Individuals with these jobs have much more coronary disease and depression than individuals in the other quadrants.

Every weekday, Brandon could ruin millions of dollars' worth of active ingredients. Most of his job relates to complying with FDA regulations. High job demands coupled with low decision latitude? I would say so.

On Saturday out we go. It's snowing heavily and from our place at the bar we can see the flakes getting thicker and bigger, mini-snowballs dropping fully formed from the sky. We tuck in, and we're chatting near the bar's fireplace. I've been telling him about all that Seligman says, the optimism, the signature strengths, the ways to make our work life more gratifying. Brandon nods, but I can tell he's not exactly taking this to heart. He's an engineer. Manufacturing plants are not bastions of flexibility where one can just throw in a signature strength.

"I can see what you mean—or what Seligman means—by needing to feel like your work is contributing to the greater good," he says.

"Does it seem different now, now that you're working on a different product?" When he started work at this company, he was working on one of the ingredients in the famous cocktail of drugs that slowed down the effects of HIV. By contrast, he now "supports," in manufacturing lingo, the factory that makes the next generation of a controversial drug that's the subject of class action lawsuits.

Brandon shrugs. "I don't know—it's a different culture now. I'm doing a different job."

We're quiet for a couple of minutes, and Brandon tells me about these gigantic vessels that are supposed to be coming over the mountain by tractor trailer in a few months.

I ask what's the biggest vessel his plant has. "It's about thirty-thousand gallons."

"Do you call it 'The Big Daddy' or something like that?" I ask. It strikes me as a good idea.

"No," Brandon tells me.

"What do you call it then?"

He rattles off a combination of letters and numbers.

"Do you have nicknames for any of the vessels?" I ask. He shakes his head. "What other vessels do you work on?"

"We have a roller . . ."

"Don't you think it would be more fun," I say, "if everybody referred to the roller by a nickname? So, instead of saying, 'Man, I have to go work on 123XYZ,' you'd say, 'Roller Girl's in trouble. I need to go check that out.' "

"There are two roller girls," Brandon says.

"That's fine," I say and take another swig of beer, which tonight I am not savoring because I find that what's even more pleasurable than savoring a beer is drinking one quickly, then ordering another. (See "Self-control," filed under "Weaknesses" above.) "You make up nicknames for both of them." I frown. I can't think of the actress's name who played Roller Girl in the Marky Mark vehicle *Boogie Nights*. "Okay, I can't remember who played Roller Girl in *Boogie Nights*, but you could call one of the vessels Tiffany. That sounds like a Roller Girl name, doesn't it?"

"It does!" Brandon says.

"And the other one, Amber," I say.

"I was thinking 'Amber,' too!" Brandon says.

Clearly we're both thinking of Tiffani Amber Thiessen, from

Beverly Hills, 90210, who took on the role of bitch after Brenda left the show, and I point that out to Brandon.

"When you go in on Monday," I say to Brandon, "you're going to tell your boss that you are now the CFO—the Chief Fun Officer."

Oh, we laugh and laugh at that one. We make up possible names for the other vessels. Brandon wants to appeal to the demographic of the plant's employees, so he suggests that the finishing machine could be called Get 'Er Done. That's a good one.

The next day, it occurs to me that naming all the vessels and trying to get other people to call them by their nicknames is something that *I* might do to incorporate my signature strengths (creativity and humor) to make the job more enjoyable. But, even with my love of learning, I don't have what it takes to be an engineer. I urge Brandon to take the signature strengths questionnaire. However, when he gets twenty-five free minutes, he declines to use them by sitting in front of the computer, which is what he does for a living.

What can I do? Not everyone joins the cult of Positive Psychology.

SELIGMAN'S CHAPTERS ON love and parenting are the weakest in the book because he bases them not on his own research, but on more widespread and, to me, more dubious sources. As a result, I can't muster up the same faith in his advice here.

Seligman claims that marriage is a "more potent happiness factor than satisfaction with job, or finances, or community." I can see some happily single people taking issue with this, but I know that I would be worse off without Brandon. I take the Close Relationships quiz online and find that my results put me in the best category: I have "secure romantic relations." Score.

But then Seligman goes on at length about the research of John Bowlby, a British psychoanalyst who studied war orphans after World

War II and drew all sorts of conclusions that have been the bane of mothers ever since,[4] and applies Bowlby's findings to happiness in a relationship.

Worse, Seligman then reports that he culled through "all the major marriage manuals" to find nuggets of wisdom. This leads him to advocating for things like passing an actual piece of floor (a square of carpet or linoleum or whatever) between lovers when each "has the floor" to speak. If I learned one thing from the marriage experiments, it's that Brandon and I do not have a communication problem, and I decline to make props for conversations with my husband.

There is one nugget I find interesting: Happy couples have all sorts of illusions about their partners. Seligman looks at the research of his colleague Sandra Murray and reports back, "Satisfied couples see virtues in their partners that are not seen at all by their closest friends. . . . Positive illusions, so Murray finds, are self-fulfilling because the idealized partners actually try to live up to them." I fill out some paperwork in a "fondness" exercise that reminds me of Dr. Phil's journaling. I try to figure out Brandon's strengths. Many of them are ones I'm lacking.

Seligman's chapter on parenting is, essentially, a love letter to his wife, Mandy. Much of what Seligman writes about in this chapter is what he and Mandy (but, okay, mostly Mandy) have done raising their children. Most of it sounds pretty familiar because most of it is what Dr. William "Attachment Parenting" Sears also recommends. It's worked well for the Seligman family—and, hey, many aspects of it work well for my family, too. But Seligman doesn't have the natural sidestepping-the-political-issues ability of most modern parenting experts and he comes out with thoughts like this: "[A]s much as I would like you to, I am going to refrain from advising you to shorten your

---

[4] See Judith Warner's *Perfect Madness: Motherhood in the Age of Anxiety* for a convincing and thorough job of how Bowlby's work is no friend of the modern mother.

work hours to spend more time with your children." Watch out, ladies! Slippery slope ahead! At the end of the chapter, Seligman reveals that he and Mandy homeschool the kids. He's careful to point out that he's not a proselytizer and I'm certainly not one to snark about homeschooling (some of my favorite contributors to *Brain, Child* homeschool), but it does reveal a parenting style that just isn't going to come naturally to a lot of people.

Still, by the time I get to the end of *Authentic Happiness*, I'm feeling about Martin Seligman the way I feel about Oprah. I like them in the way I like old friends: I can see their flaws, but I respect them and like to hear what they have to say.

Seligman ends his book with a section that may be, frankly, way above my head. That, or I just can't get into it. It has to do with evolution and theology and all sorts of esoteric matters about where God figures in. But back on page 249, he writes:

> The pleasant life . . . is wrapped up in the successful pursuit of the positive feelings, supplemented by the skills of amplifying these emotions. The good life . . . is not about maximizing positive emotion, but is a life wrapped up in successfully using your signature strengths to obtain abundant and authentic gratification. The meaningful life has one additional feature: using your signature strengths in the service of something larger than you are. To live all three lives is to lead a *full* life.

Here, I get my answer from Seligman about where Making a Difference fits in. It's the cherry on top of the good life. I decide that I'll give myself some time practicing the signature strengths before I figure out what greater cause I'll serve. Baby steps.

{6}

The People Other Than Brandon and Caleb

F OR THE NEXT WEEK, my signature strengths are foremost in my mind. I make an extra effort to use them when a situation comes a-calling. For example, one afternoon, Luna somehow unzips the sofa cushion slipcover and rips the down cushion so that when I return home, she's posed on what looks like a passel of boas, like a doggy glamour shot. I grumble, but I get right to work with the needle, the thread, and the vacuum. I'm using my Industry, Diligence, and Perseverance to take care of business.

Or, I decide that I can use my various strengths to help out with the PTO's big upcoming fundraiser. When I realize that I may have bitten off more than I can chew, instead of panicking and ditching my responsibility, I use my Creativity/Ingenuity/Originality/Street Smarts to plan to do as much as I can every day while Caleb works on his homework. If I brainstorm and make a few calls every day, I will have (neglected my hot spots, but also) accomplished the task in bite-sized pieces.

I like *Authentic Happiness* because it emphasizes what I'm doing right. This may not sound like self-help, but it is, in that my attentions are redirected.

But, alas, there are some situations where I can't think of ways to use either my signature strengths or the ABCDE model. These situations usually have to do with other people, which is unfortunate because, for most of us, that's quite a bit of what life is: dealing with other people.

Shyness isn't my problem. It's more complicated than that. I have an inability to stop myself from saying the wrong thing. It might be genetic.

After my parents' divorce, my father happened to run into a family friend whom he hadn't seen in the years since he and my mother separated. The kid had grown into a thirteen-year-old, which, you may recall, is not the best age for many of us, what with new lumps sharing space with baby fat and all manner of unpleasantness happening to the figure. "Wow," Dad said. "You've gotten so *big*!" He repeated the phrase "so big" at least twice more. *Wow! So big!* It's still unclear to me whether Dad even knew that this was a faux pas.

The next generation: I went to see the cartoonist Roz Chast give a talk here in Charlottesville last year. I had had a sinus headache, so I took a nap that day and awoke with just a little bit of time to get there. I sat on a couch in the overflow room, watched her on a large screen, and coughed into my tissues every now and then. Chast was completely charming. She has the sort of voice that makes you think of her as a friend, and she looks like you imagine a cartoonist would—small and hip-nerdy—but not as rumpled as you might expect. She spoke about what it's like to work for *The New Yorker* and revealed that she creates many cartoons, but not all of them make it into the magazine's pages. *Aha!* I thought. *She's done them anyway, and maybe she'd be willing to let* Brain, Child *publish them!* Even as I was formulating a plan to talk with her, I knew very well that I should let Stephanie take care of any matters involving interpersonal relations, but I was high on sinus medication and perhaps not thinking clearly.

I cannot emphasize enough how much I love this woman's work. She added a little commentary to each illustration in her slide show, fortifying the funny with more funny. Then she came to a slide of a cartoon with Nancy Drew all grown-up. *Oh no*, I thought. *Oh no.*

Part of my job at *Brain, Child* is coming up with cartoon ideas, which my artist friend Beth then draws. I realized that *Brain, Child* had also run a cartoon about Nancy Drew all grown up. I didn't remember that Roz Chast had even done one on the topic. But there it was, and I had to have seen it because I read *The New Yorker* like stockbrokers read *The Wall Street Journal*. I felt my face get hot. *It's okay*, I thought. *Nobody here knows.*

A true statement until I bought some books for her to sign.

"That was such a great talk!" I said.

"Thank you!" Roz Chast replied.

"I edit a magazine—*Brain, Child*—and when I heard you have left-over cartoons, I thought that maybe you'd consider sending some to us. Is there a good way to get in touch with you?" So far, so good.

"Do you have a card you could give me?"

I really should have a business card, but I never bothered to update them after we moved. "Umm . . .," I said. "No, I don't have one with me, but I'll write my e-mail address down."

I rooted around in my purse until I found an old grocery list. I carefully tore it in half, keeping the part that lists "tampons, dog food, bananas . . ." and wrote out my name and e-mail address on the other half. I knew, even as I was doing it, that I looked like a bit of a nut, so maybe my subconscious decided to take it all the way. Because I then found myself saying, "You know, we ran a Nancy Drew grown-up cartoon, too. I think I stole the idea from you." Chast looked up, still smiling but with a slightly alarmed expression on her face. "I didn't mean to. I mean, I didn't even remember seeing yours until today." I paused. "Yours was better," I continued. She finished signing quickly, but not quickly enough.

I walked down the steps, and each time my sandals hit the marbled surface, I muttered swear words to myself. I walked outside and crossed the lawn to my car, still swearing. I quizzed myself: Was there any way that could have come off as charming? No. The answer was no, there wasn't, not when you offer someone a piece of an old grocery list and announce that you stole her intellectual property. And then explain that hers was "better," as if there were such a thing as a contest between Roz Chast and yourself.

I followed up with a not-insane letter and some issues of the magazine, but not surprisingly, Roz Chast has not e-mailed me.

So, there's the inability to stop myself from saying the wrong thing. There are also the less dramatic social awkwardnesses. I don't know if this is the "human condition" that people in college were always talking about, but it's a pretty rare occasion that I feel comfortable speaking unguardedly with anyone but the closest of friends and family. So one of two things happens: I either speak unguardedly anyway and have regrets, or I speak guardedly and come across as unfriendly and cold.

And finally there's the aforementioned tendency to assume the worst about people. I actively try to fight this one, truly I do, but it seems to be my default setting.

There's really no way to get around having to deal with other people. If I want to live in the world, I have to chat with neighbors, talk with clerks and mail delivery people, interact with people through work, and perform other sundry interpersonal interactions. It's not just a matter of convenience. I—and probably the rest of the world— *need* other people so the wheels on the bus of my life don't fall off. I rely on a whole battery of neighbors, relatives, and educators to get Caleb to adulthood. I rely on my friends to help me make sense of various events. I rely on the women who work on *Brain, Child* to make work go smoothly. I rely on doctors, tax attorneys, tree specialists, other parents, etc., for all the millions of things that I cannot do myself.

I know quite well that I'm not an island, but given my set of social skills, it's too bad that I can't be completely self-reliant. Thoreau at Walden would not have had to make chitchat about real estate with other parents at the park. I'm pretty sure the Marlboro Man never had to explain to anyone the difference between a Photoshop file and an Adobe Acrobat PDF.

What's more, if I'm to figure out my greater purpose, if I'm to use my signature strengths in order to better serve the world, as Seligman suggests, I'd better start getting more comfortable with "the world."

I turn to the wisdom of the ages. I turn to Dale Carnegie's *How to Win Friends & Influence People.*

DALE CARNEGIE WROTE this book in 1936, and most of it is illustrative anecdotes culled from the gazillions of people he spoke with while teaching his methods of how to win friends and influence people. The first thing that jumps out at you—or at me, anyway—is not Carnegie's actual advice, but how much the details of life have changed since he wrote this book.

Take this example of some parents whose son has the "unholy habit of wetting his bed."

[The boy] slept with his grandmother. . . . Scolding, spanking, shaming him, reiterating that the parents didn't want him to do it—none of these things kept the bed dry. So the parents asked: "How can we make this boy want to stop wetting his bed?" . . . First he wanted to wear pajamas like Daddy instead of wearing a nightgown like Grandmother. . . .

Go ahead. Parse that out and find how many things today's parent might find objectionable or just plain odd.

In another section, Carnegie reports that "some authorities" claim that people go insane because they want to feel important. Sure, "about one-half of all mental diseases" have a physical cause (syphilis, brain lesions, etc.), but—"and this is the appalling part of the story," Carnegie says—the other half have nothing wrong with their brains at all! They know this, apparently, because scientists have looked at the autopsied brains of people afflicted with mental illness under "the highest-powered-microscopes" and found no abnormalities. I shudder a little, thinking of the faith we put in the science of our times.

But once you get past these details, the message is clearly timeless, and I can see why it's still selling briskly, seventy years after it was first published.

If there are two kinds of advice—that which you know but need to be reminded of, and that which is a novel idea—Carnegie's advice slides easily into the "Already Know" category. His "fundamental techniques in handling people," for example, are

1. Don't criticize, condemn, or complain.
2. Give honest and sincere appreciation.
3. Arouse in the other person an eager want. [Which is to say, make the person *want* to solve the problem.]

Common sense, right? Some of Carnegie's lists overlap—the first rule in how to be a leader ("Begin with praise and honest appreciation") is the same as the second rule of how to handle people ("give honest and sincere appreciation")—but he's nothing if not consistent. Basically, Carnegie rests his understanding of human nature on a few key ideas: People are interested in themselves, and not you. This is why you should be a good listener, say a person's name when you speak to him or her, and make other people feel important. With this understanding, people's intentions—the intentions that I often assumed were not good—are a moot point. They're looking out for themselves, according to Carnegie, and sometimes that'll be good for you and sometimes it won't.

Also, people don't like to be told what to do, so when you want someone to do something, the most painless way is to ask questions, let them come up with the idea, and be extraordinarily gentle in your criticism. Go hog-ass wild on the praise and be self-deprecating. There are other rules, but you get the idea.

How to Win Friends & Influence People comes with instructions on how to make the most of it. "The More You Get Out of This Book, the More You'll Get Out of Life!" Carnegie promises. For starters, I'm to read every chapter—twice. I'm also to underline the important parts, star the really important parts, be earnest in not only applying the principles but *wanting* to apply the principles, and keep notes, among other things. All do-able, I think.

Carnegie is a results man, which explains why this book is so popular among business types. He writes, "You can't win an argument," and by that he means that even if the other person concedes, you'll probably have incurred some damage. You'll be remembered as someone who embarrassed another (as Carnegie himself once did), lose truck sales (as a Mr. Patrick O'Haire did), or even lose your life (as "William Jay," the subject of a poem about a man who refused to yield the right of way, did). If given the choice, Carnegie advocates for letting others save face, even at the expense of coming across as wrong, or in some cases, not too bright yourself. *It's not worth it* would be the common refrain throughout the book if that were in the 1930s vernacular.[1]

There's also a strange tension throughout the book that I couldn't

---

[1] As it is, the vernacular is excellent and includes such phrases as "I don't give two whoops in Hades" and "you unmitigated ass."

quite put my finger on until after I finished it: I got the sense throughout that the people who were being assuaged by these rules were somehow being tricked. The cranky person who took issues with the phone
company, the old lady who just wanted someone to listen to her, the
child who wet his bed—none of them knew that the person with
whom they were interacting was applying a Dale Carnegie technique,
and I couldn't help but feel like some unsuspecting people were being
duped. (To be fair, maybe this is because some of Carnegie's techniques have been used and abused over the years. A Ken Nottingham,
employee of General Motors, discovered that by reading a cafeteria
lady's name tag and greeting her with a "Hello, Eunice" the next day
he got more ham and potato chips. I have been the Eunice in various
service jobs, and what you would get from me by reading my name
tag is a scowl for being overly familiar and a suspicion that you were
trying to con me.)

On the other hand, Carnegie is very clear about how sincere a person
has to be when applying these techniques. You cannot just pretend to
find what other people talk about interesting; you have to actually find it
interesting. You cannot pretend to understand where someone is coming
from; you have to actually understand his or her perspective. A fake
smile isn't going to cut it. Principle #8 in Being a Leader is "Make the
fault seem easy to correct," and I realize that Carnegie is using this principle on his readers. It is one thing to follow his simple and pleasant
rules; it's a much taller order to really mean it.

For all my social blundering, I actually am interested in people—
many people, anyway. It's just that I rarely seem to be able to get past
small talk to the things about people that interest me.

I RUN INTO a couple of snags early on. Unlike the myriad salesmen
and social creatures in *How to Win Friends & Influence People,* I realize
that, on a day-to-day basis, I don't have a lot of contact with the

outside world since I work at home. This means that I won't get to practice Carnegie's methods as much as other people might, and so my learning will go more slowly.

Also, one of the instructions is that I "make a lively game" by "offering some friend a dime or a dollar every time he or she catches you violating one of these principles." I'm all for lively games, but the only person who is with me enough to catch my blunders is Caleb. Caleb, who recently told Stephanie that he "collects" money, would love a dollar or a dime for helping me, but I'm afraid this would set a dangerous precedent, the child correcting the mother. Plus, the rules—thirty in all—are not especially easy to keep track of.

Anyway, I start applying Carnegie's techniques. In my case, there are two concrete things I need to do: Make more of an effort to interact with people, and just shut up and listen.

One cold January morning, Janet comes to the bus stop with her cup of coffee, and after the kids get on the bus, we stand there for twenty minutes catching up. I'm starting out small here: Janet is, after all, a close friend and I've never felt any social awkwardness with her. I decide that I will listen—*really* listen, which is Principle #4 of How to Make People Like You—to what she's saying. What she's saying is an interesting story about departmental politics; since I work at home, I get my vicarious office talk this way. This intent listening is not hard. I find Janet interesting in general, and the difference between what I normally do and what I'm doing now, my mittens stuffed in my pockets, my toes flexed to keep them warm, is that I'm not saying very much at all. Piece of cake, I think, as I walk up the steps to my house. I jot it down in the back of my book.

I continue to apply Carnegie's principles. A couple of days later, after some vigorous exercise involving a paper ball and the rug, Caleb runs into the bathroom. When he comes out, his flushed face is dripping with water. "I was so *hot*," he says dramatically. "This feels *so good*."

"Hey," I say. "You did a good job not splashing that all over your clothes." I am applying Principle #2 for handling people, being "hearty in your approbation and lavish in your praise." I'm also, I think, applying Principle #7 in being a leader: "Give the other person a fine reputation to live up to," the reputation, in this instance, being that of a non-water-splasher.

He runs back into the bathroom and emerges, soaked. His shirt is dripping, his bangs are plastered to his forehead. I start to get pissed. "I hope you didn't get water all over the bathroom," I say.

He slams the door hard and almost catches Simon in it. I am officially pissed. I open the door. "Don't you ever slam the door like that!" I yell at him. I march over to the bathroom. Water is splashed all over the walls and the sink is a wet mess, dripping onto the tile. I spin around and confront Caleb. "Why did you get water all over the walls?" I ask.

"I thought you said it was okay!" he says.

"You thought that I said it was okay to ruin the paint in the bathroom and make a big mess that someone will have to clean up," I say.

"You said that it was okay that I splashed water!" he cries.

"On your face. I didn't think I have to tell you specifically *not to ruin the walls of the bathroom!*" He's sputtering—*but, but, but!*—but I need to walk away from this. He's seven years old, old enough to know better. Like the moderately hopeless person that I'm trying not to be, I catastrophize. We will never have anything nice, I think. What is wrong with him that he thinks he can just *destroy* my home? I know perfectly well that it's not just my home, but it sounds better. Even as I'm doing it, though, I know that this is the wrong thought pattern, but I cannot help myself. This is the real me, and mercy is not my strong suit.

I fume in the living room and try to talk myself out of this extreme irritation. The problem, I think, is that we're at the point now where Caleb is such a good kid, such a mature kid that these episodes of judgment deficiency blindside me. I start to cool off. Then I apply Principle #8 of how to win people to my way of thinking—"try honestly to see things from the other person's point of view." I realize that it's possible that Caleb thought he was being given carte blanche with the splashing.

I climb the stairs to my office, where he and Brandon are playing a computer game. "I'm sorry for yelling at you," I say to Caleb and I hug him. "I can see how you thought that splashing was okay." This is Principle #3 of winning people to my way of thinking ("if you are wrong, admit it quickly and emphatically").

He hugs me back. I go downstairs and jot this in the back of the book, leaving him to play his game. I broke a few rules, but applied a few more. Pretty much a wash, so to speak.

LIFE CONTINUES IN THIS MANNER. I remain conscious of Carnegie's principles, and feel fairly proud of myself for applying them. I have not won any friends or influenced any people yet, but just keeping the principles in mind gives me a virtuous feeling.

And then something happens that gives me my own little case study.

As we get ready for bed one night, the dogs start going nuts. Caleb calls, "Someone's at the door!" No, someone's not is my first thought. It's 8:30 at night. But someone is.

"I'll get it!" Caleb says.

I spit out some toothpaste. "No, you won't," I say to Caleb. "You don't know who it is."

Before I can suggest that we not answer the door at all, Brandon and Caleb are downstairs. Brandon unlocks the dead bolt and steps out front. The porch light is off, and I stand at the top of the steps and watch. I see Brandon's figure and that of a woman. They talk. Brandon comes back in, and I hear him and Caleb rummaging around in the kitchen.

From the top of the stairs, I watch the figure on the porch. She's wearing a dark coat with the hood up. She opens her jacket. She reaches her hand inside. My legs get a little weak. She's got a gun! A knife!

No, just a drama queen watching her. She was simply hugging her coat around her. Brandon opens the door and I hear him say, "I'm sorry, we don't." He steps out front and speaks. Then he comes in and locks the door.

"What was that all about?" I ask.

"She said she ran out of gas and wanted to know if we had a dollar or two we could give her."

The three of us go to the end of the hallway on the second floor and watch her walk across the street to a neighbor's house. I can see that the woman is carrying a gas container. The neighbor answers the door and then shuts it. We watch our neighbor return with some cash and hand it to the stranger. Brandon, Caleb, and I watch the hooded woman walk down the street and out of the neighborhood into the dark.

"That's weird," I say.

"Yeah, it kind of was," Brandon says. "But maybe she did run out of gas."

We don't discuss it further there in front of Caleb. We read another chapter in the Lemony Snicket series and get him settled down in bed. He falls asleep quickly tonight, and I spring back up as soon as I can and go downstairs. I let Luna out of her crate and turn all the outside lights on.

Brandon joins me downstairs. I'm a little jumpy and I keep looking out the windows. Brandon is sticking with the possibility that she actually ran out of gas. He has this sort of faith in people.

But I'm suspicious. I'm not even entertaining that possibility. It's not that she wanted a dollar—I've been known to give money to panhandlers who are clear drunks or junkies. It's that it feels fishy; it feels invasive, this stranger knocking on my door. Some months past, a few houses in the neighborhood were robbed while the families slept upstairs, and if you want to give yourself the heebie-jeebies, think about that for a moment: a stranger rifling though your things while, steps away, you and your loved ones are unconscious and vulnerable.

"Why did she walk all the way down to the end of the street to come to *our* house?" I ask Brandon. "If I ran out of gas, I'd walk to the gas station, where I knew people had money and the gas was right there."

"Yeah, I would, too," Brandon says.

"And why wouldn't she ask to use the phone to call someone she knows to help her instead?" I ask.

"It *is* weird," Brandon says.

We talk about it some more, but there's only so far you can take an unsolved mystery. I go to bed still feeling a little uneasy. If someone really wants to cause you harm, I conclude, lying nervously in bed, there is very little you can do to stop them.

The next morning, I tell Janet about the strange visitor the night before. She raises her eyebrows. "She wanted gas?" she asks. "I happened to be over at Bruce and Anna's when the same thing happened last week. Woman, carrying a gas can? Come here."

Bruce is on his porch and Janet recounts my story to him. "Hey, she was here last week!" he says.

"What did you do?" I ask.

"I gave her some gas. I thought it was a little suspicious since her car started up without a cough or anything. It didn't sound like a car that had run out of gas," he says.

We all have to go to work, but Janet urges me to call the police and file a report.

"Eh," I say. I have plenty of work to do today, and talking to officers about a woman whom I didn't actually see and who got no money from us does not appeal.

"I would," Janet says. "Nothing happened, but she could be casing our houses."

"And she knows where people keep their money now," Bruce adds.

I'm still noncommittal. But I do send out an e-mail to the entire neighborhood, just the facts, plus Brandon's description of the woman: shoulder-length blondish hair, wire-rimmed glasses, a very thin face, lots of jewelry. People can make what they want of this, I think. I'm careful to use Carnegie's tips in my wording, specifically Principle #4 in how to be a leader: "Ask questions instead of giving direct orders."

Before lunch there are about a dozen responses from the neighbors. One neighbor mentions that he was awoken at four in the morning the Saturday before by a woman yelling. It sounded like she was calling for a lost child or pet, but when the neighbor looked outside, he couldn't see anyone. A friend tells me privately that the woman's voice sounded like mine, leaving me to wonder briefly about the sleepwalking again, but we all think this might be a coincidence and I don't have any evidence—muddy shoes, sore throat—that I was wandering around the 'hood like some sort of wraith. Brandon and I decide that it also sounds like a mildly unsatisfying ghost story. But no one was there!

The responses from the neighbors are interesting, and I get to see right there in my e-mail program who, probably intuitively, knows How to Win Friends and Influence People. One neighbor began "in a friendly way" (Principle #4 in winning people to your way of think-ing). Another talked "in terms of the other person's interests" (Principle #5 in ways to make people like you) by pointing out that everyone stands to gain if we can discourage people casing our homes. And another neighbor used a technique—a sort of self-deprecating, "this-may-seem-over-the-top" introduction—that combines a few of Carnegie's princi-ples of being a leader.

Other neighbors misstep in the winning of friends and influencing of neighbors, mostly by giving direct orders. Of this, Carnegie says, "Resentment caused by a brash order may last a long time." I notice that the people who use Carnegie's techniques are the same people who tend to have a reputation for being levelheaded and open to suggestions. The others, who stray from Carnegie's principles, tend to be a little prickly. It's a small neighborhood and these reputations matter more than one might think. Me, I'm careful not to be bossy (for once) and I keep my interjections at a minimum. I'm trying to be a leader, and leaders, according to Carnegie, seem to be extraordinarily gentle in their interactions.

No one is being an alarmist, but about half the people suggest, like Janet, that *someone* file a report. I decide that that someone might as well be me. It's the first time I've ever called the police, and I speak to an officer who gives the distinct impression that I'm closing the barn door once the horse has escaped. And also that the horse is certainly suspicious but hasn't committed any crimes.

For the rest of the day, e-mails from other neighbors come in. The strange woman, it turns out, has visited five houses in the neighborhood. The whole deal is an interesting lesson in human nature where we answer the hypothetical question: If a stranger came to your door and needed help, would you help her?

As it turns out, most of us would. We are, after all, decent people, and we'd rather be duped and keep faith in mankind than be stingy with our help. I return to my work on the computer feeling good about my little neighborhood. We talk with one another; we're watching each other's backs. We're not the sort of neighborhood that gets freaked out by strangers coming into it. It's just that, collectively, we're street smart. As one neighbor put it, "I gave her $5 just in case she really was in a bind. I figured it was a nice deed for the day if it was real." I type and sip my tea and feel glad that this is where I am: in a place where the people can find that balance between lending a hand when it's needed and avoiding being taken advantage of. I can learn things from these neighbors, I think. This is a lovely community, the sort of place a real estate agent might bill as "a good place to raise your kids." Even Caleb and Parker seemed to have gotten around their difficulties and, in fact, often seek each other out to play after school. What's that twittering on my shoulder? Why, it's a blue bird!

The warm fuzzies, I'm sorry to report, don't even make it past dinner. As I wait for the frozen cannelloni in the oven to cook into tonight's meal, I check my e-mail. And I find a whole new, albeit smaller, discussion in which this balance that I was so excited about crumples under the philosophical bulk of How We See Our Fellow Man. People extrapolate and come to somewhat extreme conclusions. One neighbor weighs in that the woman didn't seem dangerous and is probably mentally ill (read: deserving of our sympathy). A few e-mails later, another neighbor points out that he has both a Rottweiler and a shotgun if any trouble arises. My heart sinks as I watch the bleeding hearts duke it out with the macho avengers.

Because I *get* both sides of it, both extremes. I totally understand the impulse to empathize with someone so down and out that she brings a prop to your home to wring a few bucks from you. Look, I have a gas container, so I'm not lying! On the other hand, I felt intruded upon myself, standing at the top of the steps in my pajamas, watching a stranger lure my kindhearted husband out onto the darkened porch. I understand wanting to avenge yourself on whomever does you wrong.

The only person who steps into the fracas at this point is Parker's father, who notes that he doesn't think the woman is dangerous, either—just a potential thief. And he does it up Carnegie style, beginning in a friendly way, showing respect for others' opinions.

By the time Brandon, Caleb, and I eat our cannelloni and put our plates in the dishwasher, the e-mail discussion is over, and I don't send any more missives out into the 'hood. I lie to myself and say that I'm applying the principle of letting "the other person do a great deal of the talking," but I know that's not true. I'm not responding because I don't know what it would accomplish, or what I would say. In this, I fail at a principle that I starred in *How to Win Friends & Influence People*: being a good listener. I know that both the advocate for the mentally ill as well as the Rottweiler/gun owner did not feel heard. Their e-mails pretty much dropped into the void. In Carnegie-speak, they did not feel important, the single thing that people want.

I CALL MY MOM and tell her that I'm reading the Dale Carnegie book.

"How is it?" she asks.

"Oh, common sense," I say. "You're supposed to be a good listener and not correct people directly and stuff like that."

"How's that working?" she asks.

"I guess it's all pretty subtle," I admit. "I don't think I've won friends or influenced any people. Although I don't know what friends I need to win or what people I need to influence. I haven't made any social faux pas, I don't think."

"I always got the impression from you that you didn't really care a whole lot what people thought of you," she says. "Not that you're rude or anything like that. But, you know, just that people could either take you or leave you and it didn't matter a whole lot to you."

I think about this after we hang up. Could this be the root cause of all my social blundering? Could this be the thing that keeps me from the meaningful life?

On one hand, one of the all-time best things about being an adult is that popularity isn't all-important. I don't like to make an ass of myself (see Roz Chast reference), but if someone doesn't like me, it doesn't gnaw at me. I'm not an island, but I'm not an extrovert either, and there's a limit to how many opinions I can take to heart.

But is this a good way to be? Martin Seligman cites a study he and a colleague undertook in which they looked at the social lives of more than two hundred college students. They found that the "very happy" people stood out from the average and the unhappy because their social lives were hopping, both in terms of close friends and casual friends. "The very happy people spent the least time alone (and the most time socializing)," he writes. But, Seligman admits, it's a chicken-or-egg question: Is it the friends that make people happy or the happiness that attracts friends?

Carnegie, writing in the wake of the Great Depression, tends to focus more on the financial gains that await takers of his advice, but in his introduction, he points out that no school teaches interpersonal relations and "[d]ealing with people is probably the biggest problem you face." He connects popularity to happiness right there on page xxiii when he suggests his readers recite to themselves: "My popularity, my happiness and sense of worth depend to no small extent upon my skill in dealing with people." This, he says, will help you become sincere in your efforts to develop "a vigorous determination to increase your ability to deal with people." In other words, it'll help you become earnest in being interested in other people.

It's the old sincerity conundrum again. Although I'm taking Carnegie's tips and finding them useful, I just don't know if I can really muster up the wherewithal to *care* about my popularity. I do care deeply about what Brandon, Caleb, my parents, sisters, and close friends think of me, but I'm fully prepared to write off the rest of the world if they take me the wrong way, even some of the people upon whom I rely. Carnegie, of course, would see this as a very bad attitude to take. Bad for business, bad for good feelings among people, bad in the way that "unmitigated asses" are bad.

And I can't say that I disagree with him, in theory. Empathy, I'm starting to see, is going to be a key ingredient in making myself a better person. I have it on a macro level—it's wound pretty tightly into my ideals—but on the street level, so to speak, in one-on-one interactions . . . not so much.

Brandon and I used to live in a part of Virginia that was populated mostly by factory workers—the very working people that I think get so screwed over in today's America. But on an individual level, I just couldn't find a common ground with a lot of the people in the community. I didn't care much about professional sports or missionary work, and they didn't much care for . . . something about me. It became a cycle where I would try to be friendly, armed with my meager social skills, and then get shown it just wasn't going to work out, so I'd extend myself less and less, and therefore reinforce the idea that no connections could be made. I'm pretty sure it was a failing on my part. Brandon got along with everybody just fine. We spent eight years in this region of Virginia and I made exactly four friends, two of whom were married to each other. I chalked it up to culture clash.

I've chalked pretty much every situation in which I'm not well liked up to culture clash, from my inability to find my niche as an eleven-year-old in Virginia, to my Napolean-on-Elba-like existence in the Valley. But maybe it's not culture clash. Maybe it's me.

Carnegie's mantra—"My popularity, my happiness and sense of worth depend to no small extent upon my skill in dealing with people"—didn't develop in me a sincere interest in getting along with a variety of people. But I've read Dear Abby since I was a child, and I remember reading something very recently about a booklet she offers on the subject of popularity. Dear Abby is nothing if not prescriptive, no-nonsense, and blunt. I need a lash with a wet noodle; I need concrete rules that will smush the bad attitude. I look up the address, write a five-dollar check, and a few weeks later receive in my mailbox *How to Be Popular: You're Never Too Young or Too Old*.

I OPEN THE ENVELOPE and I'm pleased to see that the original Abigail Van Buren, aka Pauline Phillips, is on the front, with her kicky flip and pleasant smile. Pauline's daughter, Jeanne, writes the Dear Abby column nowadays, and while they both have their charms, I grew up with Pauline. Seeing the face I saw every morning over breakfast for years is a nice surprise.

"So you want to be popular?" Abby opens. "Who doesn't? Everybody wants to be well-liked, accepted, needed, appreciated, popular— and of course, loved." I stand in the kitchen, read this, and realize at once that Pauline, bless her heart, will not be offering tips on how to sincerely *want* to be popular. She just assumes from the get-go that a person does.

And on the face of it, Pauline is right. You gotta have friends. But how many? How far-reaching? I'm haunted by Seligman's observation that the very happy have both many close friends and many casual friends. I sit down with my cup of tea and Simon curls up on the couch with me. "*Casual* friends, Simon," I ask him. "How does one get casual friends?"

He groans a little and rolls onto his back for me to scratch his belly. *Like so?*

"No, baby, I'm not going to show people my genitals," I say.

I'm not alone in thinking that the whole concept of community has changed. I haven't read Robert D. Putnam's 2000 book, *Bowling Alone*, but I understand that he lays out an impressive array of data and analysis that shows that community is falling by the wayside. A whole mess of developments, including TV and suburban sprawl, he says, have contributed to the downfall of American community.

Community is just a good-sounding word. It's the social equivalent of bread pudding. Community means that people will be there to help you out. It means hot meals brought over when someone is born or when someone dies. It means banding together for a common cause, the village raising the child, the raising of the new barn, the simple lending of a cup of sugar. It is goodwill toward men.

But there is a price for that goodwill, and the price is having to conform to community standards, whether that means something positive—as in we all agree that we shouldn't beat our kids—or something nastier—as in we all agree that women are not good at operating any sort of machinery. I pour a bowl of cereal and think about the time my sister and I went to rent a small motorboat on a lake while living in that other part of Virginia. "It's easy to operate," the man who rented it to us said. "Even a woman can do it." (To which I smiled brightly and responded, "Talk like that can get your teeth kicked in! You'd better be careful!" easily taking home the Miss Congeniality banner.) Judgment is the ugly side of community.

In some ways, this falling apart of community has also been good for me. While I made just the four friends while living in another part of Virginia, it spurred me on to quit banging my head with people like the motorboat-rental man and to find my community of like-minded mothers: Stephanie and I started *Brain, Child*, and I got to bypass small talk and jumped right into the major issues in mothers' lives. Plus, this super-fragmentation of society has preserved me from worrying about people whom I'm just not going to like.

At the same time, I'm probably missing out on new experiences that come in the form of casual friends. I call Stephanie and ask her what she thinks about community. "Hmm," she says. "The ideal situation would be, I guess, all the benefits of community without all the judgment, right?" She points out that in England, the big issue lately is something they dub "anti-social behaviour," which is acting unneighborly and which can get you a civil court order and a jail sentence if broken.

Stephanie once told me that a clergyperson she knew said that in order to have faith, you first bend the knee. The more secular among us call it "fake it till you make it." This is the tack I'll consciously take with Abigail Van Buren. It's the tack, I realize, I've been taking all along.

. . .

IF DALE CARNEGIE was all about softening his rules with anecdotes, Pauline Phillips cuts hard to the chase. In the Dear Abby column, you can break down the letters by type: There are the people who have etiquette questions; they're either trying to settle a friendly wager, or (more often) trying to show some relative how very wrong they were in not visiting, ruining bath towels, etc. Then there are people with relationship problems, ranging from a woman suspecting adultery to a retiree disturbed that his wife doesn't shower every day. And lastly there are the serious, cautionary letters, in which someone's survivor warns Abby's readers about domestic violence or cancer.

Reading *How to Be Popular*, I realize how much Abby relies on the letters to give some sort of narrative to the column. What you get in the booklet is almost pure advice. She has rules—many rules, too many to reproduce here—and they best be followed.

Physical appearance matters, so I take care to have a pleasant expression on my face and keep my clothes, hair, fingernails, teeth, etc., well groomed. She thinks the healthy are better groomed and more pleasant to be around. She also notes, "There are plenty of heavyset people who are comfortable with their appearance. They walk with pride, wear stylish clothes that fit well, and present them-selves with confidence and dignity," which I find both patronizing (aww, look how dignified the chubby girl looks! almost human!), and refreshing, given today's cultural horror of weight. I do not flaunt my figure and I do wear a bra.

Now, I'm ready to meet people. Phillips's advice in this arena is not too far from Carnegie's—it's the commonsensical, be-friendly, don't-be-overbearing type of advice. "Not everyone can be good-looking, but everyone can be charming," she writes from 1983, an era before widespread plastic surgery. "Charm, in a nutshell, is putting the other person at ease, making him feel comfortable and important."

I learn, fairly quickly, that Phillips's advice works better with some kinds of people than others. Part of what's tricky about applying her advice is knowing when to modify it—each of America's subcultures has its own rules of decorum.

She encourages her readers to give others "a glow" by complimenting them on something; everybody has something compliment-worthy. So one morning, I tell my neighbor Lucy how great she looks. I *think* it every morning—she has this knack of looking classy and put-together, all before eight A.M.—but this time I say it. "Thank you! What a great way to start the morning!" she says and runs off to catch her bus. She looks pleased.

But when I try to spread a little glow at lunch by remarking to the sandwich maker that I like his Docs, he simply raises his eyebrows and nods. Not in an especially friendly way. Which is a bummer and immediately puts me in a cranky mood. When my sandwich is ready, I take it without a word and turn heel. *Don't try to out-cool me, you little man,* is what I'm thinking. But I don't *say* it, so I'm still in the parameters of what Pauline would approve of.

I start slipping little Pauline-isms into every social interaction I have. Talking on the phone with my sister Jill, I try to be an "up" person by finding something positive to talk about. I refrain from correcting Neil about a mismatched verb/object combination that he clearly threw together in an effort to sound authoritative and intimidating. Having drinks out with a few friends (one of whom I daresay is "casual"!), I dance dangerously close to gossiping but I stop myself before I actually do it. Whenever I see anyone I know, I greet them using their first names. I do this for weeks on end, accepting every invitation I'm offered. I was a little afraid that I would eventually morph into someone with the manner of Pauline Phillips—the sort of person who would strike up a conversation by remarking, "A dollar certainly doesn't go as far as it used to, does it?"—but once I got the hang of it, the advice worked for me, with surprisingly few modifications. "The 'key'," Phillips writes, "to being popular with both sexes is: Be kind. Be honest. Be tactful."

A MONTH IN, I'm exhausted by all this effort.

First, because even though I'm listening intently and not gossiping and introducing myself when appropriate, there are some people with whom I cannot click beyond a superficial level. "Casual friends," I'm beginning to suspect, means that you're stuck in small-talk purgatory forever, and you might be excused for not really caring since you'll never know them very well. You will never find out what the casual friend's greatest joy is or secrets from her childhood or how she and her mate act around each other when nobody else is around. You'll never know about her ambivalences or strongly held opinions regarding marriage, work, children, or any of Martin Seligman's "mansions of life." You will not be taken in confidence, and everything will always be either "fine!" or "fine."

Second, and maybe more troublingly, I don't find that applying the Carnegie or the Dear Abby tips gets any easier. I have to remind myself to use them every time I leave the house, and it's hard work—and continues to be hard work—keeping on constant watch for ways I can be better at interpersonal relations. The good news is that it's not driving me crazy, like the constant vigilance with Brandon and Caleb did. The bad news is that I'm not seeing any results, although maybe this is another one of those lessons that it takes a lifetime to master.

I decide to stop going full-throttle on the experiments with interpersonal relations one evening after I get back from a meeting. I didn't know anyone at the meeting well, and although I tried very hard to muster up the right questions to be part of the conversation, although

I listened carefully, although I kept a pleasant expression on my face, the conversation turned to art history and stayed there for a good forty-five minutes. I know that people like me are supposed to find art history interesting or at least *not* find it the equivalent of taking five shots of NyQuil one after the other, but NyQuil it was for me. I'm certain that at some point the pleasant expression drained from my face.

I come home and kick off my shoes. Brandon and Caleb are playing a card game at the kitchen table and the dogs are chewing on their toys in the family room. Brandon has the fireplace going. It's so good to be home that I stand there for a minute as if I just returned from The War instead of a supposedly pleasurable meeting with not-friends.

"Mama!" Caleb says. "Look at this card!" He rattles off some Yu-Gi-Oh trivia that he truly does find exciting—the card's a mix of something and something else, if you can believe it—and although I don't have any idea what he's saying, I listen and I am actually interested.

"How cool is that?" I say to Caleb and kiss the top of his head. He grabs me around my waist.

"How was it?" Brandon asks me.

"I think I have to face up that I am never going to be popular, or a brilliant conversationalist, or whatever," I say. "They talked about *art history*."

Brandon winces. "Can I get you a beer?" he asks.

I guess I feel a little ashamed of myself here. I have been talking the talk of empathy, but when it came to walking the walk among my fellow Charlottesvillians, I could hardly muster up enthusiasm for anything outside my regular orbit. I'm playing my role in the death knell of community, I realize. I don't care to bowl alone, but I don't want to do it with casual friends, either.

Brandon doesn't wake up after Caleb falls asleep and I come downstairs alone tonight. I look over my books on popularity. Maybe I was wrong. Maybe popularity and empathy aren't linked at all.

I'll call Stephanie the next day, and she'll remind me that plenty of people Make a Difference without being popular. "Look at Bill Gates," she says. While neither one of us has experienced whatever cocktail banter Bill Gates has to offer, we've both heard of the Bill and Melinda Gates Foundation that does indeed Make a Difference.

Or, maybe I'm just thinking of these concepts of community, popularity, and empathy all wrong. I think back to a conversation I had with Stephanie, who is consistently kind, honest, and tactful. She wondered if, maybe, community meant that everyone, no matter how different they were, had a place in their small town. Sure, Old Man Williams was bonkers, but he was Smallville's own bonkers. Yes, Miss Perkinson was a drama queen, but she was that town's drama queen. Or, Mrs. Sylvester's children were always filthy, but they seemed to be well mannered and having fun.

Neither one of us knew whether this Smallville we were imagining ever really existed, but sitting on the couch surrounded by my self-help books, Simon at my feet and Luna curled up next to me, the idea of it comforts me. In my community, I'm the lady who will probably offend you, but I often do it inadvertently. I do not care for talk of art history. I am capable of a compliment and capable of being a good listener. I tend to be suspicious and I won't always make you feel important or even heard. My kid might punch yours or he might offer one of his toys with spur-of-the-moment generosity. I'll mess up sometimes. I'll try harder to work on the mercy, so when you mess up, I can forgive you. I hope I'll get better on this front, but this is something that's going to take a long time.

I will bring you food when your baby is born.

I will not steal your recycling bin.

{7}

The Body

S PEAKING OF SITUATIONS that may or may not be imaginary . . . how can I say this?

I find myself attractive.

It's not that I find myself more attractive than other people because, really, is there anything more irritating than people thinking they're cute? Years ago, my former teacher Alex was making her first short film, and she asked me if I'd like to play the main character's best friend. I'd never acted before, but I was thrilled—seriously, so thrilled that I worked on my lines in front of a mirror and made Brandon read the main character's lines and, in complete earnestness, critiqued my performance in front of the mirror using phrases like *more feeling*. The day of the shoot came, and while Alex was setting up the camera and testing sound levels, I chatted with the actress playing the main character. She was leggy, with the sort of large white teeth that suggested milk mixed with white paint mixed with shining light from the heavens. She'd tied a red bandanna around her blond hair but unfortunately that didn't mean she was down to earth (as bandannas suggested in the early nineties). As we began to talk, it became clear that she found herself scandalously cute; while Alex focused the camera on the porch where we sat, the actress complained at length about how terribly *attractive* she was and how it made life *difficult* in all sorts of ways. Which are not problems faced by people who look very much like they could be cast as The Best Friend in a movie.

Alex began the shoot, and I voiced my lines with feeling, but later the camera revealed that while I was saying, "Oh yeah?" and "Just don't get caught!," my facial expressions were saying, "Get over yourself, sister" and "Oh, piss off." I didn't blame Alex one bit when The Best Friend became a voiceover.

So, while technically I have a face made for radio (as the old yuk-yuk goes), I'm also convinced that I look mmm-mmm good, no matter how much I weigh. In a way, it's the converse of anorexia: Instead of looking in the mirror and always seeing fat, I look in the mirror and think There I am! Good-looking as ever!

This is an illusion about myself I don't mind having. There's only one of me, and my body, for better or worse, reflects what I've done with it. I got a good start genetically. I birthed a big baby and nursed him for thirteen months. I enjoy cold Czech beer and frosted glasses of Cosmopolitans; I like smoking cigarettes. I eat foods that taste good, whether they're healthy fresh raspberries or unhealthy fried crab cakes. I don't like to exercise unless it's the having of the sex. My hair is dyed the way I like, I'm particular about my clothes, and I love how a short skirt and tall black boots feel. Sure, I have stretch marks, the beginnings of forehead wrinkles, and new creases on my torso—not things I exactly revel in— but they're the small aesthetic costs of my pleasures, my habits, my good times. I'm comfortable with the way my body looks right now.

This is all to say that my looks aren't going to be a driving motivating force here. It's all about the health, which is a whole different ball of tissue, muscle, and fat.

. . .

IF THERE'S ONE thing I've learned, it's that I'm totally justified in being skeptical of sentences that begin "Research shows . . ." When it comes to health, Research is not entirely trustworthy. Research says out of one side of its mouth that eggs are terrible for you, but then says that nope, they're okay in moderation. Years back, Research had its bowels all in an uproar about how nasty alcohol is for the body; more recently, Research has changed its tune and actually suggests that a daily glass of wine might be good for one's heart. Research does this sort of thing all the time. It's not Research's fault, really. That's the way Research is— an evolving science that sometimes gets excited and leaves behind its friends Peer-Reviewed Studies and Good Control Groups and Large Samples. (To be fair, though, with a name like "Large Samples" . . .)

Anyway, research shows that a good diet and exercise routine is linked to elevating your mood. According to the National Institutes of Mental Health, a 1999 study found that regular exercise helped older Americans fight depression. And we've all heard enough about "endorphins"—the neurochemical released during exercise that's supposed to calm and fight stress (and the accompanying flight-or-fight response)—to know that exercise can play a part in our mental well-being. Research also tells us that a healthy diet improves one's mental state, although the link is more tenuous.

I know all this. Intellectually. And I do make an effort.

I try to plan super-healthy dinners at least once a week, usually twice. And that usually means no red meat, heavy on the vegetables, light on the oil and butter. One evening, I pull out *Cooking with Rosie*, the cookbook by Oprah's one-time personal chef, from the top shelf of our pantry. Most of Rosie's recipes aren't my bag, but one I do like an awful lot is her roasted vegetable baguette. Caleb drags a chair over to the kitchen counter, steps up, and helps me chop vegetables and make the yogurt sauce. It's been a while since I made this recipe.

"A while" in grown-up years is entirely different from "a while" in kid years. Caleb has no recollection at all of this recipe. As I put his plate in front of him at the table, he shudders. Brandon and I continue futzing around with the meal, bringing the napkins to the table, making sure everyone has something to drink, adding a little lettuce to the sandwich. Caleb shudders again. His hands are even shaking a little. Finally, we bite.

"What's wrong, Caleb?" we ask.

"It's just that I *freak out* when people give me *only vegetables* for dinner," he says.

Frankly, I don't blame him. Because while I do try with the intermittent healthy eating, no one would describe the way I go about my business as a "healthy lifestyle." It's all I can do not to freak out when someone scolds me about it. I know very well what my problems are. There's the smoking, drinking, distaste for exercise, and weakness for rich foods, which have resulted in my BMI—"body mass index" (a number you arrive at after plugging your height and weight into a formula)—hovering somewhere between simply overweight and straight-up obese. I carry too much of my weight in my midsection (better to be "pear-shaped," Research says), and I don't have especially good ways of dealing with stress.

A lot of the time, I'm very good at ignoring the effects that all these bad-yet-pleasurable habits have on my health. I'm thirty-three, I tell myself. I have plenty of time to change my wicked ways before I incur permanent damage.

Except for the times when I'm not good at ignoring my health, and it occurs to me that I'm *already* thirty-three, and maybe I *have* incurred permanent damage, and maybe I'm suffering from a life-threatening illness *right this very minute*. Periodically, I'm seized with the idea that I have a terrible disease. I'm the youngest person I know to have had: a diagnostic mammogram (my "breast lump" turned out to be a normal lymph node); an MRI (my blurred vision turned out to be weak eye focus muscles, not a brain tumor); a visit to a neuro-ophthalmologist (ditto); ultrasounds (once during pregnancy and also for the alleged breast lump); and another MRI (recurrent sinus infections one year). And these are only the situations that sent me packing for medical attention. Two months ago, I pulled a neck muscle and spent an afternoon gazing at the TV and envisioning how people will shake their heads at the shame of it all: I didn't go to the doctor, even when it became clear that I was dying of meningitis.

If I were healthier, I like to think I wouldn't be seized with these visions of my impending death. I could be secure in the knowledge that I put forth my best effort vis-à-vis my health. I would be relaxed, not swigging back beer and fidgeting with a cigarette. I would calmly be taking vitamins and earning the right to wear yoga pants. I would eat salads every day and actually enjoy a vigorous walk. I am closer to having a *Real Simple* home; is it possible I could have a *Real Simple* body—pure, streamlined, peaceful?

As I see it, my two roadblocks to this healthy life are my weight and my smoking. Everybody knows that quitting smoking will lead to at least a little bit of weight gain, thus making my weight loss efforts harder, so I'm going to try to tackle the weight first. I'm not going to be crazy about it; your weight range is genetically predetermined, but I think I can get back down to the lighter end of the range, and I think I know where to turn.

IN MY OFFICE, I maintain a stack of good ideas. They're mostly in the form of magazines and, mostly, I never get around to implementing these good ideas. Still, it makes me feel good to have them around.

One of them is the January 2005 issue of *O* magazine. On the cover, Oprah, dressed in white workout clothes, is Photoshopped in next to a second Oprah dressed in a long, form-fitting gown. Girlfriend is built like a brick house these days. The issue is titled "*O*'s guide to a fresh start." This issue of *O* made it to my stack of good ideas because between the covers is both a weight-loss plan and an insert showing exactly how to carry out the plan.

Three *O* readers—Michelle, Dorine, and Susan—have written to the editors. They claim to be "doing everything right," but they're still not losing weight. The editors have responded to Michelle, Dorine, and Susan by hooking them up with a trainer, a nutritionist, and a life coach. "What were our subjects really eating?" the subhead wonders. "More important, what was eating them?"

I'd slapped this into my grocery cart back in January and, after its ten-month stay on the pile of good ideas, I pick it back up at the end of October 2005. Although I know very well that (unlike Michelle, Dorine, and Susan) I'm not doing everything right, this is as good a start as any. I put my feet up on my desk and reread the main article.

The life coach is Martha Beck, whose work I mostly know from her fine memoir *Expecting Adam*, and she begins the participants' three-month effort to lose weight by making them each throw out a full plate of food. Beck also offers some opinions on what drives each woman to sabotage her diet. Dorine, Beck says, is afraid of not having enough. Susan is stifled under caregiving responsibilities. And Michelle? Beck chalks up her problems with food to racism. This makes more sense in the article (racism begets anger begets overeating), although Michelle will decide later that racism may not be the culprit for this particular issue in her life.

Rowena "Dr. Ro" Brock is the nutritionist, and as such, she offers up her opinions regarding what Michelle, Dorine, and Susan have been eating and drinking. Dorine's nightly glass or two of wine? Dr. Ro says no. One glass once or twice a week should do the trick and save a thousand calories right there. Susan's reading while she eats? Not a good idea because Susan probably eats past when she's full.

I have to admit, Dr. Ro and Martha Beck scare me. From my years in front of daytime TV, I understand that this reaching down to find the "real reason" you're overweight is par for the course in the health world, but I truly believe that I eat the way I do because I enjoy delicious food. I don't eat fast food, and I don't really even like candy bars. But we only have five senses and to squander one of them by eating plain no-fat yogurt with a tablespoon of granola on top for dessert (as Dr. Ro suggests) strikes me as crazy talk.

Of course, this way of thinking sounds just as transparent as Dorine does when she tells Dr. Ro that she used to sell wine (ergo, she should have more than one glass), or Michelle does when she points out that a Snickers bar has the same number of calories as a regular lunch (so she's justified in skipping a real meal). Anybody—or the experts, anyway—could see that we're making excuses. Do I want to be healthy or not?

The answer, at this point, is: Yes. I most certainly do. But I would like to be healthy in the most painless way possible and I need very specific instructions, so I pin my hopes on Jorge Cruise, the exercise expert in the article. When Dorine tells Cruise on page 135, "I'm not running unless someone is after me with a gun" and Cruise responds that he doesn't run either, my heart leaps in hope.

Cruise is the author of the *8 Minutes in the Morning* series. The key to his program is that no one can make the claim that they don't have eight minutes to devote to a workout. Eight minutes is nothing!

Cruise focuses his workout on strength training. Eight minutes of cardio, or aerobic, workout will do little, but he argues that if your muscles—those body parts that make up your "structural support"— are strong, your metabolism gets a kick and helps you burn more calories throughout the day. Plus, like he said, it's only eight minutes. I can handle that.

I make my maiden voyage to a sporting goods store to purchase some free weights, weights that should range between "three and fifteen pounds." I wander around the store for a good long while. I had no idea that this world of retail existed. Who knew that the accoutrements of basketball could fill a whole section of a store? I don't even own a pair of athletic shoes, unless you count Chuck Taylors, which you shouldn't because, in my opinion, the arch support is terrible. I have to circle back to the front of the store when I realize that there's no way in hell I'll be able to transport these weights more than two feet without a cart. Finally, the weights are purchased, loaded into my trunk, brought up singly from the trunk into my family room, and placed on their special free-weight stand.

When Caleb comes home, he grabs a set of dumbbells and hoists them above his head with gusto. "Be careful!" I call to him.

"Why?" he asks.

I pause. I don't know, really. "Uh, you could get a groin injury," I say, vaguely recalling that this is something that weight lifters seem to suffer from.

"What's that?" Caleb asks.

"Never mind," I say.

Later, in a puppyish fit, Luna will pick up one of the weights and run around the room with it, leaving small tooth marks on the foam grip of the five-pounder. Everyone in my family is fitter than me, except maybe for Simon, who seems to be slowing down since Luna joined our family. Then again, he's almost sixty in dog years.

THE NEXT DAY is Halloween and I begin.

I turn to the magenta and orange "O to go" insert titled "Let's Lose Weight—Fast!" Each day, I'm to work out two different sets of muscles. Monday's the chest and back, Tuesday's the shoulders and "abdominals," Wednesday's the triceps and biceps. I'm to warm up by marching in place for one minute—"knees high, arms pumping, knuckles toward the ceiling."

As one who doesn't, as a general rule, "work out," I feel self-conscious marching in my kitchen, in front of the microwave, the timer set to sixty seconds. When the microwave sounds, I scurry over to the weights and choose the five-pounders (most women, according to the insert, will use five- to ten-pound weights to get the dumbbell that's "heavy enough to really tire out the muscle by the 12th repetition").

The insert shows the same line-drawn woman performing the week's exercises. She's ponytailed and small-breasted, and she favors tight-fitting workout clothes. She lies down on her back to work out her chest muscles, and I do the same. I'm going to do four sets of each exercise, twelve repetitions each. This is not difficult math, but I lie there and raise the dumbbells in the air. "Damn it," I say. "Was I supposed to inhale or exhale?"

I'm not a stupid person, but it's tough at first to keep all of this in mind and, at the same time, make my body do it. The prose of the instructions doesn't help:

Lie on your back, knees bent and feet flat on the floor, holding dumbbells. (Support your back and head with pillows if necessary.) With arms bent, bring shoulders in line with elbows on the floor. Exhale as you slowly press dumbbells towards the ceiling . . .

I'll tell you, it's no walking and chewing gum.

The exercising of my back muscles requires the prop of a chair, and I have the same difficulties with the breathing, but after a few false starts and stops, I have completed my reps and my sets, which are phrases I thought I might never ever use.

I spring up from the chair. There is no other way to put it: I feel pumped. I walk over to the computer to check my e-mail with a spring in my step. "Look at me," I say to Simon and Luna. "I just finished my workout."

Luna cocks her ears as if she didn't quite hear me right. *You? Workout?*

Yes, me. And this, I have to say, may be one of the better workouts I've ever experienced. Sure, my arm got a little wobbly halfway through, and the next day I will be newly conscious of the slightly aching muscles beneath my bosom. But I'm not sweaty. I'm not out of breath. And I feel, I daresay, more energetic. Whether this is psychological or physiological, I can't say, but, on the other hand, it doesn't much matter, either.

LOSING WEIGHT FAST takes three months, according to the magazine. Research has been saying lately that I shouldn't measure my health by the number on the scale—that, in fact, it's entirely possible to be a bit of a chunk and still have a healthy heart and lungs—but it would be nice to have some sort of objective measure of my progress, so, as Cruise suggests, I weigh myself every Sunday, the only day of the week I don't exercise.

And I do keep up with the eight-minute workout. The dumbbells fall into my morning routine; while my tea is brewing, I exercise. I start taking Caleb to the bus stop wearing sweatpants so as to dive into the exercising right away. For Christmas, Brandon and Caleb get me a rather psychedelic-looking yoga mat to help me with the exercises that require me to get on my hands and knees. I bring my by-now-almost-year-old issue of *O* out of town, and when I leave it there, the daily exercises are so ingrained in me that I don't need my cheat sheet with the ponytailed woman. I know that Tuesdays are the worst days (the dreaded sit-ups coupled with the shoulder exercises for which, try as I might, I can't get above a three-pound weight) and that Thursdays will bring me to reps of groin-thrusting at the ceiling.

When I'm alone—which is most of the time I'm doing the eight-minute workout—I feel a strange pride in myself as I lift my legs, crunch my stomach muscles, hoist the dumbbells. I've worked up to eight-pound weights for my chest, back, and arms. I notice that I can lift heavier things. The world of objects sixteen pounds and under is my oyster.

But when we visit Mom for Christmas, two months into this, I become suddenly aware how goofy the exercises look. It's Saturday, and the house is packed with my sisters and their families. I turn on some music one morning while the people are eating pancakes and I attempt to do my exercises. I lie on my side, propped up with one elbow, and do leg lifts. Brit, my thirteen-year-old nephew, who has achieved a level of cool I could only dream of at his age, raises an eyebrow. My mother, depositing more pancakes at the kitchen table, peers over and looks at my progress. "They used to have us do exercises like that when I went to Spa Lady back in the eighties," she remarks. It's not the first time she's pointed out that today's self-help isn't exactly revolutionary.

I take the show in the living room because I cannot bear the thought of anyone—even family—watching me exercise my outer thighs. Although the ponytailed woman in the line drawing looks unremarkable on all fours lifting her knees outward as if she's a male dog who found a fire hydrant, I feel distinctly undignified doing it in front of a group. We're not the sort of family who has assigned one sibling the role of The Fool, and I'm not interested in auditioning.

Soon, though, Caleb and my niece stand together and stare at me. "What are you doing, Jenny?" Amara asks.

"I'm exercising," I say.

She's not buying it. "When I want to exercise, I dance," she tells me.

I compliment her dancing. It goes without saying that my own dancing is only a little less embarrassing than my busting the-dog-on-a-fire-hydrant move.

Still, the audience problem with these eight-minute shenanigans doesn't come up frequently, and I finish the three months with few problems. Cruise is right when he emphasizes that you simply cannot say that you're too busy for eight minutes of his workout. I can't, anyway. For someone whose signature weaknesses include lack of self-control, I'm pretty pleased with myself.

At the end of January, I tell myself that the three-month gig is up and I don't have to do it anymore. But something funny happens: I do it anyway. I've noticed that my muscles are slightly more . . . more. Before starting the exercise routine, I would lose an arm-wrestling match to anyone; now I would lose to just *almost* anyone.

On February 5, I get on the scale. I have to face that my objective measure of weight may not be, in fact, so objective. For the past three months, I've been hovering within two pounds up or down from my original weight. You put your jiggly ass in, you take your slightly less jiggly ass out, fire up the iPod and shake it all about. I stare down past my painted toenails to the number on the scale. I'm exactly where I started. I might have lost a tiny bit of fat and gained a tiny bit of muscle. I don't know.

My clothes don't fit noticeably differently. I can carry more laundry. I have a little more energy, although this is hard to both quantify and qualify; three months in, the increased energy certainly isn't as dramatic as it was when I first started exercising. I have a weight-lifting routine. These are small, good things.

But if I'm to be honest with myself, the eight-minute workout, in my case, is like throwing a few lima beans in a hot fudge sundae. As pleased as I am that Jorge Cruise's claim that his routine is "excuse-proof" turns out to be true, I'm only a smidgen closer to the healthy lifestyle that will, in theory, bring me endorphins, energy, and happiness. And that's what it's all about.

I'M LOOKING, I think, for a bridge to somehow connect my mind and my body. The idea that the two are separate has been parsed out by so many—from Plato to porn starlets—that I find myself traveling the road to banality.

I know it's a complete luxury that, with the exception of my typing fingers and reading eyes, what I do for a living takes place almost entirely in my head. I think this every time I talk to my mother, who teaches first grade and found how difficult it was to do so when she wrenched her knee. I think about it when I talk to my sister Erin, whose husband depends on his body being healthy and strong for hanging drywall. Of course, their minds are the most integral part of their jobs. But their bodies, their health, can't be taken for granted.[1]

Mine gets ignored a lot. While I dutifully did my eight-minute workout, I didn't gain any sort of omnipresent consciousness about my body. Over those three months, I never once thought, *Hey, too much cheese on my sandwich is bad for my cholesterol, which is, in turn, bad for my heart.* If I were conscious of my body all the time, I would constantly think of death via cancer whenever I smoked a cigarette. But I didn't. I still lived mostly in my head.

I'd hoped that finding this bridge between body and mind would somehow come naturally. You know, that after some period of time, I'd become more mindful of my health, and that making good decisions regarding diet, exercise, and other body miscellany—the impromptu walk, the choosing of grilled chicken over barbecued beef, the cutting down on the smokes—would follow. It didn't work that way.

In mid-February, I find the bridge, and—if I can drag this metaphor out to its last gasping bit of usefulness—I will say that it's one that I wish I hadn't crossed.

I'LL ONLY notice this later, but when people in my life start having the accidents, it's almost a year to the day since Cleo died. By the time I notice it, though, it's after all the crap with me has begun, and I'll long

---

[1] Actually, anyone who has a job that pays hourly with no sick paid days knows how important the body is. Back when I worked at a newsweekly as the calendar editor, I was paid by the hour. I was upset about something I can't recall now. I had a cold and knew that crying would make my cold worse—maybe transform it into full-blown bronchitis—so I steeled myself not to cry because I literally could not afford it, what with rent and my student loan payments.

for the person I was last year, someone who was merely helping her sick dog die.

I'm changing some names and details here because everyone here is much more than what I'm about to describe and, frankly, there's nothing ickier than taking someone else's tragedy and twisting it so that it's your tragedy now. In any case, this is what happens, from my perspective.

In mid-February, a friend of mine—Hailie—was at work when she got the news that her girlfriend, driving down the interstate, lost control of the car and was ejected onto the road. The speed limit on the interstate is sixty-five m.p.h., and her girlfriend, Cara, had been in the left-hand lane, so she was going at least that fast. Cara was airlifted to the big university hospital an hour away.

I was supposed to see Hailie the next day, and I got a call that there had been an accident and that Hailie would probably have to cancel. "Oh, God," I said into the reciever. "I hope Cara's all right." I didn't know the details, only that there had been an accident, and as any parent or preschool teacher worth her salt knows, accidents happen. But while Caleb went outside and played with his friends and I waited for my chicken to roast, I looked up the local news online and found that the accident was going to become, to Hailie, Cara, and those who love them, The Accident, as in the single event that changed their lives. Cara had suffered head injuries. She was said to be "in critical condition."

You hear the phrase "critical condition" all the time on the news; over the next week, I'd learn what it could mean. Cara was in a coma. She'd had several strokes during her first night in the hospital. They didn't know the extent of her brain damage. They didn't know how much, if any, of the language center of her brain she'd lost. Hailie told me this on the phone, her voice wobbly and determinedly optimistic. Neither of us mentioned that Cara is a writer, but the fact hung there in the space between "language" and "center." Hailie was on Xanax, trying to hold it together for herself, for Cara, for the kids.

If you're like I used to be, you'll read this and think, Oh, that's terrible. And it is. But I couldn't get two images out of my head: Hailie at work, chatting with her clients, maybe finishing up a quick lunch, maybe thinking that Cara will drop by the office later, maybe irritated with a conversation they'd had that morning, maybe not thinking of Cara at all. And then the state trooper comes, Hailie grabs her purse, and her life is sliced neatly into two pieces that are Before The Accident and After The Accident. It's not a maudlin fantasy: This is suddenly, incontrovertibly, Hailie's reality.

The other image is of Cara herself, whom I've known for a long time but not very well. She's sitting on a stool at the sex toy party that she and Hailie threw (at which the irony-free sex-toy saleswoman impressed several times upon this group, about half of whom were lesbians, just how much our men—our *guys*, our *fellas*—will like these toys). The order forms were passed out, and the room fell silent as we all scoured our papers, our faces serious. "It's not a test, people," Cara had said, stubbing out her cigarette. "Nobody's going to quiz you on this later." A smart-ass after my own heart. That was at least three years ago. And now this funny, blunt woman might be lost, if not in body, then in mind, in language center.

I couldn't explain to Brandon just how much this was on my mind. "What's wrong?" he'd ask me as I mooned around the house.

"I'm just thinking about Hailie and Cara," I'd say.

Meanwhile, accidents were also happening to people Brandon knew. A woman of his acquaintance went snowboarding with her family, hit a tree, and broke almost every bone in her body. Another man, whom we'd seen riding his bicycle to work for years, was hit by a car and slipped into a coma. Everywhere we looked, it seemed, people's lives were cleaving into two. Snap, snap. Before, after.

These aren't the only accidents I'd ever heard about, of course. Brandon himself was in a horrible car accident when he was in high school and suffered complications from it when we were in our third year of college; he'd had emergency surgery and was visited in his hospital room by a hospital employee explaining what a living will was. Through *Brain, Child,* I'd read hundreds of essays from women about The Accident in their lives. And I read the papers; I know how much sadness there is in the world.

But here in mid-February, I finally start understanding what people mean when they say Life Is Fragile. They mean The Body Is Fragile. They mean that all those metaphors—*heartbreaking, bone-crunching, ear-splitting, breathtaking*—aren't just metaphors. They happen to the body. It crumples easier than you think.

The third week in February, I notice my vision going a little wack, and I blame it on reading for two hours in the car without my reading glasses. But, in hindsight, I realize it was my first step onto the bridge.

OF COURSE, my life has to keep on trucking. The date of the PTO's Spring Fair is fast approaching, and it's becoming clear that I'm possibly the world's worst solicitor of raffle prizes ever; in compensation, I vow to use one of my signature strengths (Creativity) to fashion attractive signs for the raffle boxes. I also agree to host a literary salon for two writers I know who are coming to town for the Virginia Festival of the Book. By the time the invitation goes out, I've invited more people to my house for this party than I had to my wedding. I try to simmer down by reminding myself that I *know* the rules of good social interaction, thanks to Pauline Phillips and Dale Carnegie. I just have to use them.

Also, you might have noticed that Martha Beck and Dr. Ro have, conveniently, slipped out of my *O* magazine program, leaving me alone for eight minutes with Jorge Cruise. You might be thinking that it's no wonder that the program didn't work, given that I ditched two of the experts. This may be true, but every time I read the article, all I got from their advice was an overwhelming feeling of denial, sometimes tinged with condescension. I suspect that this might be an effect of the article's prose—there's a certain tone service-magazine writing takes—but the sum effect is the same. Dr. Ro restricts Dorine's wine; she says "firmly" to Susan that her battle will be portion control. Ro claims that it's "all right" to "satisfy a sweet tooth" by having angel food cake. I roll my eyes. Of course it's all right to have dessert: Eating a piece of chocolate cake isn't a moral right or wrong. Meanwhile, Martha Beck issues a "politely delivered command" and gives Michelle a "knowing smile" when Michelle makes the mistake of pointing out what a waste it is to toss a whole plate of food.

I might suffer this sort of attitude if Dr. Ro and Martha Beck had *their* own inserts, complete with specifics and line drawings. But they don't.

Still, Jorge Cruise alone isn't cutting it, so I sign up for Dr. Andrew Weil's My Optimum Health program. Like the FlyLady, it's online, doses of advice parceled out via e-mail and through a Web site. My Optimum Health advice can be purchased for four dollars a week, billed to my credit card quarterly.

Andrew Weil seems to me to be the perfect storm of a health-advice dispenser. First off, he's an actual M.D. Granted, that's no warranty against crackpottedness, but it's a good start. He's also known for espousing natural and vaguely New Agey methods, a quality that, in my mind, could be either a bonus or a deal-breaker, depending on the intensity of his leanings. (A little means open-minded, a lot could mean Jerhoam territory.) But I see Weil quoted in the April 2004 issue of *Real Simple*, in an article titled "The Energy Crisis?" and this somehow reassures me. I do a quick logic problem: *Real Simple* is mainstream and *Real Simple* quotes Andrew Weil, thus Andrew Weil is not a wack job.

Best yet is the way Andrew Weil looks—and this is something you cannot miss because pictures of Weil (cooking, meditating, looking vigorous and business-casual against the backdrop of a blue sky, etc.) appear with noticeable frequency on DrWeil.com. He's sixty-ish, with merry eyes, a white beard somewhere between Santa and Jerry Garcia, and a small gut. I love this. This is my kind of fitness guru, someone who doesn't equate Hollywood bodies with health. Who'd want to take the advice of someone who's won the genetic metabolism lottery? Not me. Give me your aging, your big-boned, your dabblers in decidedly untrendy facial hair.

One Sunday, I sign up for My Optimum Health, an eight-week program with specific instructions regarding diet, exercise, and spiritual health. I get an e-mail from Dr. Weil (pictured looking upward against a blue sky background). He congratulates me on signing up for this "tool for changing [my] life." He tells me, "Optimum health should bring with it a sense of strength and joy, so you experience it as more than just the absence of disease."

By now, I'm more than a little skeptical about any expert claim of happiness, but in the next paragraph, Weil cuts to the chase:

> [My Optimum Health Plan's] ultimate purpose is to reduce your risks of premature illness and death by enhancing the performance of your body's healing system. It is certain that every one of us, sooner or later, will face a health crisis. The question is not *if* such a crisis will occur, but *when*. By making My Optimum Health Plan part of your life, you can increase the likelihood that you will be well-prepared to face life's challenges.

Intellectually, I know that it's only a sign of my relative youth that the health crises affecting the people around me are accidents, and could not have been prevented through any amount of broccoli-eating or trans-fat-avoiding. Someday, with any luck, I'll grow old and watch health crises of the variety Dr. Weil is addressing—heart disease, cancer, osteoporosis—affect my peers and me.

But my knee-jerk reaction to this e-mail is to harrumph a little at the phrase *well-prepared*. Nobody expects to fly from her car onto the interstate.

IT'S NOT MY VISION, exactly. It's something else. Am I dizzy? My balance feels a little off, although the room's not spinning and I don't feel in any danger of falling down.

I'm walking through the family room on my way to switch around the laundry in the basement, but halfway there, I decide maybe I need to stop and see if the weird balance thing resolves itself. I'd sure hate to fall down a flight of stairs onto the concrete basement floor. I can picture it; I can almost feel it. My slippered toe catches the heel of the other foot and there's a confusing moment when I tumble in a succession of thuds before I wind up irreparably damaged on the floor. I wince, ashamed—why do I have to think up these maudlin scenarios? Is it not bad enough that terrible things actually happen?

When Brandon comes into the room, I'm perched on the armchair, not doing anything in particular. "You okay?" he asks.

"I sort of felt dizzy," I say. "I think it was that reading in the car thing."

Brandon frowns. "That was like ten days ago. I'm worried about you."

"Oh, it's nothing," I say.

He looks at me an instant longer and then gets Caleb a small cup of crackers. Well, this is new, I think. Nobody has ever had to suggest to me that something is wrong.

THE FIRST THING Andrew Weil asks me to do is rid my pantry of anything with artificial coloring or sweeteners, anything made with margarine, vegetable shortening, cottonseed oil, partially hydrogenated oil, or trans-fatty acids. I print out my list upstairs and drag the trash can in front of the pantry. "Hey, Bran," I say. "I'm supposed to get rid of some things." I rattle off some of the items as I grab a box of Girl Scout cookies.

"Whoa," he says. "Hey, hold off on that. I can work my way through some of that stuff."

I laugh.

"No. Seriously."

I put the shortbread cookies back on the shelf. This is not a Martha Beck/Michelle dynamic. If Brandon says I can't just toss our jointly owned food in the trash, I can't.

The next step is to get to know the plan. Each week, Weil creates menus for breakfast, lunch, dinner, and a snack (that, with the click of a button, can be organized into a printable grocery list), and I look those over and see that I'm in major health food land. If Dr. Weil were on *The Newlywed Game*, and his bride were asked one adjective to describe his philosophy, she's do well to answer: natural. His sweeteners of choice are brown sugar and honey; a typical breakfast involves yogurt and lots of berries. Wild Alaskan salmon came under some controversy around this time—could a shopper be guaranteed that it wasn't farmed salmon?—but it's one of Weil's favorite fishes, and I could find it at the grocery store (and taste the difference) in March 2006. Nothing sounds bland, though; in fact, tonight's dinner is miso-crusted salmon with a broccoli salad. I look over the ingredients on my list. Bulgur, two kinds of tofu. It clearly spells a trip to Whole Foods.

Two hours later, I'm lugging the groceries in. I've never in my life bought this many fresh fruits and vegetables.

Five hours after that, I'm feeling sad. Beer is not in My Optimum Health Plan. It hasn't even been a full day, and I find myself thinking, *I can't wait until this is over.* Which is not an auspicious beginning for an alleged lifestyle change. I engage Brandon in a card game while we both sip water.

. . .

THE NEXT DAY, I have a physical. I haven't had one since before I got pregnant with Caleb, and I'm curious to see what the damage is, if any.

Since we moved back to Charlottesville, I haven't been able to find a doctor I like, because most health professionals are under the ill-advised impression that they can scold me into healthier behavior. (Right at this very moment, for example, I am not rescheduling my dental appointment because I dread being trapped under a sharp object poised at my gums while the hygienist lectures me—again—about smoking.)

I haven't seen today's doctor before, but when I walk into the reception area and catch a faint whiff of urine and take a gander at the other patients, I brighten. This decidedly keeping-it-real office is where I belong. These doctors aren't seeing mostly upper-middle-class patients who do Pilates every day and routinely order salads with no dressing for dinner. They're getting the McDonald's patrons, the smokers, the people who in no way have time to exercise—my fitness kin.

My doctor is a slender woman, dark-haired and pretty. We shake hands and chitchat. She starts looking over the questionnaire that I filled out this morning. I have a small list of concerns. (Of course I do.)

"I, uh, I think it has to do with reading in the car for two hours, but I've been feeling like my vision or my balance is off," I say. "But it's probably the reading in the car."

The doctor nods. "That's a form of dizziness," she affirms. "I'm glad you told me."

"Also, I have this mole on my face," I say.

"How long have you had it?" she asks.

"Maybe a year?"

The doctor takes a tape measure out of the drawer. "It doesn't look suspicious," she says. "But I'm going to have you back in six weeks just to make sure it's not growing."

We talk about birth control, which leads us to The Pill, which leads us to smoking. (By the advanced age of thirty-three, combining The Pill and smoking increases a person's risk of blood clots.) "Do you happen to know an acupuncturist you'd recommend?" I ask. Dr. Weil has suggested that acupuncture helps some people quit smoking.

She cocks her head. "I don't know—but my colleague might." She's going to make some calls, warns me that it might be a while playing phone tag, but promises me the name of an acupuncturist in the future.

BEFORE I GO SEE HAILIE, I stuff an apple and a small bag of blanched almonds in my purse, my snack since I won't be home to cook lunch. I'm feeling a little tired this morning, but I'm looking forward to seeing her. I walk down the porch steps and try to ignore that it's extraordinarily windy today, even for March.

Twenty minutes into my drive, it starts. It's my first time on the interstate since Cara's accident, and the road—with the wind, the endless tractor-trailers, the daredevil drivers, the *speed*—seems like an extraordinarily dangerous place. A gust of wind kicks up and, boom, my vision gets screwy and my balance seems off. I don't know that I'm breathing right. I blast up the air-conditioning, crack my window, and lean forward in my seat. I want desperately to cry, but that would put me in even more danger.

This puts last year's panic attack to shame.

I slow to sixty and look for exit signs. Okay, there's one. But as I get closer and closer, I think, what will I do once I get off the interstate? I don't have a cell phone. I'll have to simply get back on the interstate, and I'm not sure that I want to have to merge with these whizzing trucks in this *goddamned tornado*. I keep going. I make a promise to myself that, on the way home, I can drive to Brandon's place of employment and make him drive me home. It's not exactly close, but it's at least on the same side of the mountain as Hailie.

The panic rises and ebbs the entire rest of the drive, but it doesn't ever disappear entirely. I pull into a parking space and smoke a cigarette with shaking hands. With the soles of my shoes touching the asphalt of the parking lot—off the mountain, off the highway, standing there with everything happening at the speed of normal pedestrian life—I can see that it's actually a pretty day.

I'm still a bit shaken, though, as I go inside. I know full well that I can't hide anything on my face, but I do my best to look as chipper as I can; I can't be a voiceover in this friendship. Hailie bustles about, chatting about how Cara's doing—she was opening her eyes, but she had another setback and fell back into a coma. I'm listening, but I'm also worrying about how I'm going to get back home without another freak-out. I'm still experiencing the aftershocks of realizing that my mental health is shot to hell. During a break in the conversation, it occurs to me that I should explain why I'm acting the way I am and why I'm not being the friend that I can be. I say lamely, "Man, it was windy on the mountain today."

Then I immediately change the topic.

Here's the thing: As freaked out as I am, and as real as the panic was—really, I should not have been behind the wheel—I cannot imagine saying to Hailie that I'm having troubles and my troubles are car-related. I don't necessarily believe in a hierarchy of pain—the children starving in India don't lessen, say, the postpartum depression of a rich American mother—but I also know that Hailie is exactly the last person to whom I can parcel out my anxiety.

The rest of the afternoon is painful. Hailie wants to talk about Cara, and I listen, but inwardly flinch. Every word she says about Cara's condition reinforces my panic.

Months ago, I half-questioned that I was a "moderately hopeless" pessimist, but I know in my bones today that I am. I'm focusing on the body's fragility; Hailie, meanwhile, is focusing on its resilience. Cara is a fighter, she says. Already, she's survived what would kill most anyone.

Not surprisingly, I panic most of the way home, starting right after I pass the exit to Brandon's workplace. A big truck gets right on my ass and suddenly switches over to the passing lane, making my Honda shudder in its wake. I smile broadly, hoping for a little seratonin. No dice. I repeat aloud the most comforting words I can think of. I'm three days into My Optimum Health and up to my eyeballs in fruits, vegetables, and soy products. "Cookies," I say aloud. "Cookies, cookies, cookies." A blast of wind hits my car at a place on the mountain where the road is the highest point, sheer drop-offs on both sides. "Mashed potatoes with butter," I murmur.

I make it home, let the dogs outside, sit down, and stare blankly at the unlit fireplace for five minutes until I have to pick up Caleb from the bus stop. For the first time in my life, I want desperately to crawl into bed and stay there until the world is safe. But I can't.

Later, while Caleb and I make dinner—black bean burritos—he, tired and cranky, yells at me that he wanted to crack the eggs and, *oh my God*, I already did it. I burst into tears. "I don't want to be yelled at!" I tell him. And then I can't stop crying. Caleb decides he'd rather watch TV than cook with me; I'm not a frequent crier and he's understandably a little disturbed by my outburst. I feel horrible about this, but tears are still streaming down my face when Brandon gets home.

I found the bridge between mind and body. Unfortunately, it's between the crazy, irrational part of my mind and the uncontrollable reflex aspects of my body. I'm sorry. This isn't the turn I wanted this story to take either.

THE UNFORTUNATE THING IS, I don't have the time to fix it. Or try to fix it or understand it or whatever it is people do when their bodies start reacting in decidedly unpleasant ways to events that they can't control. I got stuff to do: the spring fair stuff, the literary party stuff, the regular parenting and working stuff, the cooking stuff.

Under Dr. Weil's program, the cooking stuff cannot be under-estimated.

First, it came as a big shock to realize that what I was eating—even the items I thought were pretty healthy—weren't all so great. I didn't know from healthy, apparently, until I started Weil's program. Whereas before, I would have considered a grilled steak, a baked potato (with a bit of butter), and some steamed broccoli not so bad, now I see that healthy really means grilled chicken, some sweet potato cakes (mashed sweet potatoes seasoned with fresh ginger and pan-fried in a tiny amount of olive oil), and about three times the amount of steamed broccoli as I was eating before. I realize that I had been eating as if every day were a special occasion being celebrated in a time of produce shortage.

Weil's daily meal plan includes breakfast, lunch, dinner, and a snack. It's a lot of food, and although none of it is the sort that sticks to your ribs (for example, no red meat, lots of fruits and vegetables, precious little baked goods), it's plenty. I've never felt hungry at all. Still, the first week of the program, I was quite unhappy with the food. It's not that it tasted terrible; in fact, Weil's chicken salad made with yogurt and salsa is actually quite delicious. (For real!) It was more that I didn't like being constrained in my choices. I felt as if my food freedom was taken from me. (And if that happens, the terrorists win, right? They hate the American food freedom!)

Eventually, I habituated to the food freedom issue, but I couldn't get accustomed to the sheer amount of time I spent—and am still spend-ing—in the kitchen. I started eating breakfast sporadically back during the Jorge Cruise epoch, but now I was to prepare it every day; some-times the prep's minimal (throw together some berries, low-fat yogurt, and granola), but sometimes, as when I prepare a breakfast quesadilla, it's more work. I'd never properly prepared lunch at all, but now I spend a half hour in the kitchen arranging a salad or creating a "mayo" out of silken tofu, mustard, vinegar, etc. Dinner takes me, without fail, at least an hour to prepare. All this cooking generates dirty dishes, and some days I run the dishwasher twice.

Diet's probably the biggest lifestyle change Weil institutes, but it doesn't stop there. Each week on My Optimum Health, Weil issues a variety of assignments, ranging from walking a certain amount of time each week, to getting some info on a water-purification system for the house, to drinking some antioxidant-rich green tea.

Or taking Weil's special vitamins. You can order the vitamins through his website (and a "Vitamin Adviser" quiz will also direct you to what other vitamins and supplements to purchase),[2] but I decide to visit a store in town that sells Weil products. I'd passed it many times before, struck by the poster of Weil's head blown up to at least three times the size of a normal head.

I drive nervously to the store. My anxiety has certainly not improved, but I park and walk through the shopping center, the ongoing to-do list on a loop in my mind. After I buy the vitamins, I need to stop by the post office, and then I need to go home and make a list of what I need to buy for the party, and then I need to check in with the spring fair co-ordinator about some detail. This week, people, more people than normal, are counting on me not to mess up.

I enter the store and gaze around. Lots of lotions and other bottles of beautification products. I hear someone in the back office on the phone. "I have to go—I have a customer out front," she says. A woman with long brown hair appears, smiling enthusiastically at me. Uh-oh. This doesn't help with the cult-like image the store is dancing dangerously toward, what with The Leader's pictures everywhere. "How can I help you?" she asks.

---

[2] The profits go to the Weil Foundation, a nonprofit organization that Weil founded to support integrative medicine.

"Do you have vitamins here?" I ask.

They do. She leads me to a shelf behind the counter and picks up a bottle.

"That's the multivitamin?" I ask since she doesn't hand it over.

"Yep," she says. I just want to continue on with my errands, but she's holding my vitamins hostage until I suffer through a sales pitch. She holds them in one hand while gesturing with the other to another product on the shelf. "This one is *so* good for your skin," she tells me. "He thinks that inflammation is what damages the body, and this calms your skin down. Rosacea, acne—" she peers at my face—"well, you don't have any problems with acne, but this really cleared my skin up. We're all on it here!"

I look at her blankly. Why would she bring up my skin tone, I wonder in one beat, then realize in the very next beat, because she thinks something is obviously wrong with it. Oh, for Christ's sake.

I don't want a repeat of the whole discount card debacle, but here I am, going about my business, trying to handle driving my car, preparing for two big social events, just trudging the path to My Optimum Health, and out of nowhere, I get a little reminder that my skin is ruddier than average, a fact that hadn't registered on my list of five million things to do something about. I run through a quick ABCDE; this has nothing to do with me, I conclude.

She clearly has no idea that she's crossed a line. But I don't have it in me right now to be the bigger person, to give her a glow, to make her feel important.

"I just want the vitamins," I say.

She chatters on about some lotion that *also! reduces! redness!* dabs a little on my hand, and I resign myself to smelling like a Phish concert for the rest of the day. She presses on me a sample of the lotion, and I write a check. The vitamins cost over forty dollars for a month's supply.

. . .

DR. SELIGMAN WAS RIGHT: Our powers of habituation are astounding.

Less than a week after having the major panic attack, the anxiety balloons to now include all driving situations. One Sunday, I'm due to hit the grocery store for the week's worth of My Optimum Health fuel. I get dressed, put on my shoes, and stand there with the keys. I'm like those barnyard animals before a tornado, I think. Something feels off to me. I put my keys on the counter and kick off my shoes. I just can't drive today, I decide. We have enough healthy food for one more meal, and maybe I'll feel better tomorrow. But I cannot do it today. It's amazing how easily that fact goes down, how I barely blink before accepting the limitations on my life.

If only I could embrace My Optimum Health this fully, habituate entirely to the program.

On Friday, Brandon, Caleb, and I go to see a lawyer about setting up a will, something that David Bach and Suze Orman had been haunting me with for over a year. By the time we leave the meeting, all three of us are hungry, and this mother's cupboards are bare. We go to a restaurant where I order a grilled portobello sandwich—on a white kaiser roll (bad choice), smothered with Brie (another bad choice), and served with a side of buttery mashed potatoes (perhaps I'll take up the sport of sumo wrestling). Tonight, I'm a member of the clean-plate club. I also order two lagers and drink them down one after the other. By the time we leave, I'm stuffed and surprisingly buzzed. Before Dr. Weil, this meal would not have fazed me.

This is the end of week one. I don't beat myself up too badly for falling off the wagon—after all, in the scheme of things, this sandwich wasn't the worst thing I could order and, moreover, I'm still shocked at how, after just a week of My Optimum Health, my body reacted to overindulgence.

The next week, though, brings the party, to which about fifty people have RSVPed in the affirmative. Many of them are *Brain, Child* subscribers, whom I consider my people yet at the same time strangers. I spend one day cleaning the downstairs; although I still keep up with my FLYing to some degree, it's not the degree that, say, keeps the dust off the baseboards in the bathroom. I spend another day cleaning more and figuring out what to serve, and after consulting with Stephanie and Janet, both seasoned party planners, I decide on wine, beer, limeade, cheese, fruit, sliced baguettes, and pastries from a local bakery. I place the orders.

Like "in critical condition," "nervous exhaustion" is a phrase that I didn't used to understand all too well. And I'm still not certain that I actually do, but I know for sure that this week, I'm very nervous as well as very exhausted, to the point of having trouble keeping my eyes open, to the point of being unable to focus on my actual work. This is the week—with much of my self-help in full bloom, the decluttering, the getting the will in order, the anticipation of winning friends and influencing people, the healthy eating and daily exercise—that I reach the point that I simply don't have time to work. I get not a single lick of work done this week, and experience no "flow" whatsoever. I'm much too busy being the best me I can be.

"What can I do to help?" Brandon asks me, as I check my e-mail compulsively for any more RSVPs.

"I don't know, sweetie," I say. And I don't. I'm putting too much pressure on myself, I know. But I also know that if I were to go to a party thrown by the editor of a magazine I enjoy, and the editor was a little strange in person, I'd think differently of the magazine. I would enjoy it less. I would be less likely to renew. Intellectually, I know that the very future of *Brain, Child* does not hang in the balance here, but it feels that way.

At the bus stop, I'm telling Janet about my cluelessness regarding wine. "I could go to Market Street and get some for you," she offers, just like that.

"Oh, my God, I'd love that," I say. "Really?"

"Oh, no problem," she says.

I could kiss her. It's not just the wine, although being assured of serving decent booze is a comfort. It's the feeling that someone who doesn't have to have my back has my back anyway.

It all buoys me, and on the night of the party, in my mind, I feel slightly calmer. The house looks great. The food and drink are plentiful and delicious-seeming. Caleb has fashioned signs ("This is the house. Jennifer's party! Come on in.") and set up a table for people to make name tags for themselves, along with instructions ("Put your name right here. And put it on your shirt. ok? grate.") Stephanie arrives and opens wine while I slice limes for the limeade and Brandon and Caleb put the last of the food on the table.

But somehow, my body has decided that we're in survival mode and all bets are off. I have a beer and greet the incoming guests. I have another beer. I mingle, coming across as maybe a little socially awkward, but I don't, for example, offer my contact information on a ripped grocery list or note how *big* anybody is. The guests seem lovely. I have another beer. I refresh the food and drink, but see that Brandon and Caleb have already been keeping up with it. Soon, the writers begin the discussion of their books, and I stand near my kitchen sink, have another beer, and internally debate (1) whether I'd look drunk if I tried to sit on the counter and (2) if I really could get up there in these jeans. I sneak into the dining room for a hunk of cheese and a slice of baguette. I sneak back in to have a key lime mini-tart. And then again for a chocolate one. I sneak onto the porch for a cigarette. Four times. These most certainly are not things Dr. Weil is pictured doing on his website.

This fall off the wagon had a heavier thud to it, but I tell myself that hosting a large party is a one-shot event for me, and it's no wonder that I took in extra, empty calories with the beer and the baked goods.

But by the weekend, nearing the end of week two in my eight-week program, I have to face the truth: I need to build in some allowances for myself if I'm to continue this program. Call it lack of willpower, or call it My Optimum Justification Abilities, but I cannot follow Dr. Andrew Weil to the letter much longer. The time spent cooking is a big factor; the weekends are also problematic. Eating out and going to bars with Brandon are two things that reliably make me happy, and I just cannot justify giving that up for the promise of being able to handle whatever health crisis comes my way.

That Saturday morning, I decide I need to be the liver again. I need to take what I can from Dr. Weil and leave the rest. It's scary, in a way, because my faith in my own judgment has been shaken; I only need to remind myself of the sort of meals I was preparing pre-Weil to know that my perception of doing the healthy thing and actually doing the healthy thing are not the same.

But I think back to my dealing in the finances period of my self-improvement, and realize this is the same deal. Just as there are only two ways to have more money—spend less or earn more—there are only two ways to lose weight—take in less calories or burn more of them. I hang on to this as I filter through My Optimum Health. I'm eating out on Friday and Saturday nights, but I'll choose the relatively healthier dish. (For example, I order the sweet-potato gnocchi with marinara sauce instead of the Parmesan gnocchi with blue cheese cream sauce one night.) I'm going to feel free to have beers, although I'll cut back. Black tea with milk and sugar need not be replaced with green tea with honey and soy milk. I'm going to follow Weil's walking instructions to the letter. The other advice—taking a "fast" on news (i.e., not reading the paper or watching the news on TV), drinking only filtered water, putting an air filter in the bedroom—I'll consider on a case by case basis.

THE EXERCISE COMPONENT of My Optimum Health doesn't seem that dramatic in the first weeks: Walk ten minutes a day, walk fifteen minutes a day. It starts feeling like you're taking care of business, though, when you get up to twenty minutes.

My sister Krissy calls, and I tell her that I'm walking every weekday morning after the bus picks up Caleb. "Do you feel better?" she asks.

"Yeah!" I say. "I think I do." With the party and the fair (which went off just fine, although I'm not sure that I actually pulled my weight) behind me, the walking seems to me to be a manageable, good thing.

"Do you take the dogs with you?" she asks.

"Oh, no," I say. "No. I'm not as scared of other people's dogs as I used to be, but dogs attract dogs, and I don't want a strange dog coming up to me."

We chat some more, and she tells me she's coming up to visit Mom in a week or so. "You should drive up," she says.

"I've been having these issues. I sort of have been freaking out while I drive," I confess. I pause. "Don't I sound like a delicate little flower! 'I'm scared to take the dogs. I'm scared to drive.' "

We both laugh at the idea of me as this fragile thing.

But the truth is, I am afraid to take the dogs with me. I am afraid to drive. Crap. I am a delicate little flower.

I LOOK AT one of my objective measures of my health, and I can report that, four weeks in, I've lost about seven pounds, even with the modifications I've made to My Optimum Health. More subjectively, I can also report that my body just *feels* healthier; some of the creases on my torso have disappeared, and although I don't look noticeably slimmer, I have to keep hiking up certain pairs of jeans. There's something uplifting about both the exercise itself—even though the walk causes sweating, good iPod-delivered music on a crisp spring morning is definitely a pleasure—and about watching my BMI slowly shimmy down into a more cardiovascular-healthy category.

And yet I'm troubled by two things. One is that I was unable to stick to My Optimum Health, word for word, for longer than ten days. (And the only reason I lasted ten days was not so much my commitment to Dr. Weil or my health but my commitment to these experiments.) The second and more troubling issue, though, is that I continue to have the anxiety.

Although I learn to like the daily walks and found more to admire in Weil's food, I don't at all feel like I'm, as Weil puts it, experiencing a sense of strength and joy. I wake up one morning with a weird spasm in my lower lip and a general feeling of nervousness. It lingers past the morning activities—the lunch-packing, the breakfast-giving, the shower-taking—and when I start off on my walk, I remember what I called the twisted-glove feeling. What I wouldn't give for a little twisted glove now, I think. Even last year's sleepwalking and constant sense of how much I suck would be preferable to this anxiety.

I wonder where I should look to fix this new problem.

And then, as I start up the hill, my big toe of duh stubs against a gigantic log of irony: Um, what the hell have I been doing for the last year and three-quarters? *Trying to make myself better.* I've been consumed with the improvement of myself, and yet here I am facing a condition that finally isn't just vague dissatisfaction, not feeling right in my own skin, lingering crankiness. I'm doing all this self-help and for the first time in my life, I'm faced with a condition outlined in the *DSM-IV*: anxiety.

I round the corner and realize that this can say nothing good about my experience with self-help. On one hand, I can't blame the experts for my anxiety. Regular life has gone on: Cleo suffered and died, Luna joined our family, Caleb has had to find his way socially and otherwise, Brandon escaped the ax of downsizing twice, Hailie lost the Cara she knew, the earth kept rotating. All these events had an effect on me, for better or worse, and it'd be ridiculous to suggest that there's anything my experts could have done to prevent the effects.

But then again, after all my immersion in advice, I'd have hoped that these exercises in self-improvement would have buffered me somehow against these events. Maybe they have, I think as I smile and nod at the retired couple I pass each morning. There are no control groups here. Maybe I would have wound up with worse than anxiety if I hadn't been taking all this advice. But I doubt it. I doubt the experiments had any positive effect on my mental health at all. My retirement account, yes. My social interactions, when I want it, yes. But not my happiness, despite their promises.

The truth is, I'm tired of thinking about myself. I'm tired of so many first-person pronouns in my head. What are *my* thoughts about *me*? I don't want to think about my mind, my body, my anxiety, the way I do anything at all. As I reach the end of the block, it occurs to me what role all these experts have played in my anxiety. While individually harmless and occasionally helpful, the experts and their constant pushing for self-examination foster a super-heightened awareness of self. And a heightened awareness of self makes for a heightened sense of burden. It's the flip side of empowerment; I know all too well all that I'm responsible for, what I can—and have to—control in order for life to happen. Which is not good for the average non-megalomaniac person. Which is terrible for this average non-megalomaniac person, anyway.

I'm at the overpass, the part of the walk I hate. The sidewalk bears the broken shards of someone's beer bottles and dried patches of gritty dirt, washed in from the latest spring storm. Stained concrete rises up on each side of the road to a small dark space at the top where the concrete doesn't quite meet the overpass. The sounds of cars speeding on the road overhead echo noisily, no matter how high I turn up the iPod. It smells of the exhaust from the traffic. I've taught myself not to look at the dark spaces at the top because if I do, I'll think of all the things I'm afraid of: zooming cars, unattended strange dogs, rodents of almost all manner, people whose minds are broken in such a way they would do me harm, people whose minds are broken in such a way they'd voluntarily go up into the small dark spaces. I walk more quickly, as if I can—if I just hightail it enough—escape the fearful person I've become.

THIS IS NOT to say that the experimentation is over. I'm liking Dr. Weil's program well enough, and I don't see any reason why he or I should suffer for the sins of the self-help genre at large. Besides, it's all well and good to have an epiphany, but, to my disappointment, I find that it doesn't cure anxiety.

"Mama!" Caleb pulls his folder out of his backpack when we get back from the bus stop. "You won't believe this!"

"What, babe?" I ask him.

He rustles through the papers until he finds the one he's looking for. "We're going on a field trip," he says, "*and you can drive me there!*" Caleb hands me the paper and looks at me expectantly. I read it over; the field trip is to Richmond, an hour away on the interstate.

I lied when I said that it's easy to habituate to anxiety. It's only mostly easy, as when you're faced with chores or some other dull task that you'd rather put off in favor of reading. It's very, very hard when you're faced with the chipped-baby-teeth smile of a seven-and-a-half-year-old boy who has ketchup in the corners of his mouth and, in his heart, the sort of innocent expectation that you forgot existed until you became his mother. He truly can't imagine that I could fail to be as excited as he is.

"We'll see," I say, but I know that the door has swung shut on the field trip. I just can't.

"THIS IS INSANE," I say to Brandon. "On one hand, I think I should just be able to buck up and go. On the other hand, I'm scared that I'll be driving with Caleb and a few of his friends in the back and I'll have a freak-out." What I don't say is that it's not just the freak-out itself that I'm afraid of in this scenario; it's that I'll cause a scene, embarrassing myself in front of the teachers and other parents, and possibly embarrassing Caleb in front of his classmates. Because even *I*'m thinking it: Just *drive*, for God's sakes. Quitcher bellyaching.

"I wish I could go," Brandon says. "But I'm already taking days off for Caleb's spring break."

After my fuss regarding the snow days I had to take, Brandon has decided he'll take off half of whatever holiday Caleb has. But I'd be lying if I said that part of me didn't wish that Brandon would just say to hell with work—Caleb wants a parent to drive him to Richmond and since I can't (won't?) do it, he will.

We're on the back porch, and I take a long drag on my cigarette. The doctor hasn't yet called me back with the name of an acupuncturist to help me stop smoking. It's just as well. I don't think I can handle one more project at this point, particularly a project that will strain my already raw nerves.

"What am I so afraid of?" I ask quietly. I'm not trying to be melodramatic, but I'm keeping my voice down so the neighbors won't hear me. I don't want this anxiety to become part of me, my image: the actual crazy woman in the attic.

"Oh, doll," Brandon says and touches me on the small of my back.

That was a good answer. There are two other answers, though.

One is that some subsconscious part of me has realized that my life is actually pretty good and that I'm afraid of losing any small part of it. This subconscious wants to bubble wrap everyone and keep us safe. Or freeze time so that we never get old, never divorce, never grow apart, never have larger worries, never die, never have the slightest chance of being in an accident. I want things the way they are, or the way they were before I became anxious. This, of course, is a stupid way to think, the personal philosophy equivalent of covering your couch with plastic. Life changes.

The other answer to what I'm afraid of, I'm sorry to tell you, is this: the Honda. This thought pops into my head as I idle at a stoplight and listen to the engine sound a little choky when I press the gas. In the next few days, I nurture my blame of the Honda until I'm fully convinced that it can be fingered as the source of all my troubles. By Thursday, I've talked myself out of getting a gas hybrid, which is what I've been saying for years that I wanted after the Honda goes. No more. I want a Volvo station wagon, one of the the safest cars in the world,[3] its gas mileage be damned.

Friday, I screw up my courage and test-drive five used Volvos, with Brandon in the passenger seat as a safety device to be deployed in the event of a panic attack.

Saturday, the three of us drive up to the dealership in the rain and buy a V-70 model.

I assuage my considerable guilt—at giving in to these crazy thoughts, at having the sort of money that allows me to just *buy* a used Volvo, at owning more cars than we have drivers—by giving the Honda away to a good cause. I feel a twinge as I watch it go. Intellectually, I know it was a good car. But somebody had to take the fall.

IN MY NON-DRIVING HOURS, which is most of them, I'm trying on a new identity, although I can't help but try to mitigate it. There is something distinctly unpalatable to me about appearing to be a health nut. So I'm Fast-Walking Woman, but on my headphones, I'm listening to Modest Mouse's "Tiny Cities Made of Ashes." I'm The Tofu Chef, but on the weekends, I still get enough of a buzz on to have to walk home. I know these immature actions are perhaps unbecoming to a woman my age, but I'm taking baby steps out of my irresponsible behavior regarding health.

[3] According to the manufacturer.

Funnily enough, though, in my car, I am Safety Lady. Keep it orderly, drivers. No sudden moves or my mental health gets it. "Curtain airbags," I murmur to myself. "This is the safest car in the world." These are some sweet, sweet words as I drive the Volvo around town, on the twisty road that leads me to the grocery store, on the crowded streets in downtown rush hour, on the main drag where reckless young men weave in and out of their lanes. I actually think of them as "reckless young men."

My own young man, meanwhile, goes on his field trip to Richmond. He comes home excited and chattering about all the wildlife at the park. "Guess what I saw?" He begs me to guess. As it turns out, many things, wildlife of all manner.

"Did you get to ride on the fancy bus?" I ask.

"Yeah," he says.

"Did you sit next to Patrick?"

Caleb's face falls. "No," he says. His best friend rode with two other boys in the backseat of a car driven by a braver mother. Caleb was on the bus, not chosen for the car ride.

This image eviscerates me.

I need to get over this problem.

That night, I turn to a book called *The Happiness Hypothesis: Finding Modern Truth in Ancient Wisdom*, by Jonathan Haidt. It's not a self-help book; it's a book that appeals to my signature strength of love of learning. In it, Haidt—one of Seligman's positive-psychology homeboys—takes a look at the wisdom of the ages, East and West, and sees how it squares with the findings of positive psychology.

I settle in with the book and I like what I see. Haidt starts the book with one truth that Research has substantiated: The self is divided. It's split up in many ways (mind/body, left/right, etc.), and here Haidt introduces a metaphor that he'll have cause to revisit throughout the book. It's about why we humans make bad choices, irrational choices, even though in our rational minds we know better.

The image that I came up with for myself, as I marveled at my weakness, was that I was a rider on the back of an elephant. I'm holding the reins in my hand, and by pulling one way or the other, I can tell the elephant to turn, to stop, or to go. I can direct things, but only when the elephant doesn't have desires of his own. When the elephant really wants to do something, I'm no match for him.

Whew! Jonathan Haidt, where have you been all My Optimum Health? Haidt goes further to explain that the rider is "conscious, controlled thought" while the elephant is "everything else . . . [including] gut feelings, visceral reactions, emotions, and intuitions that comprise much of the automatic system."

I chew on this a little while and find that it rather handily provides an answer to the troubling question of why I couldn't stick with Dr. Weil word for word for more than ten days. My elephant, I think, can only handle being denied black tea with milk and sugar, or beer, or eating out, for so long before it protests. If there's one thing my elephant doesn't like, it's being denied its creature comforts.

For the more troubling question of my anxiety, Haidt waits for chapter two, in which he addresses changing one's mind. The problem with changing one's mind, the way we normally think of it, is that we focus on changing the rider's mind while the elephant remains set in his ways. "The elephant reacts before the rider even sees the snake in the path," Haidt writes. "Although you can tell yourself that you are not afraid of snakes, if your elephant fears them and rears up, you'll still be thrown."

Snakes, driving, what have you.

Haidt is the sort of writer who gives the impression that he's laying out all your options on the table here, which is comforting.[4] He

---

[4] If not always exactly true—like Seligman, he brings up old John Bowlby and his attachment theory without even acknowledging that the research has not kept up with the realities of modern families.

claims that to calm your elephant, your subconscious, the part of you that you can't just *decide* to calm, you have three simple options: meditation, cognitive therapy, and Prozac (or a drug that works similarly).

I HAVE A DECISION to make here. Haidt calls it calming the elephant, but I see that his three options—meditation, cognitive therapy, or Prozac—can also be seen as better bridges between the mind and body. I need to build a better bridge, but there are some factors I have to consider.

- Brandon has a job with health insurance now, but the way the downsizing—or, as they're calling it lately, "separations" (nice euphemism, with its *sorry, hon, it just didn't work out* vibe)— is going, we may be doing some insurance shopping in the future.
- I've lost about nine pounds now, which is dandy and good for the heart, but I'm still what one might consider a chunky girl.
- I know three women who were deemed virtually uninsurable— either denied coverage or were quoted an astronomical sum— because they were overweight and being treated for depression with an SSRI.

In a more just world, I could consider my options based entirely on what's best for my mental health. I could consult a doctor to help me make the decision. But since we Americans rely on corporations to provide health care to the country's citizens (and a visit to a doctor would go down in my records), I don't actually have three options— not if I want affordable medical care for my yearly Pap smears, occasional need for antibiotics, and (God forbid) the catastrophic accident. I can't have an ongoing mental illness on my record and weigh what I do. I have one option: meditation. It might have been the first one I tried anyway, but if it doesn't work, I'm screwed. Given my self-help track record, this scares me.

I'M NOT MESSING AROUND HERE. There are roughly a hundred billion jillion gazillion books, DVDs, tapes, and classes on meditation and its more athletic sister, yoga, and I'm pretty sure that I read a little something about all of them as I scour the Internet. I need the cream of the crop here. I need some meditation manual that makes sense to me. Too many times in my research, I run across sentences that spiral upward into abstractions—*consciousness, chakra, energy, transcendental*—that mean exactly nothing to me.

Finally I settle on the one-two approach: A DVD put out by *Yoga Journal* aimed at relieving stress and the best-selling book *Wherever You Go There You Are: Mindfulness Meditation in Everyday Life*, by Jon Kabat-Zinn, which was recently reprinted. *Yoga Journal*, I reason, is a fairly mainstream magazine, which means that they'll likely use a regular vocabulary that I understand. Kabat-Zinn's book has been lauded for its down-to-earth quality.

I order them online, and the *Yoga Journal Yoga Step By Step* DVD arrives first.

In two days, I'm slated to drive over the mountain again to visit Hailie, and I can feel the anxiety building up. I've been checking the weather compulsively, wanting reassurance that no storm or sudden windiness is making its debut in the forecast. One April afternoon before Caleb gets home, I pull the coffee table to the side of the room, spread out my yoga mat, and pop in the DVD.

My instructor is Baxter Bell, M.D., a slim man with a pleasant, frank manner. His voice is soothing. I ignore the man-ponytail because if I start to fixate on it, I'll be reminded of all the groovy folk here in Charlottesville with their *consciousness-transcendentalism-chakra-energy* talk and hemp-fiber clothing and love of bluegrass music, and realize that this—and by extension, Bell—is not my crowd. Instead, I focus on Bell's doctor's license. Later, I'll listen to an interview with him in which he describes how he gave up his traditional medical practice and reinvented it, incorporating some Eastern healing methods, including something called "tongue evaluation." He'll admit that the stresses of life aren't going to go away, and the best he can do is change his reaction to said stresses. Again, it strikes me how much of self-improvement has to do with making do within the parameters of our culture.

I start with the second session on the DVD, "Yoga for Stress Relief," figuring that it's a little late for "Yoga for Stress Prevention." Bell introduces viewers to his two assistants: Allison, who does the more advanced moves, and Betty, who does the poses for the less limber. I watch Betty.

Nobody's home but the dogs and me. It's too cold for the AC but not cold enough for the heat, and the house's vents and machinery are quiet. Bell starts off with some simple breathing and stretching and works his way up to more advanced poses, talking calmly all the way. I have to say, it's soothing.

He suggests that I hold certain poses for several minutes, so I reach for the remote and pause the DVD. I breathe. I'm supposed to be noticing, all along, what muscles are tense, how I'm carrying my stress, what feels good. I stay in the Child's Pose—forehead to the floor, butt resting on my heels—and breathe. In. Out. In. Out. In.

"ARGH ARGH ARGH ARGH ARGH ARGH!"

I immediately stiffen as the dogs bound across the yoga mat, jump to the back of the couch, and bark out the window at the neighbor's loose dog across the street. Luna catches my pinkie toe with her nail, and a sharp pain puts me into the fight-or-flight mode the DVD is supposed to be easing. "Simon," I hiss, my forehead still on the floor. "Luna." They continue barking. "Stop. It," I say. "Right. Now." They don't listen to me. Eventually, the neighbor's dog wanders out of sight and they quiet.

I keep the DVD paused a few minutes longer and resume the practice. You end in the Queen's Pose, the most relaxing pose they have.

There. I finish. While it was certainly nice, I'm not sure how this is going to help me on the road. I'll be unable to close my eyes. I certainly won't be able to touch my head down on the dashboard or twist the stress out of my spine. I hit menu on the remote and choose the guided meditation.

During meditation, you close your eyes. I see Betty sitting in a chair and I get comfortable on the love seat. Bell starts talking. I am just going to focus on my breath, he says. That's it.

I breathe, making sure to get all of my breath out of my lungs. I'm breathing. I'm breathing. I'm focusing on the expansion of my rib cage. I'm focusing on the . . . I wonder what time it is. I wonder what time I'm going to have to leave to get to Hailie's. Will I have time for my walk?

Man. This is crazy hard.

Baxter Bell tells me, "Instead of getting caught up in the content of the thoughts that arise, allow yourself to release them as soon as you feel or sense that they're coming up. . . . See if you could just let it drift away like the child letting go of the string of a helium-filled balloon."

I love this image. There is a hand and it's releasing a string and the string flies up into the air. The thought is gone for now. In my mind, it's a short film, the hand and string in faded color, a little grainy. I like this. This film of the hand is my version of the portrait of Dorian Gray: my anxiety magically displaced into art.

I'M SLIDING a little on My Optimum Health here in week six. My in-laws are in town, and Brandon's mom invites us over for brunch. We chat about real estate and why she tends to paint her walls green while I tend to paint mine yellow and other nonsense. She makes me a cup of tea.

Then she serves me a three-egg omelette cooked in margarine with lots of cheese and ham. It's garnished with more cheese, chopped tomatoes, and scallions. On the side is some bacon. It looks delicious.

What am I supposed to do? On the one hand, she knows that I'm following a health plan because she and Brandon's father came to dinner a night I made fusilli with roasted red pepper and smoked salmon sauce with a salad, and served a crustless berry tart for dessert. On the other hand, what kind of prima donna insists that other people serve a specific kind of food in their own homes? Not this kind of prima donna, that's for sure.

Last week, I turned down Liz when she suggested we grab some bagels for dinner and hang out with the families. "I'll make a tofu and veggie stir-fry?" I suggested. But to have this sort of diet restriction is to be a pain in the ass. We wound up not eating together because breaking this particular sort of bread was simply not part of My Optimum Health and she felt uncomfortable making me cook for eight people. I decided at that time that social ties bring me more happiness than healthy food, and I wouldn't make the same mistake in the future.

"This looks great," I say. I dig in, but I decline the coffee cake.

IT'S A SMALL WORLD. The evening before I have to drive over the mountain, I receive Jon Kabat-Zinn's *Wherever You Go There You Are* in the mail, and flip to the back flap. What do you know? Kabat-Zinn, in addition to founding the Stress Reduction Clinic and the Center for Mindfulness in Medicine, Health Care, and Society at UMass's medical school, has worked with one Dr. Andrew Weil to make a CD program called *Meditation for Optimum Health*.

I start reading while Caleb's in the shower and Brandon's putting away his laundry, and I can see at once why people like this book. Kabat-Zinn's big contribution to meditation's reputation is to make it seem like a normal thing. You don't have to fast or wear specific clothing or give up your TV or listen to bluegrass music to use it. It's a way of remaining "mindful," he says, the meditation crowd's term for living in the moment.

Kabat-Zinn breaks the book up into very small chapters, each less than four pages. "Each chapter is a glimpse through one face of the multifaceted diamond of mindfulness," he writes. Thoreau is quoted liberally throughout.

But although Kabat-Zinn is fairly down to earth, I still encounter passages like:

> We can apprentice ourselves to this work, knowing full well that non-doing is truly the work of a lifetime; and conscious all the while that the doing mode is usually so strong in us that the cultivating of non-doing takes considerable effort.

Huh? As I sigh, Brandon comes down the stairs. "What's up?" he asks.

"I think I really need a book called *Meditation for Smart-Asses*," I say.

THE SELF IS DIVIDED. Part of me—the scoffing part, the one that finds fault with "consciousness" being used metaphorically—does actually need the book titled *Meditation for Smart-Asses*. However, the anxious part of me, the elephant, is really grooving on parts of *Wherever You Go There You Are*.

The morning I'm supposed to drive over the mountain, Caleb's grade is having their Spring Sing. After I take him to the bus stop, I come home, feed Simon and Luna, and hurriedly eat a bowl of cereal with blueberries and soy milk. I don't have time to go on my walk this morning. I don't have time to meditate or do yoga. I throw *Wherever You Go There You Are* in my bag and head up to Caleb's school.

As usual, I'm early, so I take a seat in the front row and shrug off my coat. The kindergarten and second-grade classes are filing in, and I wave at Caleb's teacher. I pull the book from my purse and open it against my coat, balled up on my lap, so nobody sees the title. I read Kabat-Zinn's "This Is It" chapter, where he describes the meditation philosophy of just accepting things as they are at this moment. I look up. At this moment, the auditorium is loud with kids' chatter, and I'm about to see my child sing songs that he's been practicing all season. He takes it seriously; as we were falling asleep last night, he worried whether the girls were enunciating *beets* and *beans* well enough and remarked, "We really should practice some more." This, according to Kabat-Zinn, is unlike meditation, where one should have no expectations of achieving results. Just doing it is the result. At the end of the chapter, Kabat-Zinn urges me to ponder something: "Is it possible for you to contemplate that in a very real way, *this* may actually be the best season, the best moment of your life?"

It certainly is possible for me to contemplate this. But it's difficult because as soon as these moments of sitting in the auditorium are over, I'll have to get on the interstate.

Soon the first-graders file down the aisles and make their way to the risers on stage. I concentrate on enjoying the moment, putting off for a little longer my worries about driving. The children open with a song in which they claim that they are all flowers and would enjoy the sun's warmth. Caleb is in the first row under the warmth of the stage lights. The message of the song is that they're all unique and beautiful. At last year's concert, I teared up watching these children sing so earnestly about how special they were, and I don't do any better this year as I look at each one now: Liz's daughter singing as if this is a difficult test, the tall boy with his hair in cornrows looking like he doesn't know what to do with his hands, the wild child of the class who's belting it out at full volume, the pretty little girl with Down syndrome who keeps looking at the other kids for cues. Caleb, meanwhile, has his poker face on.

They end with "It's a Small World After All." Next week, Caleb will point out his objections to the lyrics—the world actually is gigantic—but today we all applaud, and I try very hard to just focus on Caleb's small smile and the feeling in my hands as I clap them together. On my way out, I make the sign-language I-love-you sign to him, and he gives me a barely perceptible nod.

The moment has arrived.

So, between my meditation DVD and Jon Kabat-Zinn, I think I may have built a better mind-body bridge. Now, as I pull the Volvo out of the parking lot and ease it across town to the interstate ramp, I will see if the bridge holds.

Ten minutes in, I'm a little nervous, but I'm doing okay. Although the speed limit is sixty-five, I keep it around sixty. My window is preemptively cracked in case of troubles breathing. I inhale through my nose and whoosh the air out through my mouth. It's a little trick I learned from Dr. Weil.

A maroon pickup truck is coming up fast on my left. I pay attention to my body and can start to feel it going into the panic spin. What if the truck nips my tail end and sends me spinning off the road? Hand! Release the balloon! It does.

I'm not even quite to the next town over and by the time I reach the bottom of the mountain, I've envisioned the hand far too many times. I'm afraid of it losing its power, of my habituating to the helpful vision of the balloon/thought's release. I sing along with the music a little. I press the pedal to the floor and drive up the incline.

As soon as my ears start to feel the pressure of the higher elevation, I feel my anxiety ratcheting up exponentially. "What if this is the best moment of my life?" I say aloud, simultaneously thinking (a) am I kidding? and (b) all things considered, I am lucky and it could be a good period in my life. The panic abates a little, but I know it'll be back and will grow into a full-on attack if I can't figure out a way to help myself here even more.

And then it occurs to me: This is the same route I took when I was eighteen visiting a friend who was at another college. It was spring, and the first long trip I had ever taken by myself, on a busy interstate no less. Then—fifteen years ago—I looked at the mountain that I was driving up, amazed at how small my car and I were on it. Back then it exhilarated me. Look at me! I wanted to shout. Look how adventurous I am! I was going to visit Beth, one of my oldest friends. We were going to a keg party at someone's house. The weekend promised flirting, drinking, good conversation, and getting away from the mess of my college friends. It was warm and I had the windows open and "Near Wild Heaven" was playing on my boom box in the backseat.

Today, I play a little game of make-believe. I'm going to a keg party with Beth, not to see a friend who, as the result of a terrible accident, has a much different life than the one she made for herself. I'm adventurous, not anxious. I am the person I was at eighteen, not this fearful thirty-three-year-old who took her mental health for granted, who took self-help too seriously, who (embarrassingly enough) is using herself as an inspiration to herself. This is the same body, I tell myself. This is the same mind as then. For this trip at least, I believe it.

I open the window a little wider and, using a combination of make-believe, the hand, and the concept that *this is it*, I make it there and back, listening with genuine care to Hailie, only a little scared and more than a little proud.

I'D LIKE TO REPORT that the driving anxiety is gone, that the bridge held and I'm better than new. It's a bummer, but I'm not. There is no magic here. I'm working hard on calming the elephant. Maybe by the time you read this, I'll be driving like a normal person.

Please note that this is optimism.

The Soul

CALEB'S FRIEND SOPHIE, for the time being, is done pretending she's a superhero. She's taken off her cape and put down her plastic star. As Brandon and I scuttle around the kitchen, one of us paying the babysitter who had been minding the dynamic duo, the other rooting around in the fridge for dinner, Sophie wants to talk God.

"Do you believe in God?" she asks me. If you know Sophie, then you know that this isn't delivered so much in a plaintive, little-girl voice as in that of a graduate student with a point to make.

"Um," I say. "Well, it's a complicated question, Sophie." I open the vegetable bin and pull out some iffy-looking broccoli. "A lot of people believe different things about God. Some people think he's like a guy in heaven. Other people believe God is in everything—"

Sophie doesn't want that sort of answer. "*I* believe in God."

"Okay," I say cheerfully.

"My *mom* believes in God."

"Uh-huh," I say cheerfully.

"My *dad* believes in God."

I pull the salmon out of the fridge.

"*Bobo* believes in God," Sophie says. Bobo is her cat.

"Bobo believes in God?" Caleb asks.

"*Yes*," Sophie says, exasperated.

Our little clan throws up its collective hands when this sort of religious talk comes up. On one hand, we live in a country founded on the principle of religious freedom and in a neighborhood where even short-haired tabbies can be said to have religious convictions. We know that religion is very important to certain people and we're not curmudgeonly enough to inject big doses of doubt into a little girl's faith.

But on the other hand, it's a gray area for us, and we can't pretend to share Sophie's religion. We're not even church-on-Christmas-and-Easter folk. Even at the height of my anxiety, it never once occurred to me to pray for help.

OF COURSE, the traditional way to offload burdens, like anxiety, is through religion. Let go and let God, as the bumper sticker says. Which sounds great. But.

I call Stephanie and, as we often do, we wander to the subject of Did You Read . . .? and Did You Hear About . . .? We're like the Bush administration, our own internal newsfeed.

"Did you hear about Naomi Wolf?" she asks.

"No," I say. "Does she have a new book?"

"In some interview, she said that she had a vision of Christ," Stephanie says.

"Isn't she Jewish?" I ask. "And meaning what? Like she actually saw him? Or did he *talk* to her? What did he say?"

"I guess she saw him," Steph says. "Actually, I don't know—I can't remember. But she says that she was overcome with this feeling of calm and peace."

I sit there on the phone for a minute, trying to envision what it would be like to just be hanging around your house, turn the corner, and . . . there's Jesus! Ack! As I'm thinking this, I say slowly, "I hope that never happens to me."

Stephanie laughs.

"Oh, God," I say. "I knew that sounded stupid even as I was saying it."

Stupid—because this sort of peace and calm is *exactly* what I'm after—but true. Sure, I play cute with Oprah on the TV and the dogs talking to me, but I know it's not real. I'm already feeling a little shaky vis-à-vis my mental health, and a *vision* that didn't spring from my imagination would not make me feel better. Besides, what would I do with that sort of experience in my life? It has to be life-altering, right? I would have to get really *into* Jesus and somehow explain this new son of God in my life to all my loved ones. And then Brandon would have to figure out how to be married to a born-again wife and we'd have fights about whether I could put a Jesus fish on the car and Caleb would rustle out of bed early on Sundays to go to church and I'd have to reconcile for myself all these things like Christ Dying for My Sins.

Still, Research shows that religious people are happier. I remind myself that, clearly, not all religious paths involve a vision. Or even Judeo-Christian thought, for that matter. Why, I'm even meditating—true, it's in a pretty secular way. But the helpful doctor Baxter Bell throws out clearly Eastern spiritual phrases like "Brahmarandra." Jon Kabat-Zinn has latched onto a pretty Buddhist idea. The whole world of spirituality is open to me. Kind of.

I'M SUPERSTITIOUS. Not so much that it actually stops me in my tracks, but just enough that I pause. For example, I could barely finish writing the section above, because I kept thinking, Oh, no—I'm totally going to have a vision of Jesus Christ now that I revealed that the thought of it scares me. And now. I just wrote that sentence and I'm thinking, Oh, no, I just made fun of having a vision of Jesus Christ, and now I'll go straight to Hell if it exists. So, preemptively, just in case, and semi-sincerely: Please forgive me.

Although I was baptized Catholic (thanks to my persistent paternal grandparents), I was raised Presbyterian. I suppose you could call me a cultural Presbyterian, like there are lapsed Catholics and cultural Jews. For a long time I wished I were a lapsed Catholic or a cultural Jew. As a lapsed Catholic, you get out of all the hard work of being Catholic (the rosary, the no-contraception rule), but you still have the cool rituals, the knowledge that you can be absolved of your sins with a simple visit to a booth, and kooky relatives who in all seriousness believe that they feel the presence of angels/the Virgin Mary. As a cultural Jew, you get out of all the hard work of being Jewish (the fasting, the Friday night observances), but you have the delicious food, the lefty politics, and the right to use the funny Jewish mother voice like my friend Liz does.

Being a cultural Presbyterian, though, is virtually indistinguishable from being, say, a midwesterner. There are no escape hatches from your sins, just barreling ahead striving striving striving to be the most decent human being you can be. You have no big city affiliation, and you tend to enjoy pot roast and badminton. None of your Presbyterian relatives have ever participated in things like full-body baptisms (Baptists), speaking in tongues (Pentecostals), or going church-sanctioned wild for a period of time (old-order Mennonites). Your memories of church are nothing over the top, just mildly grating: The music always seemed to be dominated by some trilling show-off and her tone-deaf husband, although they were nice enough. Disapproval was tamped down with pressed-together lips and reminders that WE ARE ALL PART OF THE LORD'S FLOCK.

There's nothing really wrong with Presbyterianism, if you're fine with Christianity and down with Protestantism. In the Presbyterian churches with which I'm familiar, everyone seems reasonable enough. (We don't need wine and special wafers—croutons and grape juice will do just fine!) With these sort of moderate religions, though, you only have two routes of rebellion: You can become more hard-core[1] or you can leave quietly.

I went to Sunday school and vacation Bible school and, when we moved to Virginia, even became a member of the church sometime in middle school, a harrowing experience in which I answered every single question the confirmation-class leader asked the group because he had eyes that peered in two different directions and I could never tell if he was directing the questions at me or someone across the circle. But I left quietly sometime shortly after that for reasons that had 75 percent to do with the congregation, 25 percent to do with God, and, in any case, are less than 5 percent interesting.

I don't really think about religion too much now, and when I do, it's often all mushed together with politics. I know enough devout people now to know that religion can be a source of great strength and guidance, in terms of both a personal relationship with God and a personal relationship with members of their congregations. And I respect that, but in the way I respect someone's right to go hunting. I can see the good in it, but I can also see the harm it can do. Take Jimmy Carter—he fulfills a deep primal need and Makes a Difference with it. Pat Robertson might fulfill a deep primal need, too, but he also fulfills another, baser urge (like power-grabbing). If Carter is figuratively thinning out the deer population so they don't starve to death, then Robertson is trophy hunting Siberian tigers to mount in his office.[2]

Me, I don't even know if I have the primal need, period. Part of the problem is that religion is not rational, and I don't mean that in a

---

[1] The only exception I can think of to this rule is Debie, who joined a more liberal church where, for example, anyone can take Communion. Then again, she's the preacher's daughter.
[2] Or South American dictators. You know, figuratively.

condescending, smarty-pants way. Religion's not supposed to be rational. It's something that you feel viscerally. But viscerally, in the years since I left the church, I've developed a great many secular convictions. In other words, at this point in my life, I'm not going to be able to think my way to a religion, and for any religion to take, it's going to have to dovetail with my other convictions.

SPIRITUALITY is last on my list to cross off, but I'm treading lightly here. I'm going to be honest with you: I think it's pretty unlikely that I'm going to undergo a religious conversion. As such, I'm going to kick up the filtering—this means seeking out the experts with whom I already have some common ground. This means, for example, no weirdness with women's roles and a commitment to keep the line between church and state distinct.

I look up some books on the best-seller list that truck in matters of the soul. I find *The Purpose Driven Life*, by Rick Warren, and *Your Best Life Now*, by Joel Osteen, both wildly popular, but both penned by evangelical preachers in mega-churches. In other words, they both preach to believers. They're also both politically conservative. Am I going to be able to erase from my memory associations with other conservative religious figures? Nope. I am not. I keep on searching.

Stephanie tells me about a website, BeliefNet (beliefnet.com). She thinks it's the best spirituality site on the Internet, and they offer something called the Belief-O-Matic. The Belief-O-Matic is a twenty-question quiz that will, at the end, offer a variety of faiths that you might consider. I like this. I don't have to reinvent religion; other people have been pondering it for aeons. Maybe there's a faith out there that's tailor-made to my own personal philosophies. I also like that the name betrays a good sense of humor, something that most faiths could use a little more of, in my opinion.

I take the quiz one morning while the menfolk are at school and work, and, although it's just some online deal, it becomes pretty clear that it requires some sophisticated thinking. About half the questions are simple statements—about abortion, say—that you either agree with, disagree with, or have no opinion about. But the other half deal with things like where you can find God. Is he embodied somehow? Where? In everything? In nothing? In, say, a certain fellow with the stigmata? Do you feel that you don't know or that it doesn't matter?

This makes the good student in me feel squirmy. Worse, I feel like I knew the "right" answers at one point, but I don't anymore. I muddle through the twenty questions. I click the button that will tell me which faith squares best with my own beliefs.

And I, the cultural Presbyterian, am . . .

Mainline to Liberal Christian Protestant! 100 percent!

The Belief-O-Matic gives you twenty-eight other, lesser matches, and my top ones include Unitarian Universalism (91 percent), Liberal Quakers (88 percent), Secular Humanism (80 percent), the Baháí' Faith (75 percent), Neo Pagan (73 percent), and Reform Judaism (70 percent). I'm emphatically not a Seventh Day Adventist (22 percent) or Hindu (17 percent).

BeliefNet has a fact sheet on each of these faiths, and I click around. Mainline to Liberal Christian Protestants don't believe in a literal interpretation of the Bible, or in original sin. They don't believe Satan causes suffering; some believe that suffering is part of God's plan and others believe that suffering doesn't really have a spiritual dimension at all. It's important that you do good on earth.

I scoot back from the screen after looking at some of my other options. My profound thought? *Huh.*

I open a new screen and check my e-mail. Something's bugging me, and that something is that I'm not sure that I filled out the Belief-O-Matic entirely honestly. I saw phrases like "The Father, the Son, and the Holy Ghost," I think, and had a Pavlovian reaction to them.

What would a good Christian say? My brain reverts to thirteen and suddenly I'm being called upon to give the correct theological answer (or am I?).

I go back to the Belief-O-Matic and retake the quiz, giving answers that are closer to my professed superstitious agnostic beliefs, which often boil down to *I don't know.* I answer the last question and click the button for my results. The real me is . . .

Mainline to Liberal Protestant! 100 percent!

I scan down the list. By answering as the real me, I excluded Neo-Paganism from my top matches, and introduced nontheism (which is atheism or agnosticism). Huh.

I MAKE BRANDON take the quiz a few days later. Brandon's spiritual beliefs are rather hazy to me; this sort of thing doesn't come up that often between us.

The Belief-O-Matic spits out that my husband is a Unitarian Universalist. But a close second for him is Liberal Quakers. And since we had mojitos with lunch and a few beers already, please forgive us when we conflate the Quakers with the Puritans of old. Goodman Brandon gets Goody Jennifer a beer. Goodman Brandon is skating on thin ice wearing such finery as a zipper. Oh, ha ha.

After we have our fun, though, I start to wonder what we're supposed to do with this information. "So, now what?" I ask him. "Are we supposed to go to church because we know that there are people who share our beliefs?"

Brandon winces. "You know how in that one Malcolm Gladwell book, he said that most people's personal universe is fewer than a hundred people?" I nod. "Mine's about twenty."

"Yeah," I say. "It sort of reminds me when people in my dorm started rushing sororities. I could barely stand my suitemates, let alone a whole houseful of sorority sisters."

I imagine that there are some differences between sororities and liberal Christian congregations, the main one being that the phrase "hot Lutheran choir members" yields no matches in a Google search. But for those of us who aren't joiners, there is one important similarity between the two: They both require group participation. There will be "casual friends" to be made.

"Should we try it?" I ask Brandon.

"I don't see why," he says. "We belong to a lot of communities already. Probably too many." We landed in most of them via parenthood: the neighborhood kids and their parents, the elementary school community; then there are the actual friends we chose all by ourselves. Caleb recently joined Little League, so we've been sucked into that, too.

"The point of religion isn't *socializing*," I say. "For us, anyway," I add, thinking of the people I know for whom socializing is an important part of their faith.

Just because I learned some tips on how to interact better with people doesn't mean I find it enjoyable or even worthwhile. I'd just be distracted by all the strangers at church, I think. I tell myself I'm just delaying the church decision. But the truth is, the thought of it fills me with dread, the opposite of that peace and calm Naomi Wolf's been talking about.

WELL. I barely know what to do with myself. For the past many many months, I've had some manner of self-help up my sleeve, at the ready. But here, when it comes to religious instruction, I'm at an impasse, and as a result, I have no experts in my life. It feels good, in the way that the days following a fever feel good. I'm a little worse for wear, but free with the sense that I can cut myself some slack. The house gets a little messy. Caleb and I spend an afternoon getting him a haircut and browsing at a bookstore. I read magazines and books like they're going out of style, as in fact Research says they are. Brandon and I have perfectly pleasant conversations about nothing important, like whether the plots of *Medium* have gotten weaker or not. I get outside of myself—I don't have any expert to define myself with or against. I don't have to have an opinion about anything in particular.

In fact, I feel like I'm living my life in the way Hillary Clinton did when she went on her listening tour. All ears, my friends. I'm trying anyway.

Since I've almost completely given up the hope of church (on the grounds of the socializing) or popular religious tracts (on the grounds of conservatism being sneaked in), my new tack is trying to get believers to tell me what they like about their religion. I am not interested in hearing what the Pat Robertsons of the world have to say about religion, but I am interested in what people I respect have to say on the subject. Because even though the religious right gets a lot of press, there are people who actually walk the walk, people, like Jimmy Carter, whose faith leads them to take admirable actions.

I start casting about for religious talk. I'm listening, but sometimes people need a nudge.

So when some neighbors come over for after-dinner drinks on the porch one evening and the conversation turns to Passover, and when it's revealed that one neighbor was pretty devout in his twenties, I try not to pounce on it, but I'm afraid I do.

"So what was it about Judaism that really spoke to you then?" I ask.

"It just made sense to me," my neighbor replies.

"But you're not religious anymore?" I ask.

"No," he says.

"And when did you leave it?" I ask.

"Other things just started making more sense to me," he says.

It's pretty clear that this is not a conversation he wants to have. "So, do you want to talk to me about your sex life and credit history now?" I ask. We laugh, but I let it drop.

If it were just this one neighbor, I might be able to chalk it up to his own reticence. But again and again, with friends and "casual" friends, family and neighbors, I try to bring up religion—I'm ready to *listen!*—but no one wants to talk with me about it in depth.[3] Maybe I'm too jokey and blunt, and nobody wants to pluck their gods from inside themselves and hold them up for me to examine with my critical eye.

Or, maybe, I think, it's just that people don't have good words to describe what it's like to have a faith that really speaks to you. If you try to keep it simple, as my mother does, you use words like *comfort* and wind up describing the Golden Rule. It makes sense, but it doesn't make me *feel* that faith for myself. If you go deeper, you wind up using words like *transcendence*, *awe*, and possibly *energy*. And my eyes glaze over.

How do religions do it? Clearly, people would stop going to their place of worship if, week after week, they were staring down an hour or more of abstractions. Then I remember an essay I edited by Tracy Mayor, a longtime contributor to *Brain, Child* who was raised Catholic. In her essay "Losing My Religion," she writes that she *could* give up her faith entirely. "But then I'd have to give up the New Testament stories that I really do love, and I'm not ready for that, any more than my son wants to stop listening for the sound of hoofs on the roof." She concludes that the stories of her faith—especially those of the Virgin Mary—help her make sense of, if not God, then at least the world around her.

This essay won a prestigious award, so that makes me a little less embarrassed to admit that it was the first time I'd ever read that questioning God's power—why the Holocaust? why do little kids get cancer?—is a cliché. (What did I think before? That I was especially clever?) It was also the first time that I encountered anyone suggesting in such a blatant way that one could actually relate to the folks in the Bible. Unlike Tracy, I'd only ever thought of Mary as a choice Nativity play role, a flannel board figure, or an icon. I just couldn't

---

[3] I did glean that Sophie's parents aren't as devout as she might lead you to believe.

ever find myself in Bible stories, peopled as they are with God and his son, his saintly disciples, or the no-good-niks who wouldn't do what God told them. It's only in retrospect that I can acknowledge that I might have been approaching Sunday school as if it were a writing workshop. Okay, so Zaccheus was a "wee little man." But you've got to give us more *character* than the fact that he was a little person who enjoyed tree-climbing and wanted to see The Lord. Where's the emotional connection here?

If religion is built on stories, I reason, I need stories for our times. I don't have Tracy's ability to find an emotional connection in the Virgin Mary's story—but I do have the ability to find an emotional connection in Tracy's story. This, actually, is my job at *Brain, Child*: to identify the essays that are both intellectually interesting and have that certain component that makes the essay emotionally visceral.

I turn to the memoir genre. Reading people's stories has never once done me wrong. I want to viscerally feel what it's like to be a believer.

AFTER AN UNSUCCESSFUL TRIP to the bookstore, where I found myself in the unfamiliar (and, in this instance, unpeopled) bookstore territory of "Christian Inspiration," I come home and start ordering online. By Friday, I have a stack of books on the kitchen table. I think of it as my little pile of faith. I plan to submerge myself in it this weekend.

I start with Anne Lamott, whose work I know from her columns on Salon and her memoir *Operating Instructions: A Journal of My Son's First Year*, a book about motherhood that's credited with kickstarting a whole mini-genre of writing on motherhood. On my little pile of faith are her collections *Traveling Mercies: Some Thoughts on Faith* and *Plan B: Further Thoughts on Faith*.

Lamott's story is fairly well known to anyone who's read her work: She grew up the daughter of lefty parents. She spent some crazy years as a drug addict and alcoholic before becoming a born-again Christian and a single mother to Sam. She's fiercely liberal in that particular West Coast way.

I start *Traveling Mercies* on Friday afternoon, and I have to say that Lamott's writing cadence all by itself is soothing. Check this:

> More than anything else on earth, I do not want Sam ever to blow away, but you know what? He will. His ashes will stick to the fingers of someone who loves him. Maybe his ashes will blow that person into a place where things do not come out right, where things cannot be boxed up or spackled back together but where somehow he or she can see, with whatever joy can be mustered, the four or five leaves on the formerly barren tree.

How does she do that? Take the topic of her son's eventual death and actually make it a *comforting* passage? By the time Brandon gets home for dinner, I'm ready to write Anne Lamott and politely ask her to please finish writing this book for me because she seems to possess the sort of let-go-and-let-God attitude that I'm not able to cough up.

And that attitude and how it plays out is the overriding theme of her book: just how her faith allows her some modicum of peace and lets her off the hook in some way. Not in a moral or political way—she's too conscious of social injustice for that—but her belief in God lets her off from trying to rationalize and intellectualize all the troubles she finds herself in. Some troubles are large: the death of her best friend Pammy, for example. Others are more petty; she dedicates a whole essay to dealing with a particularly irritating mother of a kid in her son's class. No matter the size of what's troubling her, though, Lamott has a method. She stops, she prays, she waits to understand what she's supposed to do next, if anything. This is, of course, the definition of faith—believing in something even though you have no empirical evidence that it makes a whit of difference—and Lamott has it in spades.

I guess you can call what's happening to me as I read Lamott's work "flow," because I read in the armchair while Brandon and Caleb watch the Friday night lineup on Nick, and I lose myself in her work. Or I suppose you could call it a sort of empathy born of good writing. At some point, in bed that night, I sit up half-asleep in the dark. I hear some rustling downstairs. It's probably Luna licking her paws in her crate, but I'm so immersed in Lamott's faith that, before I can stop myself, I think, "Oh, that's just Jesus." I'm not kidding.

The next morning, we take Caleb to his baseball game. Through Lamott, I feel like I'm starting to understand what it means to really have faith. Not that I have it myself. But I try to channel her a little. When another parent on the team tries to boss me, I take a moment and consciously decide to be tactful instead of pointing out that if she wants someone else to parent, she could consider having another child. I say cheerily, "Oh, I'm his mother, not his coach!" which hardly qualifies as Christ-like behavior, but it's a start.

But then after the game, it all falls apart. We get home and I pick up *Traveling Mercies* again, only to rediscover the distance between Lamott the believer and myself.

In her essay "The Man Who Was Mean to His Dog," Lamott describes a morning when she and her son went to the beach. The beach was empty except for another woman and her kids, and a man with a golden retriever. Then, "the ugliest real-life thing Sam has ever witnessed" happened: The man first hit his dog in the ribs with a large stick; later, he yanked the dog up in the air by the leash, "like something on a meat hook." Everyone watching was horrified, and it speaks to Lamott's writing that I could feel this internal debate a million miles a minute along with her: Do you say something, even to someone who'd do this to his dog, not knowing what he'd do to two women and their kids? Or do you keep quiet? What's the right thing to do?

As it turns out, the other woman tells the man that she's calling the authorities and Lamott echoes her, but weakly.

And then I guess that I forget that this is a book heavy on Jesus because I feel this injustice so viscerally that I want some Old Testament eye for an eye here. I want somebody—even a person as yet unintroduced into the story—to rise up out of the ocean and smite the bad man, so the dog can run free and maybe joins one of the families. The phrase "tender smiles" should figure in somewhere. Instead, Lamott writes about how Jesus loves this man, too, just as much as he loves anyone else.

Later, I'll be able to recognize that it's Anne Lamott's essay after all and if the conclusion she wants to draw is about Jesus' love, well then, that's the way it is. But I have to say I get a surge of outrage when I read it. Viscerally, I feel this is *the wrong conclusion to draw, ANNE.* It's not the time to let go and let God. The man who was mean to his dog should have gone down, if not in truth then symbolically.

Which, of course, would transform an essay on faith into a fairy tale, where the bad guy gets punished and the good guys can feel righteous and possibly get a fluffy new pet. In this sense, Lamott is doing what the writers of the Bible were doing by including stories about Abraham (who was asked to kill his own son) and Job (who loses everything for reasons unclear). She's trying to make sense, or come to some kind of peace, with the hard questions. Her conclusion, ultimately, is that there are things she simply cannot know.

I'd agree that certainly there are things I cannot know, but in this particular instance, it's a deeply unsatisfying sentiment. So I'm back to where I started, holding my own burdens, arms aching.

EVEN IN A HEATHEN household like ours, good and evil, reward and punishment, pop up on a surprisingly regular basis. Like all children, Caleb is drawn to the extremes. We try to rein him in.

The developer of our neighborhood is kind of a prick, and, as the three of us get ready for bed one night, I tell Brandon about an e-mail

I saw in which he wrote something nasty to one of our neighborhood friends. "Who was he mean to?" Caleb asks.

"Christina," I say.

"We should punch him!" Caleb says and demonstrates some kung fu.

"We don't punch people" is my line as a mainstream twenty-first-century parent, so I say it.

"But he's bad," Caleb says. "He's mean."

"He *is* mean," I say. He's also immature, calculating, and demands to be emotionally coddled—and at the same time, he's given to acts of generosity. He offered one of his properties, rent-free, to a family displaced by Hurricane Katrina, and he travels abroad every once in a while, volunteering his construction expertise and labor. I continue to Caleb, "I don't know about 'bad.' He's no Count Olaf."

Count Olaf is the main bad guy in the *Series of Unfortunate Events* books we've been reading every night for several months now. The three of us, teeth brushed, pajamas on, line up in bed, and I start reading from the twelfth book. The main characters are three orphans caught up in a world of secret organizations, greed, and arson. The author, one Mr. Lemony Snicket, describes the good guys—"volunteers" in their organization—as "noble." The bad guys are "treacherous" and "villians." In these last books of the series, Mr. Snicket introduces a large swath of gray area where even the volunteers sometimes act treacherous and the villians can let fly with a little nobility, or at least humanity. Caleb's listening, but he's antsy tonight. As I read, he lies back and makes fart noises with the pits of his knees.

I know that he likes the idea of true good and true evil, and it's fine by me if he wants to hang on to that a little longer. We—Brandon, Lemony Snicket, and I—are preparing him for the gray area, but, really, it's sort of a mess to deal with.

NEXT UP IN MY little pile of faith is a classic: Harold S. Kushner's *When Bad Things Happen to Good People*. Kushner's bad thing was, in my opinion, possibly the very worst thing. His son, Aaron, died in his early teens after living through progeria, an illness that caused him to age rapidly. Kushner, a rabbi, dedicates this book to uncovering the answer to this most troubling question of belief: Why me?

There are, I suppose, people out there who haven't yet received the message, but most of us can thank Kushner for, in 1981, laying out the reasons why the only acceptable thing to say when someone experiences misfortune is, *I'm so sorry*. (Wrong responses include *It's for the best* and *God needed him/her more than you*.) It's a terrible thing, Kushner says, to suggest to someone that he or she could have done something to prevent a tragedy—prayed harder, loved more, had more faith.

It's a Saturday night when I read *When Bad Things Happen to Good People*, Brandon and Caleb tucked away in bed, Simon and Luna snoozing on the couch next to me. I'm enjoying my time with Rabbi Kushner, who seems wise, levelheaded, and far above resorting to pat answers. Like Anne Lamott, his faith in God is unswerving, but he picks at it a little harder and a lot longer than she does. To believe in God, he says, we have to give up this idea that God is all-powerful. God can't control things. Why do bad things happen to good people? Well, sometimes tragedy is man-made. Sometimes, though, bad things just happen. Kushner writes, "[C]haos is evil; not wrong, not malevolent, but evil nonetheless, because by causing tragedies at random, it prevents people from believing in God's goodness."

I underline this passage.

In short order, Kushner gets to the purpose of God. Praying, he writes, is worthwhile because although God can't change events, he can give you the strength to deal with the events. Also,

Our responding to life's unfairness with sympathy and with righteous indignation, God's compassion and God's anger working through us, may be the surest proof of all of God's reality.

I'm not so sure that I can believe that. Are my morals proof of the existence of God? If anything, they seem to me to be proof of the existence of my mother. But I keep reading.

Kushner ends with a reframing of the question. What's important, he decides, is not puzzling out *why* a tragedy happens, but what you do with it. (Hailie, by the way, says the same thing next time we get together.) The key is being able to love and forgive—the world, the people in it, God—despite their limitations, despite their flaws. He's not glib about it. He'd give up everything he's learned in the course of Aaron's illness and death if only his son could be alive and well. But he's not, and Kushner's left with having to both make peace with his son's death and make good out of the tragedy.

By the time I finish the book, it's well after midnight, and even the dogs are past pretending that they're close to conscious. I head upstairs and turn on the bathroom light. Caleb's lying flat on his back, exhaling noisily through his nose, and I, thinking of Rabbi Kushner's Aaron, creep over to the bed and kiss my son's damp forehead, smelling his health, his existence.

I SPEND SUNDAY stewing in other people's faith. We're not at church—in fact, we're eating brunch at a theme restaurant Caleb requested, we're planting flowers and herbs in decorative pots, we're writing out bills—but nonetheless God is very much on my mind.

I've spent all weekend with believers, and I think I know how being a believer feels: It's a calm feeling of being connected to Something Larger than yourself. And this Something Larger helps you bear burdens. Which is great—I viscerally understand that feeling.

But, try as I might, I can't experience true belief myself. I cannot will myself to actually believe in the type of Something Larger that Anne Lamott and Rabbi Kushner are talking about. I'm not saying it doesn't exist. But I'm not saying it does, either.

On Monday, I call Stephanie, she who has studied religion. "Would you like to talk about God?" I ask.

"Sure," she says.

I describe my big God-a-palooza weekend: Lamott and her calming cadence, Jesus in Lamott's houseboat, the evil man at the beach, Kushner's son, his rejection of pat answers, his reworking of the "why me?" question. I take a breath. "But I can't *make* myself believe," I say.

"Hmm," she says, and there's a pause. "I think you're worrying too much about belief. Christianity emphasizes belief. A lot of other religions focus so much more on practice."

"Okay," I say.

"There are two pieces here: There's belief and then there's just doing what you're supposed to. Your actions count a lot more in, say, Judaism."

"So that's what I'm going to have to do," I say. "I'm just going to focus on moral behavior and forget about the belief."

"Well, there are people who would say that the two are tied together—that you can't have moral behavior without the belief."

I consider this. "Yeah," I say. "But I'm not going to pay attention to those people."

OKAY, so research shows that the religious are happier than the non-religious. But what is it about religion that makes people happy? If Steph's right (and she almost always is), then for many believers, it's both the belief and the practice, two parts of the Something Larger equation.

But what about the rest of us—the doubters, the *I-don't-know*-ers, the *probably-not*-ers, the *no-way*-ers? Is there a parallel for the secularly inclined?

According to *The Happiness Hypothesis*'s Jonathan Haidt, there is indeed. Just as the religious cultivate a personal relationship with God *and* also participate in the group dynamic of church, Haidt points out that the divided self means that everyone—even an atheist like him—needs to focus on both the self and the Something Larger. "We were shaped by individual selection to be selfish creatures who struggle for resources, pleasure, and prestige," he writes, "and we were shaped by group selection to be hive creatures who long to lose ourselves in something larger." Happiness, he hypothesizes, can be found in the balance between the two, within and without.

Haidt isn't the first person to say this. In fact, he's not even the first expert I've encountered in my quest to say it. David Bach dedicates two pages to telling his readers to have a "greater purpose beyond the two of you." Dr. Phil takes the religious tack and suggests that couples who pray together stay together.[4] Lawrence Shapiro devotes a chapter to encouraging empathy in your children—and just telling them to be empathetic doesn't cut it; parents need to practice empathy. Still, with most self-help advice, the Something Larger gets short shrift.

In hindsight, I've been trying, subconsciously maybe, to balance the focus on myself with contributions to various outfits larger than myself. While we were taking financial advice, Brandon and I funded Christmas for two families affected by HIV or AIDS. Shortly after trying to improve my interpersonal interactions, I joined the board of our homeowners' association. After my freak-out about driving, I gave the car away. Karmically speaking, it's been one for me, one for Something Larger.

It's all part of a midlife crisis I've been having since I was in my teens, knowing that what I'm best at has to do with language, but also knowing that language cannot be served up for dinner for homeless people, used to cure cancer, or to provide affordable, high-quality child care for working Americans. In my last year of college, I remember sitting in my adviser's office, wretched and wondering what I had

---

[4] Whether this is someone's anecdotal observation or a real study is unclear.

gotten myself into with this *English* degree, of all things. I hung out with people interested in doing good in the world. In a few years' time, Brandon would make part of a drug cocktail to combat AIDS. My friend Kathy would live in Mexico with nuns, teaching literacy in a rural area. My friend Emily would work at a Head Start program in Colorado. At that moment, I was planning on continuing my job with the local alternative newsweekly, writing up press releases into a calendar of events. Cracker is playing at Trax! There will be art openings on the first Friday of this and every month! Here is a new play that the paper's theater critic finds well lit and nicely costumed! "Shouldn't I be doing something that does good in the world?" I asked my adviser.

She considered this. "If you want to do good in the world, you're going to do it anyway," she finally said. "Whether or not it's your job."

True enough words. But my striving inner Presbyterian looks at my recent good deeds and finds them, well, a little *random*. It's time to get serious about my Something Larger, and I'm not talking about my ass again.

HERE'S A CHEMISTRY QUIZ for you: Take religion. Separate out the moral behavior from belief in God. Then add to the moral behavior something vaguely spiritual although not at all religious. What's this new compound?

I'm going to say it's something like secular spirituality. This is where I am now, my Belief-O-Matic results and lessons from Kushner and Lamott notwithstanding. But where does the secular spiritualist—a non-religious person who wants to Make a Difference—turn these days? Especially if she's a woman who happens to be home at four o'clock on the East Coast? Especially if she likes her seeking presented in an entertaining format?

Oprah.

Even people who don't watch daytime television or read self-help know that there's something that sets Oprah apart—above—her compatriots. She's been on the air longer, of course, and her set, with the buttery leather furniture, is classier than everyone else's. There's the book club that lends a certain literary gravitas to the show, and she's the only one who has the pull to give away a parking lot worth of cars.

But, really, Oprah could be filming in the showroom of a Rent-a-Center and giving away ballpoint pens, and I suspect she'd stand out. I know someone who knows someone who was on the show, and it was reported back that Oprah Winfrey is, hands down, the most charismatic person ever—you just want to be around her. For a good long while, I chalked up my attraction—why I'd keep watching even as Oprah would mystify me by tossing off phrases like Honoring Your Truth—to this charisma.

But now I'm thinking it's something else: Her show is the only one on daytime TV really committed to examining both the self and the Something Larger. She gets within and without. One day, you'll be learning how to get the best pair of jeans for your booty; the next, you'll be learning about organizations in Africa that aim to end the frighteningly common women's health problem of fistulas. One day, you'll be hearing about how bad body issues get transmitted from mother to daughter; the next you'll be examining class in the U.S. It's the full equation of bettering oneself.

Plus celebrities!

If there's any secular expert who knows about the Something Larger, it's Oprah. She's even coined a handful of catchphrases that get at matters of the spirit, like, for example "Remembering Your Spirit."

I go to Oprah.com. I'm looking for a path to Something Larger, and I keep clicking until I land on "Oprah's Angel Network." If you're like me, you'll wonder why it's call *Oprah's* Angel Network—don't the angels themselves get some credit? The answer is that Oprah matches whatever her angels contribute, and she's the one with name recognition, so there you go. According to the website, the network has raised more than fifty million dollars for various causes, including Christmas in Africa and help for those affected by Hurricane Katrina.

There's a page titled "Start Making a Difference" with a quote from Oprah: "Think about what you have to give, not even in terms of dollars because I believe that your life is about service. It's about what you came to give to the world, to your children, to your family."

There was a time when my child, my family, was all the service I could manage. And it's plenty, especially if your child is an infant and you spend most of the day pinned under him breastfeeding. Or if your child is an exploring toddler and you spend all your waking hours foiling his tendency to kill himself. Or, as it happens all the time, if your parents are in the foggy area between independent and dependent and you're charged with filling in the gaps: driving them to appointments, making sure there are groceries in the house, gathering medication. This caregiving service is nothing to sneeze at. It's rude to sneeze at it, anyway, and shows a certain arrogance, a certain sense of entitlement. We've all been dependent and likely will be again, and the people who take care of the dependents make the world go round. Clearly, Oprah knows that.

But I'm in a period with a more independent child and still independent parents. I can turn my attention to the world.

Also, I like that Oprah calls it "service." I feel comfortable with this image of me, just trying to be a good helper. I'm the gum-chewing waitress, kindly asking, "Can I get you some crackers for the baby, hon?" I'm the friendly nurse, offering more warm blankets. I'm the honest mechanic, saying, "Save your money—those tires are good for another five thousand miles."

Service is good. Charity—as Suze Orman emphasized—is more fraught. Just as I don't want to be an ass regarding money, I don't want to be one regarding service either, sacrificing another person's dignity to fuel the good feelings about myself.

To start making a difference, Oprah offers some questions I should ask myself. They're ones that Jackie Waldman, author of *The Courage to Give*, came up with. I look at the computer screen and ponder who I work best with (kids, people my own age, older people), which issues really concern me, what I love to do. It's a lot to ponder.

I figure the methods for Making a Difference fall into two basic categories: the person-to-person approach, and the more sweeping but more bureaucratic institutional method. The person-to-person method might include teaching literacy, becoming a foster parent, working at a battered women's shelter. The institutional method involves stuff more removed—the organization is Making a Difference and you might find yourself filing, writing press releases, handing out flyers. One's not better than the other, in my opinion, and they're both necessary and good. I'm open to either.

"Whew! When we're in charge, we'll have a lot of work to do!" is how my grandfather and I tend to end our bemoaning-the-state-of-the-union conversations, and I see that it's truer than ever while pondering my service options.

As I sit down with Oprah's questions one morning, I get at one of the underlying issues: Who do I want to help? As it is, Brandon and I give money to the food bank, the free health clinic and Planned Parenthood, and Habitat for Humanity, figuring that, at the bare minimum, people need food, health care, and a home. (They also need child care, which is an enormous expense, but there isn't a nonprofit dedicated to that, so I try to address that through my job at *Brain, Child*.)

According to the local paper, the people who use these services aren't unlike us in any significant way. Many of these people at the food bank already work, sometimes two jobs. But the cost of living here, even in the worst part of town, is crazy expensive. Brandon and I are really just a few turns of bad luck away from needing these services ourselves. On one hand, we have college educations; on the other, the big joke is that you move to Charlottesville because you like your bartender to have a Ph.D.

I make myself a cup of tea. I load the dishwasher. I think about my "passion to give back," and as I jostle a stack of plates a little hard, it occurs to me that my passion is firing up my righteous ire. In our country, working people should not have to be the recipients of charity. I'm glad that the food bank, the free clinic, Planned Parenthood, and Habitat exist—but they shouldn't have to serve as many people as they do. Even twelve-year-olds know the basic rule of capitalism: You work, you get paid—it's not a favor.

Except capitalism isn't working, for a lot of people, for a lot of reasons. Actually not a lot of reasons. Just two: greed, and the lack of a system of checks and balances against that greed. And don't give me that malarkey about the poor small-business owners. I myself am a small-business owner, and we could pay our employees the minimum wage. But we don't.

IT'S ONE THING TO FIND your passion. It's another to walk around with your passion cocked, ready to go off at the slightest provocation. Oprah.com offers some tips on starting your own nonprofit organization, but I think that's a little more than I need. I'm fairly sure that someone else has thought of this sort of thing already. Enough money for food, health care, housing, child care. This is not revolutionary. No one will be printing my face on T-shirts a generation from now.

When you're trying to get pregnant, the world is filled with babies, and when you're buying a certain type of car, traffic seems jam-packed with them. I'm hoping that in this way, with this new awareness of my passion, an organization will suddenly appear. I'm having a little faith, if you will.

Meanwhile, I take Oprah up on her challenge to start a "kindness chain," which is simply remembering to be nice to other people. "Performing acts of kindness is one of the best and quickest ways to improve your life," according to her website.

Brandon and I take Caleb to baseball practice one night. It's a city league. Twenty-five percent of Charlottesville's citizens live in poverty, and while the team doesn't reflect that breakdown, it's not uniformly upper middle class, either. One of Caleb's teammates is a boy I'll call Marcus. We've never seen his parents. He doesn't have a baseball mitt. Our neighbor Kathleen, shoring up her own link in the kindness chain, picks him up and brings him home for every practice and every game. Marcus is the only kid without the special polyester baseball pants. I don't know what specific issues his parents are facing—lack of transportation, lack of money, lack of time, lack of child care, lack of good health, lack of giving two whoops in Hades—but I'm pretty sure his family is part of that 25 percent.

Marcus's lack of a mitt becomes apparent pretty quickly—he didn't *forget* it, he doesn't *have* one—but still parents scramble around at every practice and game. Maybe there's an extra in the car? Maybe so-and-so could lend Marcus his? This makes me increasingly uncomfortable, this fresh pointing out of what Marcus does not have at every game.

"Maybe we should just buy some extra mitts," I say to Brandon.

"That sounds like a good idea," he says.

So in the days between a game and a practice, Brandon stops on his way home from work and buys two extra mitts. "So," Brandon says. "I was thinking about what Suze Orman said about just handing a person a dollar. . . . How are we going to get this to Marcus?"

"Good point," I say.

"I mean, I don't want to be like, 'HERE WE ARE, MARCUS, GIVING YOU THIS BASEBALL GLOVE THAT WE BOUGHT FOR YOU!' " Brandon says.

"Maybe we just give it to Kathleen to give it to him for him to keep?" I ask. But then I think a little harder: Would I be happy to have Caleb show up at home with a glove someone donated? No, I decide. My dignity would get quite a pinch from this material evidence that I couldn't provide a twenty-five-dollar baseball mitt for my boy, and some Richie Riches sent one home and made him a charity case.

In the end, we just bring the mitts and discreetly distribute them to whoever needs them at each meeting. We tell Caleb they're extras. He and everyone else seems to buy that.

Inwardly, I'm slapping our backs, busting out the cigars. Such good, kind people Brandon and I are! But in order to not be an asshole, I wear my poker face. Hey, man, we're just the family that brings a plastic grocery sack of two mitts to every game and practice. Need one? We got 'em. Nothing unusual about that.

THOUGH LET'S NOT be too self-congratulatory here, too much of a martyr. Let's remember that when our much-loved mother and much-loved baby sister Jill were down visiting, we said, "Fuck all y'all" to them for a minor teasing. Let's remember that we wasted a good half hour of this somewhat rare visit in irritation. Let's remember that we are not even approaching a Jesus-like empathy here, but simply balancing our questionable karma with good deeds.

I'M READING Barbara Ehrenreich's blog when I find it, the organization whose values and goals more or less match mine. It has the bonus feature of appealing to the policy wonk in me. It's called the Virginia Organizing Project, a grassroots nonprofit organization with offices in Charlottesville. They work for getting Virginia's minimum wage raised above its current $5.15 an hour, finding affordable housing solutions across the state, and changing the state tax code that currently punishes the poor and rewards the rich, among other issues. Their mission statement reads, in part: "The Virginia Organizing Project is a statewide grassroots organization dedicated to challenging injustice by empowering people in local communities to address issues that affect the quality of their lives."

I read it as, "You can't change your luck, but we're working to change things we can control." As Kushner says, some tragedies are man-made.

I e-mail one of the directors, asking how I can help. I say that I'm willing to help in whatever way, but I do have some experience with publications. A few e-mails later, I have an appointment to meet with the executive director next week.

It seems silly to say that this is a big step for me. After all, I volunteer with some regularity at Caleb's school. And, clearly, I'm not the sort of person who finds it difficult or embarrassing to state her opinions publicly. Politics informs a lot of my everyday decisions, but now I'm stepping into Big-P Politics. Maybe it's this way for everyone, but especially as someone who was once a journalist of sorts, I get a little nervous. This *is* a big step. It's me publicly saying that there are issues I care more about than any attempts at impartiality. It's saying that I'm choosing a side. It's saying that I'm not just critiquing policy anymore—I'm hoping to change it.

Me, me, me. "Isn't it ironic," I ask Brandon, "that I'm finally taking steps to do something outside of myself, but I'm still caught up in what it means to me?"

"But you *are* you," Brandon says. "It's impossible to completely erase yourself from your actions."

"Hmm," I say. "That's true." I push back on the porch swing. "I'm excited to meet with the guy."

"What do they do again?" Brandon asks.

Since I've been studying the website, I can tell him pretty comprehensively all the social and economic justice issues they take up.

"But how do they accomplish it?" he asks. Because this is the sticky part. This is what makes it a big deal to get involved in Big-P Politics. Brandon and I are both rule-followers. We're not big fans of the protest rally or the protest demonstration, particularly the ones that seem fringe. You can recognize the fringe ones because they always seem to involve large puppets.

"A lot of ways, I guess. They work with a bunch of different groups, so I guess it depends on the issue whether they meet with delegates and get them to sponsor a bill, or bring some issue to a school district's attention, or whatever. They *were* involved with the living wage protest," I say, referring to a controversial student protest at our alma mater regarding the wages of the university workers, about which Brandon and I have complicated feelings. "But there were no puppets."

"That's good," Brandon says. "Puppets would not make you happy."

IT'S NOT A LARGE PUPPET sort of organization. After my morning walk, I drive to the Virginia Organizing Project's offices, located on the first floor of a converted house near the train tracks. I meet with Joe Szakos, the executive director of the program, and he explains what they do, which is, as the name suggests, to organize. By design, he says, they're diverse in terms of race and class. They're also diverse in terms of the specific issues they address, but the way it works is that, say, the people who are working on health care issues don't have to fight the gay rights issues. They just promise to help out at key moments in a gay rights campaign, and the gay rights people will help the health care people when needed. Joe recognizes that not everyone's going to be really jazzed about everyone else's campaign. "But when you say it's about dignity, people respect that," he says. "And if there are problems, we talk about them. We don't pretend to know all the answers, but we try to face issues head-on."

We're about fifteen minutes into the meeting, and while I'm enjoying myself—see Love of Learning, filed under signature strengths—and while I viscerally feel that the VOP is the sort of Something Larger that I can support, I'm not quite sure how I can fit into this work. Joe's work sounds an awful lot like entering into situation after situation rife with the possibility of socially screwing up. I have a quick vision of me dropping an f-bomb in front of a group of rural, elderly churchgoers who want to help with homelessness. Oh, not good.

"So why are you here?" Joe asks rhetorically. He pulls a thick manuscript off the desk beside him. "What we do is organize, and none of us here have the time to go hide away for days or even hours to work on something like this."

"This" turns out to be something called "The Virginia Housing Primer 2006" by an organizer named Larry Lamar Yates. The manuscript is intended to be a little booklet to get people up to speed on housing issues in Virginia. More specifically, it's intended for people who might be experiencing housing crises themselves—from a lack of a water system to a dearth of affordable housing—to learn and take action on behalf of themselves and their communities.

I'm to edit it and use my layout skills so it can be printed and distributed. Oh, my, I think excitedly. Oh, my. The work with language can actually Make a Difference. And I get to indulge my policy wonkery. And I get to design a publication *from scratch*. I feel a burst of adrenaline, or maybe it's seratonin, at the prospect of my task. I'm relieved that I don't have to be a different person from who I am in order to be of service. I'm charged that the geeky little things that bring me flow are actually going to put me in service land. I slide the manuscript into my purse.

And just like that, I can see the little speck in the Something Larger that has my name on it.

I SPEND TWO DAYS in service of editing the housing primer. Editing work is not the most exciting work in the world to read about and the author's prose was pretty solid as it is, but let it suffice to say that where there was jargon, there is jargon no more. Where there were unsupported statements, support has blossomed. Where there were inappropriate en-dashes, there are now em-dashes. I've been on leave from *Brain, Child* for some months now and I miss the editing work, this polishing of other people's ideas.

For the record, I'm aware of the irony that this primer might be described as something like self-help. I get a brief sinking sensation when I realize this—*I've crossed to the other side!*—until the big dif hits me: This whole idea of the primer revolves around collective action, not just one individual saving the world by herself.

And then there's the other, subtler dif. For the past two years, I've tried to picture myself as someone different: a relaxed lady who lives in a Pottery Barn catalog, the competent whiz who can work an investment interest calculator, a gentle good role model of a mother, an optimist, the life of the party, a cheerful helper of humanity.

But in the days that I work on the housing primer, visions of myself stay submerged. Instead, I imagine the people to whom my small contribution might make a difference. There's the woman who can't find affordable housing within a two-hour radius of where she works. There's the family out in the country who doesn't have reliable water and sewage. There's the guy who's worried about his homeless brother. There's someone's grandma who hasn't been able to afford her real estate tax bill since her neighborhood got cappuccinos and tapas.

These people want to do *something* about these housing issues but they don't know where to start. *But what's this?* (It's a little fuzzy in my imagination how they happen upon the booklet, but let's just say it somehow appears in their hands. Poof!) *Why, it's the Virginia Housing Primer 2006! Why, it's just the tool I need to find help for this housing crisis! And look how well it's edited!*

Oh, shut up. I know that editing is invisible work, but it's my fantasy.

Will the primer change lives? I don't know for sure. I know that these projects sometimes get lost in red tape. But I have a sort of faith in the Virginia Organizing Project that my work won't be for naught. For those of us who truck in secular spirituality, maybe this is all faith means: You're not responsible for everything, but you do your small part and you have faith that others will do theirs, and with effort and a clear goal, it'll all come together in the end.

"I REALLY LIKED working on the primer," I say to Brandon as we load the dishwasher.

"That was really cool to work on that housing primer," I say on the back porch.

"So, I turned the primer in today—I hope Joe likes it," I say to Brandon as we prepare to read this night's chapter from the Lemony Snicket book to Caleb.

"Yeah—that's what you were saying. You seem really happy about it," Brandon says.

"What's a primer?" Caleb asks.

"It's a booklet with information. The one I was working on is for people who want to learn more about how we can make it so that everyone can afford a place to live," I tell him.

"I thought you were working on a book," he says.

"I am," I say. "But this is something extra I volunteered to do."

Caleb sits up straight and grabs my arm. "Wait! You're a *volunteer?*" He's looking at me as if I divulged my superpowers. "That means you're a *noble person!*"

Well. I have some serious flaws. I invest in corporations that put the bottom line above all else. I let Cleo suffer longer than she had to. I sometimes offend, either inadvertently or advertently. "Noble" is pushing it.

But, for this minute anyway, before the three of us drift off to a knees-in-the-back sleep, while I still have the feeling of calm all up in my Brahmarandra, I allow that I might be okay.

The Thrilling Conclusion

WHAT IF, two years ago, I got up from the rug in the family room where I was cleaning Cleo's mess, washed my hands, thought better of my little self-improvement scheme, and put the list back in the recycling from whence it came? Would I be a different person now, two years after the fact, if I hadn't embarked on my experiments?

I don't know. A person with more faith in action and consequence would say yes, that in this alternate universe in which I steered clear of experts, I would be different. The main events wouldn't change, of course—for example, Cleo would still be dead. (If *God* can't steer the world's events, surely self-help can't, either.) But other things might have turned out differently. This other Jennifer would live in a messier house than I do and she'd still be putting off setting up a retirement account. She wouldn't have examined either herself or her menfolk as closely as I did. She'd be more socially awkward and about ten pounds heavier. She might not have had panic attacks or anxiety. She'd get squirmy with most talk of spirituality, and she might be Making a Difference but in another, probably smaller, way.

But I wouldn't necessarily say that things would turn out this way for the alternate universe Jennifer. Two years has indeed changed me, but two years changes everybody. I don't think that self-help is necessarily the only way I would have, say, lost ten pounds. By the same token, I can't say with any certainty that I could have avoided the panic attacks if I'd steered clear of self-help. I think chances are pretty decent that self-help contributed to both these positive and negative turns of event, but after all this, I still believe too much in luck, too much in randomness, to say that there's a simple, direct correlation between self-help and the person I am today. You can choose your own adventure, but it might not turn out the way you thought it would.

PEOPLE NOTICED AS my house got cleaner, as Brandon and I went on a vacation alone, as my jeans became ill-fitting. They wanted a verdict from me. I was actually following the advice, not just buying the book, unlike many in the civilian population. Everyone who knew about my experiments asked. For real, yo—does it work?

At first, I'd respond gaily, "I'll let you know!"

Later, I'd say darkly, "Not in a good way."

Finally, I'd stammer. "Well . . . um, kind of. It's complicated."

It's complicated. The problem, across the board, is that the experts promise way too much. Truly, I would have been plenty satisfied if they'd simply promised me, say, knowledge of the stock market or how to use good manners in dealing with other people. But they overreached.

In hindsight, I did, too. I took the experiments too far. The reason, I suspect, that most people don't take self-help as literally as I did is that we all have some internal thermostat that tells us to abort the mission if self-help leads us into dangerous territory. Of course, this usually comes out as *I failed at this self-help exercise*. But most of the time, the real answer is that the advice couldn't work for us.

I had plenty of signs along the way that something was wrong. It started with the wack vision and progressed to the sleepwalking, to the feeling that I generally suck, to the panic attacks. It wound up with anxiety. Why did I ignore all this stuff? Probably because I still can't say that the experts caused all this—I had a life going on at the same time. Also, I have to admit that I became more than a little impressed with the amount of willpower I could exert. (What a Miss Thang I am! Working it for thirty minutes every weekday!) On the flip side, the amount of introspection the experts were asking me to undertake was bad for me. The level of self-awareness that I reached—thinking about every single thing I said or did with my family, my friends, even in my own home—was crazy-making. And the thing is, once you establish that habit, you cannot escape from your own brain.

I agree with Jonathan Haidt, Oprah Winfrey, and Martin Seligman when they emphasize—*really* emphasize—that you need to do for yourself and for others. If I had it to do over again (which I won't, believe you me) I would have focused more on the doing for others: the without, the Making a Difference. I would have tried to better balance the self with the world. That said, just as I took the focus on the self too far, I bet you can probably take the Making a Difference too far, too. But at least you can escape it. At least your loved ones will have some concrete thing to pull you away from. No, you don't have an extra twenty hours a week. No, we're not equipped to take in a foster child at this stage of our lives. No, you may not give away all our money to Oxfam.

As it was, though, I thought I could save myself from bad advice if I could just devise some sort of equation, a litmus test, a Good-Advice-O-Meter. For a time, I thought I'd hit upon it! The rule was simply to steer clear of advice in areas that require other people's—your mate's, your kid's, your casual friends'—cooperation. That's a losing game, trying to change other people.

Later, I thought that the best idea was to steer clear of advice that asked you to buy into a worldview that didn't make sense to you.

But the thing is, they *all* offer their own worldviews, and no matter what the particulars are, the experts have one thing in common: They believe that, with enough hard work, you can fix what ails you. By definition, experts' worldviews promote the extraordinarily optimistic idea that you *can* help your self, by yourself. They have extraordinary faith in the individual.

Most of the experts are completely sincere. I even feel a tenderness toward some of them because of this sincerity, and I wouldn't be surprised if most of them, when they sat back and contemplated their own lives, saw their advice as how they Make a Difference. But, in my experience—perhaps unfortunately—the experts' conviction that people can follow simple steps to make their lives better . . . well, believing in it doesn't make it true. In my experience, there are too many barriers against self-help actually working.

FOR INSTANCE: I actually sat down with my husband and pondered which animal he's most like. I actually walked around my house and clapped my hands in the corners. I was asked to stop reading the newspaper. I think about one night in particular after Brandon and I sat in the kitchen and did Dr. Phil's *Relationship Rescue* exercises. If Phil were a religious figure—and let's acknowledge here that some of the experts would in fact like to be seen as such—these exercises of his could only be explained as A Test for His Followers. How much faith do you have to have in order to undertake these rituals, night after night, unable to understand where they'll lead?

I found that sometimes even if the advice is solid, though, you can still fall into the experts' huge blind spots regarding the practical considerations of time and money. One day, I looked at myself and realized that I had become, in many ways, the stereotype of an upper-middle-class woman who was going about her business as if feminism never happened. I stood in my spotless and well-organized kitchen, cooking breakfast, still in my workout clothes. The day to come was going to be busy, although I'd be neither parenting nor working. I had reached a point that working on myself could literally take up all my hours.

Even one program can be difficult to carry out. Take the simple act of walking for exercise, something that actually did seem to be a positive step in my life. I lose either a half hour of work or sleep to do it. And I can only do it when Caleb is at school or otherwise supervised. When I first started, I talked to my mom and listened as she thought through how her life would have to change in order to start walking herself: She'd have to do it either early in the morning or at night; she doesn't have the option of blowing off a portion of her workday. And she'd have to drive to her walk because she lives in a suburb without sidewalks, putting her in traffic's way. Also, she has concerns about the safety of the neighborhoods in a fifteen-minute pedestrian radius from her house.

Sure, you can figure out ways to get around these limitations, but my point is that taking the advice becomes exponentially more of a pain in the ass.

ME, I was in a pretty good place for self-help to work. When I was armed with reasonable advice, a flexible schedule, plenty of money, and the desire to try the advice, there wasn't any good reason that the self-help would fail.

Except, I found out, the reason of my own personality. It's hard to change who you are, if it's possible at all.

By way of example, let my pettiness and my recycling bins make their final appearance: Recently, some of my neighbors[1] hired a few

---

[1] Amazing coincidence: the very same neighbors whom I suspected of lifting the recycling bin two years ago. Oh, Karma.

college students to landscape their front yard. It was a Thursday (trash and recycling day) and I'm walking down to get the mail when one of the guys says, "Hi! How are you?"

I slow down and look closely at the yard. My recycling bins *are right there*. With dirt piled in them. "Fine," I say slowly. "Except I think you're using my recycling bins."

"Oh, we're just borrowing them temporarily," the guy says.

I furiously flip through all my self-help tools. Is this really such a big deal? No, it's not, I decide. They're recycling bins, used for refuse anyway. "Okay," I say. And then I trudge up the stairs into the house and stew for two hours. On the one hand, the bins are just plastic containers. On the other, you don't just *take* someone's recycling bins and then pretend that it's fine that they get all *dirty* with red *dust* so that the owners of the bins will go to work with filthy hands and clothes. And pretend that there's something *wrong* with the owner of the recycling bins if she doesn't agree to this "temporary" borrowing. Oh, I was pissed, at them and at myself for not being more forceful in my disapproval.

In other words, I reacted in the exact same way I would have before I'd started my quest in self-help and before I knew what I know now. Both Dear Abby and Dale Carnegie offer good advice on how I could have dealt with this man. Martin Seligman offered good advice on how I could have used optimism and his ABCDE method to avoid letting this bother me. Even my spiritual advisers—Anne Lamott and Rabbi Kushner and Jon Kabat-Zinn—offer some larger philosophical thoughts on how you have to accept the flaws of the world.

But I couldn't do it. I could intellectually understand how one might, in theory, combat these feelings. I could even, when reading, viscerally *feel* how one might approach this situation with a little more forgiveness and calm. But actually feeling something other than serious irritation myself? Wasn't happening.

. . .

AND YET I'm unwilling to write off the whole genre because there did come a time—when just the thought of getting behind the wheel made my heart pound, when I really felt as if I were crazy, and when I believed I had no control over this craziness—that Jon Kabat-Zinn and Dr. Baxter Bell offered tools that undeniably helped me.

Oh, I know the pop psychology answers:

a. I "hit bottom" and was open to a solution.
b. I was not "getting something" from my anxiety so I had no reason to "hang on to" it.
c. These are the best experts.

Eh.

The truth is, I think Kabat-Zinn and Bell worked in tandem with an idea I got from Jonathan Haidt: You can calm the elephant, but the elephant is there and no matter what you do, you can't make it disappear. Paradoxically, my anxiety abated when I got the message that the anxiety was as much part of me as my pettiness, my Love of Learning, my sense of humor. I couldn't get rid of the anxiety, but through meditation and mindfulness, I could placate it, melt it into a smooth puddle at the bottom of my mind. You can't amputate parts of yourself—at least I couldn't—but you can manage them.

Oprah? Correct me if I'm wrong, but I believe this might be considered something like Honoring My Truth.

THE SKY IS CLAY GRAY and trees are bowing this way and that in the wind. The air smells like earthworms. A big thunderstorm is about to let loose.

Brandon, Caleb, and I are turning the rocking chairs over and gathering up our drying swimsuits, towels, and various detritus from the porch. "Looks like a Nor'eastah, Ma," Brandon says in his fake Maine accent.

"Bettah tie up the dinghy, Pa," I respond, the wind untucking my hair from behind my ears.

"Bring in the lobstah pots," Caleb says. He, almost eight years old, can finally participate in our inside joke.

An hour from now, I'll be cranky from being housebound and listening to Simon's incessant barking at the thunder. But for right now—dry and energized and relaxed—I'm about as happy as a moderately hopeless girl can get.

But enough about me.

The Gratitude Appendix

IT'S NO LAMINATED SHEET, but I offer a heartfelt thanks to the following people.

It's a long, long road to becoming a writer, and I'm indebted to those who taught me how: Katherine Greig, Arlene Edwards, Sylvia Leidigh, Susan Beasley Brown, Norma Bornarth, Ruth Keiper, Alexandria Searls, Sydney Blair, and especially Hawes Spencer.

It's a shorter—but very important—piece of road before starting a book, and I'm grateful for the early support of my work from Neva Grant, Betsy Reed, Tai Moses, Leslie Falk, Jill Schwartzman, Caryn Carmatz-Rudy, and Kathy Belden.

This book is a million times richer for the following people's involvement in it: Anna Brickhouse, Ruth Candler, Mike Fietz, Beth (Hannon) Fuller, Christina Hendricks, Bruce Holsinger, Janet Horne, Dick Holway, Kelly Howe, John Pepper, Kathleen Rodriguez, Marlee Ryson (with the blessing of Mr. John Marriot), Heather Sykes, Joe Szakos, Debie Thomas, Trisha Thompson-Willingham, Dan

Willingham, Liz Wittner, all of the people in my neighborhood, and the talented women of *Brain, Child*.

The careful reader may have noticed that when the plot called for some smart, commonsense thinking, I dialed up Stephanie Wilkinson. She belongs in a category of her own, that category being friend/ business partner/reader/fount of wisdom.

The whole Putnam experience has been wonderful. I'm grateful to Ivan Held, Catharine Lynch, Marilyn Ducksworth, Kristin Ilardi, Stephanie Sorensen, Carolyn Morrisroe, Tova Sacks, Allison Hargraves, and the rest of the crew.

I offer up enormous thanks to the dynamic duo: my incredible agent, Daniel Lazar, whose talents are vast but include uncanny insight, good humor, and telling it like it 'tis; and my excellent editor, Jackie Cantor, whose intuition and smarts are spot-on and whose phone calls were always the highlight of my day.

Q: How lucky am I that the following people are *my* people? A: Very lucky. Thanks to Bob Niesslein, Connie Ghrist, James Ghrist, Lois and Larry Rose, Millie Benning, Jeff Feaster, John Espey, and Brit and Amara. An extra big thank-you with hugs and kisses on top to my mother, Karen Niesslein, and my sisters, Erin Niesslein, Krissy Espey, and Jill Niesslein.

And, finally, the biggest thanks of all to Brandon C. Rose and Caleb Rose, who are indeed practically perfect in all the ways that matter. I love you fellas.

The Material

Bach, David. *Smart Couples Finish Rich: 9 Steps to Creating a Rich Future for You and Your Partner*. New York: Broadway Books, 2001.

Beliefnet.com. Materials from the Belief-o-Matic page, Beliefnet, Inc.

Carnegie, Dale. *How to Win Friends & Influence People*, rev. ed. New York: Simon and Schuster, 1981.

Craker, Lorilee. *We Should Do This More Often: A Parents' Guide to Romance, Passion, and Other Pre-child Activities You Vaguely Recall*. Colorado Springs: WaterBrook Press, 2005.

Dominguez, Joe, and Vicki Robin. *Your Money or Your Life: Transforming Your Relationship with Money and Achieving Financial Independence*. New York: Viking, 1992.

Ehrenreich, Barbara. *Nickel and Dimed: On (Not) Getting By in America*. New York: Metropolitan/Owl Books, 2001.

Ezzo, Gary, and Robert Bucknam, PH.D. *On Becoming Baby Wise: Book II: Parenting Your Pre-toddler, Five to Fifteen Months*. Sisters, OR: Multnomah Books, 1995.

Flylady.net and e-mails from the FlyLady Listserv April–July 2004.

Gray, John, PH.D., *Men Are from Mars, Women Are from Venus: The Classic Guide to Understanding the Opposite Sex*. New York: HarperCollins, 1992.

Haidt, Jonathan. *The Happiness Hypothesis: Finding Modern Truth in Ancient Wisdom*. New York: Basic Books, 2005.

Hinnant, Amanda. "Act Like You're Moving . . . and six more innovative strategies to kiss clutter good-bye." *Real Simple* (May 2004): 184–88.

Kabat-Zinn, Jon. *Wherever You Go, There You Are: Mindfulness Meditation in Everyday Life*, 10th anniversary edition. New York: Hyperion, 2005.

Kingston, Karen. *Clear Your Clutter with Feng Shui: Free Yourself from Physical, Mental, Emotional, and Spiritual Clutter Forever*. New York: Broadway Books, 1999.

Kushner, Harold S. *When Bad Things Happen to Good People*. New York: Avon Books, 1981.

Lamott, Anne. *Plan B: Further Thoughts on Faith*. New York: Riverhead Books, 2005.
———. *Traveling Mercies: Some Thoughts on Faith*. New York: Anchor Books, 2000.

Lavin, Christiane. "A Cure for Bad Conduct." *Child* (November 2005): 72.

Leach, Penelope. *Your Baby & Child from Birth to Age Five*, 3rd ed. New York: Knopf, 1997.

Leeds, Regina. *Sharing a Place Without Losing Your Space: A Couple's Guide to Blending Homes, Lives, and Clutter*. New York: Alpha Books, 2003.

Mayor, Tracy. "Losing My Religion." *Brain, Child: The Magazine for Thinking Mothers* (Winter 2003): 46–48.
———. *Relationship Rescue: A Seven-Step Strategy for Reconnecting with Your Partner*. New York: Hyperion, 2000.

Medline Plus. Materials from The U.S. National Library of Medicine and the National Institutes of Health. nlm.nih.gov/medlineplus/ency/article/000808.htm.

National Sleep Foundation. Materials from sleepfoundation.org/sleeptionary/index.php?id=22.

Oprah.com. Materials from "Oprah's Angel Network." Harpo Productions, Inc. http: www2.oprah.com/uyl/oan_landing.jhtml.

Orman, Suze. *The 9 Steps to Financial Freedom: Practical & Spiritual Steps So You Can Stop Worrying*, rev. ed. New York: Three Rivers Press, 2000.

Putnam, Robert D. *Bowling Alone: The Collapse and Revival of American Community*. New York: Simon and Schuster, 2000.

Schlessinger, Laura. *The Proper Care and Feeding of Husbands*. New York: Harper-Collins, 2004.

Sears, William, M.D., and Martha Sears, R.N. *The Baby Book: Everything You Need to Know About Your Baby—From Birth to Age Two*. New York: Little, Brown and Company, 1993.

Seligman, Martin E. P., PH.D. *Authentic Happiness: Using the New Positive Psychology to Realize Your Potential for Lasting Fulfillment*. New York: Free Press, 2002. authentichappiness.org.

Shapiro, Lawrence E., PH.D. *How to Raise a Child with a High E.Q.: A Parents' Guide to Emotional Intelligence*. New York: HarperCollins, 1997.

Shelov, Steven P., M.D., FAAP, ed. *Caring for Your Baby and Young Child, Birth to Age 5* (The American Academy of Pediatrics) rev. ed. New York: Bantam, 1998.

St. James, Elaine. *Simplify Your Life with Kids: 100 Ways to Make Family Life Easier and More Fun*. Kansas City, MO: Andrews McMeel, 1997.

Van Buren, Abigail. "How to Be Popular: You're Never Too Young or Too Old." Phillips-VanBuren, 1983.

Virginia Organizing Project. Materials from virginia-organizing.org.

Warner, Judith. *Perfect Madness: Motherhood in the Age of Anxiety*. New York: Riverhead, 2005.

Warren, Elizabeth, and Amelia Warren Tyagi. *The Two-Income Trap: Why Middle-Class Mothers and Fathers Are Going Broke*. New York: Basic Books, 2003.

Weil, Andrew. Materials from drweil.com and affiliated My Optimum Health site. Weil Lifestyle, LLC.

Yoffe, Emily. "I'm Doing Everything Right—Why Can't I Lose Weight?" *O: The Oprah Magazine* (January 2005): 132–35, 164–67, and insert.

Yoga Journal's Yoga Step By Step (DVD). Executive producers Martin Kupferman and Steve Michelson. Yoga Journal, 2004.